THE WORLD COURT
WHAT IT IS AND HOW IT WORKS

The Peace Palace at the Hague

THE WORLD COURT

WHAT IT IS AND HOW IT WORKS

by

SHABTAI ROSENNE

Ambassador of Israel

Legal Adviser of the Ministry for Foreign Affairs

Member of the International Law Commission
of the United Nations

SECOND REVISED EDITION

A. W. SYTHOFF – LEYDEN
OCEANA PUBLICATIONS – NEW YORK
1963

LIBRARY OF CONGRESS CATALOG CARD NUMBER: 62-9743

© 1962 BY A. W. SYTHOFF, LEYDEN, THE NETHERLANDS

Illustration I-II: United Nations
Illustrations III-V: Daniel Rosenne
Photographs as credited

Printed in the Netherlands

FOREWORD

EVERY year two or three cases come before the principal judicial organ of the United Nations—the International Court of Justice. Every year some discussion takes place, both within the United Nations and outside it, about whether to refer one case or another to the Court's verdict. Some of these cases can affect the lives of millions of human beings. All of them relate to important matters of State. Yet surprisingly little is known about the Court outside that small group of international lawyers—practising advocates and teachers—and others whose duties or particular interests require them to familiarize themselves with the Court, with its theory and practice.

The present book is intended to serve the politician, the diplomat, the member of parliament, and the enquiring members of the public at large, all who are interested in international affairs and the organs through which they are conducted, as a guide and introduction to the main factors which make the Court what it is and cause it to work as it does. I also hope that members of the legal profession, international lawyers and others, will find it of use and interest to them. I have tried as far as possible to be descriptive rather than contemplative, to depict the Court as it is and as it works, eschewing theoretical and purely historical digressions and philosophical analysis. However, I have felt obliged to treat the subject here in accordance with my fundamental belief, that proper presentation of the material must place in due perspective the interplay of political and legal factors which together bear upon the Court and its role in modern international intercourse—which affect the Court as it is and how it works.

Beth ha-Kerem, Jerusalem   SHABTAI ROSENNE
August, 1961

ADVANTAGE is being taken of this new printing to correct a few errors in the first printing, and to bring Chapter VI up to date.

September, 1962   SH. R.

TABLE OF CONTENTS

WHAT THE COURT IS

CHAPTER I: THE FORERUNNERS   11
Early beginnings, 11; The Nineteenth Century, 12; The Hague
Conferences of 1899 and 1907, 14; The Permanent Court of
Arbitration, 16; The League of Nations, 19; The Permanent
Court of International Justice, 22; Notes, 27.

CHAPTER II: THE UNITED NATIONS AND THE COURT   31
The War and the San Francisco Conference (1945), 31;
Principal Organ of the United Nations, 36; The Court and
the Specialized Agencies, 41; Execution of the Court's Decisions, 42; The Court's Finances, 44; Notes, 45.

CHAPTER III: THE JUDGES   48
The Judges' Qualifications, 48; Regional Distribution of Seats,
49; Nominating Candidates, 55; The Elections, 56; Case
Study, the Elections of 1960, 59; The Independence of the
Judges, 61; The President, 62; Judges ad hoc, 63; Chambers
of the Court, 66; The Registrar and the Registry, 67; Diplomatic Privileges, 67; Notes, 68.

HOW THE COURT WORKS

CHAPTER IV: JURISDICTION   73
A Court for States, 74; How Jurisdiction is Conferred, 76;
Jurisdiction by Unilateral Declaration (Compulsory Jurisdiction), 80; Continuity of Jurisdiction between the Permanent Court and the present Court, 84; Interim Measures of
Protection, 84; Disputes over Jurisdiction (Preliminary Objections), 85; Advisory Jurisdiction, 89; Notes, 95.

CHAPTER V: HOW A CASE IS TRIED   98
The Right of Passage case: Background, 98; The Institution
of the Proceedings, 101; Official Languages, 102; Represen-
tation of the Parties, 102; Steps following the Institution of the
Proceedings, 103; The Written Pleadings, 105; The Prelim-
inary Objections, 108; The Case ready for Hearing, 109;
The Hearing, 110; Final Submissions, 112; Interim Measures
of Protection, 115; Closure of Oral Proceedings, 115; The
Bench, 115; The Court's Deliberation, 116; The Judgment
of 26 November 1957, 118; The Separate and Dissenting
Opinions, 120; The Resumed Proceedings on the Merits, 123;
Must a State Appear? 126; Settlement out of Court, 127;
The Law applied by the Court, 127; The Final Submissions

on the Merits, 130; The Judgment of 12 April 1960, 131; Costs, 134; Interpretation and Revision, 134; The Extra-judicial Function, 135; Notes, 135.

CHAPTER VI: THE WORK OF THE COURT 138
The Corfu Channel, 138; Membership in the United Nations, 141; Reparation for the United Nations, 143; Fishing in the North Sea, 144; French Nationals in Egypt, 146; A Case of Diplomatic Asylum, 146; Questions of Human Rights in Certain Peace Treaties, 148; The Question of South-West Africa, 150; Rights of U.S. Nationals in (French) Morocco, 152; The Genocide Convention, 152; A Greek Citizen's Claim for Damages for Breach of Contract, 153; The Anglo-Iranian Oil Co., 154; Whose are the Channel Islets: Minquiers and Ecrehos? 156; A German National Claims Restoration of his Sequestered Property, 157; Gold Looted from Rome in 1943, 157; France's Difficulties in the Lebanon, 158; The Adminis-trative Tribunals, 159; The Iron Curtain Overflown (I)—Military Aircraft, 160; The Antarctica, 161; Some Norwegian Loans, 161; Right of Passage, 162; Who shall appoint a Guardian over an Infant? 162; The Interhandel Company's Assets, 163; The Iron Curtain Overflown (II)—Civil Aircraft, 164; Baerle-Duc and Baarle Nassau—Belgian or Dutch? 166; The Frontier between Honduras and Nicaragua, 166; The Affairs of the Barcelona Traction, Light and Power Company, 167; The Maritime Safety Committee, 167; The Temple of Preah Vihear, 168; The Northern Cameroons, 168; The U.N. Budget, 169; Evaluation, 170; Notes, 175.

Appendix 1. Charter of the United Nations 179
Appendix 2. Statute of the International Court of Justice . . . 200
Appendix 3. Composition of the Court, 1922-45, 1946-61 213
Appendix 4. Judicial Statistics, 1922-45, 1946-60 217
Appendix 5. Authority to Request Advisory Opinions 219
Note on Bibliography 222
Index of Names 223
Index of Cases 225
General Index 227

Illustration I.   The United Nations and Related Agencies . . .   37
Illustration II.   Reproduction of an actual Ballot Paper. . . .   65
Illustration III. The Contentious Jurisdiction   79
Illustration IV.   The Advisory Competence   92
Illustration V.   How a Case is Tried 100

Table I.   The Court's Finances   47
Table II.   Distribution of Seats by Continents   51
Table III. Distribution of Seats by Regional Groups   52
Table IV.   Representation of Principal Legal Systems   53
Table V.   Nationality of Judges   54

WHAT THE COURT IS

In the last resort, recourse to international justice depends on the will of governments and on their readiness to submit for legal decision all which can and should be preserved from the arbitrament of violence. As for the Court, it means to accomplish to the full the duties incumbent upon it; and it will not weaken in that resolve—Judge J. Gustavo Guerrero, President of the Permanent Court of International Justice (1936-45) and of the International Court of Justice (1946-49), on 4 December 1939.

CHAPTER I

THE FORERUNNERS

THE idea of resolving international disputes through disinterested third parties deciding the dispute on the basis of law and justice, as an alternative to direct settlement of the dispute by means of violence after diplomacy has failed, is a deep-rooted human aspiration. Its origins can be found in religious sentiment which tended to recoil from the horrors of war and seek other ways of eradicating conflicts of international interests. At times the idea was expressed in Messianic terms, as by the Prophets Isaiah and Micah: "And it shall come to pass in the end of days . . . And He shall judge between the nations, and shall decide for many peoples; and they shall beat their swords into plowshares and their spears into pruning-hooks; Nation shall not lift up sword against nation, neither shall they learn war any more."[1] At others, it is cast in the language of political programme, as by Hugo Grotius, the father of modern international law: "Christian kings and states are bound to employ this method [arbitration] of avoiding war . . . And for this and many other purposes, it would be helpful—as a matter of fact, necessary—for the Christian powers to hold conferences, where those whose interests were not involved might settle the disputes of the rest, and even take measures to compel the parties to accept peace on fair terms."[2]

EARLY BEGINNINGS

As an ideal, this concept seems to have been widespread: in practice, however, its application was far from general. It was found, for instance, in the early periods of Middle Eastern history and in sacred codes of the Far East,[3] and it is encountered in the experience of Islam.[4] But it was in Europe that the concept most took root. Its attraction for the European mind was that it sought to transfer the absolute values of the discipline of the law, on which the well-being of the national society in Western Europe was thought to depend, to the problems of the international community. The Greek city-states, for instance, possessed a well-developed system of third-party settlement of their disputes, within the framework of their own Hellenic culture, especially through the instrumentality of the Delphic Amphictyonies.[5] Here, indeed, there is something approaching true disinterested third-party judgment between nominally equal political units—the city-states—on the basis of a rudimentary system of law or custom by which the correct behaviour of those political units might be judged. With the growth of the big empires—Macedonia, Rome, Byzantium—this form of third-party settlement fell into disuse, partly, no doubt, because of the impossibility of finding any true disinterested third party, and partly because the general imperialist and expansionist tendencies of those super-Powers, and their centralized system of government, would not easily be reconciled to the idea of the settlement of *their* disputes by application of "law" (however rudimentary international law might have been at that time). On the other hand, the classical historical writings contain many circumstantial accounts of those Powers "deciding" disputes between their various clients and vassals through a procedure which resembles partly a system of arbitration, and partly a system of mediation and conciliation—and partly a mere concealment for force.

In medieval Europe, too, both types of "arbitration" are found. For instance, in Switzerland, where peculiar geographical conditions impressed their stamp on the political organization in a manner reminiscent of that of ancient Hellas, several cases are known in which disputes between two or more cities were arbitrated by disinterested ecclesiastical and secular authorities, who tried to reach a settlement by a combination of methods of persuasion and of decision.[6] Something similar seems once to have existed for the city-states of Italy. On the other hand, the tradition of the Roman Empire was largely continued by the Popes and Emperors, whose system of government contained built-in machinery for resolving disputes between their vassals and subordinates. Here it has been said that the major premise was that the church knows what is right and wrong, and that the peace-maker, if he is the delegate of the church, must begin by judging, not by conciliating, the parties.[7] It was in this period too that the theologian-jurists began developing the theory, that the existence of central institutions in the Papacy for the settlement of disputes implied that the princes were not entitled to take the law into their own hands—an idea closely connected with the theory of the just war and the unjust war or (as we would say today) the war of aggression.

THE NINETEENTH CENTURY

The origins of modern arbitration are usually traced to the so-called

Jay Treaty of 19 November 1794, between the United States and Great Britain, putting an end to the American War of Independence. This provided for the setting up of three different commissions for the settlement of outstanding questions. Two of these commissions successfully completed their task, but the third ran into difficulties which were only resolved later by direct diplomatic means. The commissions were composed of American and British nationals exclusively—a fact which negatives any idea of third-party settlement. However, the proceedings before the commissions were conducted on the model of court actions, and the commissioners tried to reach their decisions by applying rules of law.[8] This type of proceeding was in substance diplomatic rather than judicial in character, since there was no impartial arbitrament between the two parties represented on the commissions. But the Jay Treaty and these processes led to a renewal of general interest in the possibilities of using legal and judicial techniques as a method of resolving certain types of international conflict, especially, though by no means exclusively, when there is involved in the international dispute a large number of private and individual claims. Occasionally instances are found, in the early part of the nineteenth century, in which true third-party settlement of a dispute is invoked—the third party being nominally either the Head of a State or one of its organs, acceptable to the two litigants. When this happened, the process begins to lose its purely diplomatic character, and to assume that of true judicial arbitration.

A major development in the history of international adjudication occurred in the well-known *Alabama* case, arising out of the American Civil War. This, commonly regarded as the watershed of modern international litigation, was a spectacular affair, which, because it involved fundamental questions of the law of neutrality and of warfare at sea, touched upon serious political interests of Great Britain, the defendant. The dispute, which originated in the departure of the *Alabama* from the Merseyside shipyards on 29 July 1862 to join the Confederate Forces and prey upon U.S. shipping in the Atlantic, caused great political bitterness on both sides. It was not until the Washington Treaty of 8 May 1871 that the two countries agreed to submit it to arbitration. The significance of this act lies in the nature of the tribunal, which was composed of one national of each of the two parties, together with three neutral members—nationals of Italy, Switzerland and Brazil. The Treaty also contained another innovation: it specified some (though not all) of the basic legal rules concerning the duties of neutral states, which the Tribunal was to apply. After complicated proceedings held in the Hôtel de Ville at Geneva the Tribunal handed down its award (reached by a majority of four to one) on 14 September 1872[9]. Despite the dissent of the British arbitrator, the British Government paid the damages to the tune of over $ 15,000,000 within the time stipulated. The spectacle of two important countries submitting a dispute of this character to impartial third-party settlement on the basis of law, and then complying with the terms of the award, naturally gave a great fillip to the development of the concept of international arbitration as an alternative to allowing political tension to smoulder indefinitely.

THE HAGUE CONFERENCES OF 1899 AND 1907

The experience of the Geneva Tribunal, and other important instances of arbitration proceedings in its wake, provided the point of departure for a new development which came to a head, on the initiative of the Tsar Nicholas II of Russia, in the First Hague Peace Conference of 1899, and which was consummated in the Second Hague Peace Conference of 1907.[10]

Among other things, these conferences attempted to find a way of repairing a number of obvious cracks in the system and practice of international arbitration, as it had been developing during the nineteenth century. The agreements to have recourse to arbitration had all been reached *ad hoc*. All the instances of international arbitration up to this time, even when successful in settling the political dispute, had been marked by acute political difficulties in reaching agreement on the composition and procedure of the arbitral tribunal and on fixing precisely the point or points on which it was to be asked to decide. This was because no standing arbitral machinery existed, and no clearly accepted concepts of international arbitral procedure, and it is rarely easy to reach agreement on these highly complicated and at times extremely technical aspects in the heat of a political controversy which may leave little room for manoeuvre. This added to the difficulties of invoking disinterested third-party judgment and increased the psychological obstacles which, in the nature of things, always make it difficult for a government to empower outsiders to reach binding decisions on delicate matters of direct concern to it. This had the consequence that if political passions became too inflamed, the governments concerned might find it politically impossible to agree to settle the matter by arbitration even if they wanted to, or, what was worse, they could make illusory agreements, or frustrate their declared intentions by other means. For reasons such as these, enlightened persons, and governments, began looking for a method by which permanent arbitration machinery could always be at the disposal of States: some went even further, and began thinking of the possibility of making it *compulsory* for States to have recourse to arbitration, if not for all then at least for certain types of international disputes.

At this point two almost insuperable problems made an appearance. They are mentioned here because they have dogged the whole history of international adjudication and their influence is felt in the International Court. The first was the composition of the Tribunal. The second was how to define *in advance* its jurisdiction. Neither of these problems were fully solved by the Peace Conferences of 1899 and 1907.

On the question of composition, the experience of the diplomatic arbitrations of the nineteenth century showed that even if the balance in an arbitral commission should be held by neutral arbitrators or a neutral umpire, States, for reasons which are essentially psychological, could not normally be expected to agree to submit their disputes to a tribunal in which there was not a single national of their own. This aspect was the easier to resolve, basically on the principle that the balance in an arbitral tribunal, in which the parties too should be represented, should be held by "neutral" members. More significant, however—and it was this which really made it impossible then to establish a permanent arbitration court —was the attitude of the Great Powers of the time. Loosely organized in the Concert of Europe, these felt that their international interests and responsibilities (including their general responsibilities to preserve the peace between the Small Powers and to maintain the balance of power between themselves) were sufficiently heavy and universal to justify a demand that if any permanent international court were created, they should be represented on it. Experience showed—and this was no more than a matter of political reality—that it was one thing for Powers, even Great Powers, to agree to settle their existing disputes through arbitrators of their own choice: it was quite another thing to expect them to agree *in advance* to submit their future disputes, with parties and on matters unknown, to a permanent tribunal whose composition was already fixed and on which they might not be represented.

The difficulty of setting down in advance and in general terms the jurisdiction of a tribunal had its roots no less in experience and political realism. It derives from the view which is firmly held and valid as a matter of political doctrine (however repugnant it may be to legal theory) that not every international dispute, especially when it is one involving a serious clash of interests, or of aspirations, can be said generally and in advance to be suitable for settlement through disinterested judges applying legal techniques and criteria exclusively. Many of the most intractable and dangerous international disputes are born out of a desire to alter the law, for instance when the law is embodied in an unpopular, but legally binding, treaty. This difficulty, which is a real one, has led to a long series of attempts to define the types of disputes which can be inherently regarded, in advance, as suitable for settlement by arbitrators or judges, to set down the tests for the "justiciability" and "non-justiciability" of disputes, to employ a common term (borrowed from the experience of the United States Supreme Court in dealing with certain constitutional matters). These attempts may be regarded as satisfactory technical advances: it would be an illusion to think, however, that they have solved the problem, as can indeed be seen by the frequency with which defendant States challenge the jurisdiction of the Court (see p. 87 below).

In 1907, no workable solution was found to either of these problems (partly because German militarism thought that an effective system of arbitration would give their enemies a useful instrument for delaying political events, and thus enable them to overtake the German superiority in armaments). As a result, a compromise was adopted. The idea of compulsory arbitration, even for limited categories of disputes, was for the time being dropped. It was replaced by a system of voluntary arbitration which required, for each instance, the consent of the States concerned, both to the composition of the Tribunal and to its terms of reference. On the other hand, it was recognized that certain types of disputes were probably more suitable for arbitration than others. The value of the institution of arbitration had proved itself, and there was a widespread desire to transform it from an exclusively *ad hoc* diplomatic process into one having elements of permanency. The attempt was made to formulate the main lines of arbitration procedure (which, nevertheless, States were free to modify at will). This technical aspect was important as a step towards simplifying the drawing up of arbitration agreements and thus reducing the opportunities of frustrating a political decision to resort to arbitration.

THE PERMANENT COURT OF ARBITRATION

The element of permanency was created by the establishment of the Permanent Court of International Arbitration. In fact this institution is misnamed, for it is neither a court nor permanent. It consists of a panel of arbitrators nominated by the contracting parties (they may each nominate not more than four persons, of known competency in questions of international law, of the highest moral reputation and disposed to accept the duties of arbitrator).

From this panel the States may choose a Tribunal to decide their particular case, the balance in the Tribunal being, of course, confided to neutral arbitrators. The Permanent Court of Arbitration has an Administrative Council, consisting of the diplomatic representatives at The Hague of the contracting parties, and a small Secretariat. Its headquarters were established at The Hague (where they still are).

The First Hague Convention of 1907 for the Pacific Settlement of International Disputes (replacing the First Convention of 1899), therefore contains an elaborate code covering a number of processes for the settlement of international disputes, in the event of failure of diplomatic negotiations to produce satisfactory results, and arbitration is included among them. Others are the procedures of good offices and mediation, and arrangements for international commissions of enquiry, essentially for the elucidation of disputed facts. The Convention defined the object of international arbitration as "the settlement of disputes between States by judges of their own choice". It imposed no obligation on the Parties to have recourse to arbitration, but Article 38 stated that: "In questions of a legal nature, and especially in the interpretation or application of international conventions, arbitration is recognized by the contracting Powers as the most effective and at the same time the most equitable means of settling disputes which diplomacy has failed to settle". Consequently it was desirable to have recourse to it in that type of case. But it was never obligatory, even after arbitration had been decided upon, to have recourse to a panel of the Permanent Court of Arbitration: that was maintained primarily as machinery to facilitate recourse to arbitration.

These difficulties, above all, made it impossible, at The Hague, to establish any general obligation to have resort to arbitration. All that could be done was to create machinery, and to lay down a series of general rules, for the conduct of arbitration proceedings,[11] leaving their actual application in a concrete case to the unfettered will of the States concerned. Therefore, in order to set arbitration proceedings in motion, there must be a special agreement for that purpose (sometimes called technically, even in English, a *compromis*) —whether an agreement, bilateral or multilateral, providing for the submission of certain types of disputes to arbitration, or one providing for the submission of a specific dispute to arbitration.

Even before the 1899 Conference, two other developments in the practice of States started to make an appearance. The first was the inclusion in general treaties of a "compromissory clause"—a stipulation to refer disputes arising out of the particular treaty to arbitration. The second was the conclusion of general treaties of arbitration, as distinct from special agreements, sometimes coupled with other machineries for the settlement of disputes, between pairs of States. In these treaties too the problem of defining in advance the type of dispute which they were intended to cover was found to be extremely difficult. Usually they excluded from their scope disputes involving the vital interests, national sovereignty, independence or honour of the contracting parties, and in so far as this formula granted the State concerned a right of unilateral determination that a given dispute came within that category, the treaty was to that extent illusory.

Despite these weaknesses, the Hague Conferences gave a great impetus both to the process of including bilateral arbitration treaties, and to the invocation of arbitration proceedings. It has been estimated that between 1900 and 1914 more than 120 general arbitration treaties were concluded between pairs of States. Between 1902 and 1920, fourteen disputes were handled by panels of arbitrators chosen from the Permanent Court of Arbitration and more than fifty other disputes were arbitrated in some other manner.[12] Since the end of the First World War to date, some forty-one cases of arbitration have been held, of which nine were before panels of the Permanent Court of Arbitration, and the balance before *ad hoc* arbitration tribunals.[13]

By the outbreak of the First World War, the main lines of international arbitral procedure were firmly drawn. From the starting point of the voluntary character of the whole process, the following are the principal features that may be noted:

Firstly, it had become accepted that if in the course of the proceedings a dispute should arise concerning the Tribunal's jurisdiction, *that* dispute should normally be settled by the Tribunal itself, and should not be referred back to the diplomatic channels, unless the arbitration agreement provided otherwise. Thus one way of frustrating the work of the arbitration tribunals was blocked.

Secondly, it was accepted that the arbitrators should all be persons of recognized competence and of the highest standards of integrity. Where the Head of a State was appointed arbitrator, as was frequently done, he was entitled to delegate the actual work to his own officials, but the award was promulgated personally and under his own authority. The mixed diplomatic and judicial quality of international arbitration was generally preserved by the appointment of national arbitrators (who in the Tribunal tended to cancel each other out), leaving the real power of decision in the hands of a group of neutral arbitrators or even a single Umpire.[14]

Thirdly, accepted elements of the normal judicial techniques, including features such as the equality of the parties, the right of

both parties to an equal hearing, and, of course, the independence
of the arbitrators, were fully incorporated into international practice. International political thought began to appreciate the implications of the maxim, that justice must not only be done but
that it must be seen to be done.

Fourthly, the outlines of fairly regular patterns of procedure
began to establish themselves. These included both written and oral
pleadings, closed deliberations of the Tribunal, the promulgation
of its award (unless for any reason the parties desired to keep the
whole arbitration secret, which they were entitled to do), the duty
of the Tribunal to give reasons for its award, and the right of any
member of the Tribunal to express his dissent (this latter was not
invariable: the custom of dissenting opinions is essentially of a
"common law" origin, and is not familiar to continental jurists).

Finally, it became established as a rule of law, not requiring to
be specifically written into arbitration agreements, that the agreement to have recourse to arbitration automatically contained the
obligation to abide by the Tribunal's award, and to carry it out in
good faith. The award was "final" and "binding" as a settlement
of the dispute. It is this which distinguished arbitration from other
diplomatic processes such as conciliation and mediation, in which
the binding quality was not always present.

These essential features of international arbitration have been
preserved to this day, and have exercised a potent influence on the
development of international adjudication proper, through the
International Court.[15]

THE LEAGUE OF NATIONS

One of the reasons for the difficulties which attended all the earlier
attempts to establish permanent international tribunals of general
jurisdiction was the absence of any central political administration
for the international community. Before the First World War, no
regular international machinery existed, neither on the political-
diplomatic level nor on the administrative level. The so-called
Concert of Europe of the time was an informal system of consultation between the Great European Powers of the epoch; it
lacked all the attributes of system and constitution, and its machinery was that of the traditional techniques of diplomacy.

The establishment of the League of Nations by the Peace Treaties
of 1919 changed this. Especially significant was the differentiation
between the Council and the Assembly. The Council was conceived
as a small executive body in which the political responsibility and
power were concentrated. It was composed of a number of perma-

nent members, who were the surviving Great Powers which were members of the League, and elected members. On the other hand, the Assembly, which met once a year in regular session, was the general deliberative body of the total membership. The League was equipped with an administrative organ, the Secretariat, and a regular budget. Obviously, the existence of such a pattern of international organization opened new perspectives for a permanent international judicial organ.

The relative success of the 1907 Conference—which only served to highlight the obstinate political difficulties in the way of true international adjudication—inspired a significant movement which was not satisfied with the partial solution and looked forward to the day when a permanent tribunal with compulsory jurisdiction would exist. The Hague Conference itself had adopted a resolution admitting the principle of obligatory arbitration as well as a project for the creation of a court of arbitral justice, but nothing had come of it. Important bodies, however, kept hammering away at the theme, including the Institute of International Law (resolution of 1911) and others. During the War, the Scandinavian neutral States prepared a joint plan for the organization of an international judicial organ, and this was followed by other plans prepared under the aegis of the Swiss (1918) and Netherlands (1919) Governments. The movement also had powerful backing in the United States, and among the Western Allies in general. It was a movement which, therefore, could not be ignored by the peacemakers of 1919.

By the time the early drafts of the constitution of the League of Nations were circulating at the beginning of 1919, the notion that permanent machinery for international adjudication must be included seems to have been accepted. It was perceived that the establishment of the League, in which the Principal Allied and Associated Powers would have a predominant position (they would be permanent members of the Council), opened the way to a solution of the problem of the composition of such a tribunal. It was also felt that the existence of a regularly established international organization might facilitate a solution for the question of the extent to which the principle of compulsory arbitration could become feasible. Obviously, however, a great deal of work was required before these ideas could be translated into the language of reality. Article 12 of the Covenant contained a general obligation to submit to arbitration or settlement by the League Council any dispute likely to lead to a rupture, as well as provisions for the execution of decisions, and Article 13 contained a general declaration about the types of dispute which were regarded as generally suitable for submission to arbitration.[16] These included disputes as to: *(a)* the interpretation of a treaty; *(b)* any question of international law; *(c)* the existence of any fact which if established would constitute a breach of any international obligation; or *(d)* the extent and nature of the reparation to be made for any such breach. The first of these categories had appeared in Article 38 of the Hague Convention of 1907. The others, however, are new, and indicate the extent of the intellectual advance achieved since 1907. If the matter could be disposed of merely by means of definitions and classifications, the four categories together are broad enough to cover every international *dispute*, though not necessarily every type or instance of international tension which might occur. This formula has come to exercise a significant and on the whole fruitful influence on the work of the International Court.

Articles 12 and 13 contained general obligations binding on the Members of the League, obligations which were vague and of indefinite scope it is true, but nonetheless obligations. That was as far as the Peace Conference could go in the time at its disposal. It could not establish the permanent judicial organ, and it therefore decided to leave future developments to the organs of the League. Article 14 of the Covenant consequently imposed on the Council the duty of formulating plans for the establishment of what was termed the Permanent Court of International Justice, which would be competent to hear and determine any dispute of an international character which the parties thereto submit to it. This Article also introduced a completely novel idea into international practice, by providing that the Court might give an advisory opinion upon any dispute or question referred to it by the Council of the Assembly. This is discussed on pp. 89 ff. below.

The Council lost little time in getting down to work and already at its second session in February, 1920, appointed a committee of ten eminent jurists (several of whom had participated at The Hague in 1907), from allied or neutral countries, to submit a report to the Council. The Committee's attention was called to the plans which had been drawn up in the meantime, and to certain assurances that had been given to the German and Austrian Governments in the course of the Peace Conferences. By July it adopted its draft scheme which was promptly discussed by the Council, and after modifications was forwarded to the First Assembly of the League. The Assembly, after further amendment, then adopted the Statute of the Permanent Court of International Justice, and opened its Protocol of Signature on 16 December 1920. It decided that the Statute would come into force as soon as it was ratified by the majority of the members of the League. This process was completed by the beginning of September the next year, and the Statute then came into force. The first election of judges took place in 1921, and the Court was formally inaugurated in January 1922. The first case to come before the Court—an advisory opinion—was filed in May, 1922, and the first contentious case was instituted a year later.[17]

Thus was the concept of a permanent international judicial organ translated into reality. On the other hand, the concept of compulsory jurisdiction was not yet accepted into international practice.

THE PERMANENT COURT OF INTERNATIONAL JUSTICE

Despite Article 14 of the Covenant, the Permanent Court, which was in existence from 1922 until the dissolution of the League on 19 April 1946, was strictly speaking not an organ of the League. The fact that a State was a Member of the League did not automatically make it a party to the Statute of the Court, although, as laid down in the Statute, it could participate in the elections of the judges, and had to bear its share of the Court's expenses. This meant that what is sometimes known as the "international judicial community", i.e. the States which are parties to the Statute, was not identical with the international political community organized in the League. All members of the League were *qualified* to become parties to the Statute, but so too were other States provided certain conditions were fulfilled. Furthermore, under given conditions even States which were not parties to the Statute could litigate their differences with other States before the Court, whether as plaintiffs or as defendants. The Court was created to serve the whole international community. Not for nothing was its seat established at The Hague, alongside the Permanent Court of Arbitration, and not at Geneva. The Court never became "tainted" with the "Geneva spirit".

Yet the Court was closely connected with the League—so close in fact that its fortunes were undoubtedly tied to those of the League, and it could not survive the disappearance of the League. This meant that developments in the general international situation, which prevented effective action on the political level by the League, could not leave the Court unaffected, and that the progressive disintegration of the post-War political system had a direct impact on the Court. That was inevitable. On the other hand, that bond made possible solutions to some of the problems which had prevented the earlier establishment of any permanent general international judicial organ. For instance, the difficulty over the composition of the Court was neatly solved by confiding the election of the judges to the two principal organs of the League, the Council and the Assembly, an ingenious device which ensured not only the presence of the Great Powers on the Court, but also a balanced Court from the point of view of the representation on it of the principal legal systems and the major political trends in the world. This tie also overcame difficulties in financing the Court's expenses. All this has now been taken over by the United Nations, and will be described more fully in the following chapters.

Although, as stated, the concept of the compulsory settlement of all, or certain types of, international disputes was not incorporated into either the League Covenant or the Statute, the general political climate of the early period of the League lent encouragement to the idea that States should voluntarily take upon themselves more precise obligations for submitting disputes to the Court. That objective was further facilitated by the Statute of the Court, and even more so by its actual practice. Nevertheless, the fundamental principle which had underpinned the international arbitrations of the nineteenth century, that the consent of the litigating States is the *only* basis for the exercise of jurisdiction, remained firmly enshrined as the *only* basis for the exercise of jurisdiction by the Permanent Court. The many, and far-reaching, changes which in the course of time international practice has assimilated, have never departed from that fundamental principle.

The Permanent Court, after an experimental and tentative start, also made tremendous advances in international judicial procedure. Using as its point of departure the models of procedure in the domestic courts (especially the highest courts), international judicial procedure is today a completely autonomous institution of international law and practice having only superficial resemblances to domestic legal procedure. The Court's procedure became crystallized by 1936 with the adoption of the last version of the Rules of Procedure. Together with the Statute, these Rules have been taken over, virtually unchanged, by the United Nations and the present Court (see Appendices 1 and 2). How these procedures were developed and applied by the Permanent Court is now a matter of historical and professional interest. Naturally, there is a continuous process of development to meet the constantly changing requirements and patterns of international life and experience, and in later chapters of this book the attempt will be made to describe their essential features as they are today.

It is of greater importance to try and evaluate—or more accurately re-evaluate—the work of the Permanent Court, because now, with the passage of time, its achievements can be looked at more dispassionately and from a distance. What can be learned from its experience, that will be of value today in understanding the potentialities for, and the limitations on, the international judicial function?

The judicial statistics of the Court (see Appendix 4) show that in the 18 years of its effective life, from 1922 to 1939, a total of 66 cases were brought before it. Thirty-eight were contentious cases and 28 advisory cases. Of those, 12 were later settled out of Court. In the fifty-four cases left for decision the Court delivered 27 advisory opinions (all at the request of the League Council) and 32 judgments (two cases were pending when the Second World War silenced the Court). There were in addition a number of substantive pronouncements couched in the form of orders. This gives an average of nearly four cases filed per year, and a slightly smaller number of major judicial pronouncements—figures considerably in excess of anything experienced by international arbitration.

What were these cases about? What were the realities of the disputes with which the Permanent Court was called upon to deal? For as a matter of form by far the greater part of them superficially dealt with technical questions of law, indeed mostly the interpretation of treaties. But let us not confuse the form with the underlying causes of the disputes.

Their subject-matter, as their political context and background, varied. But looking back on these affairs we may notice some interesting, and perhaps unsuspected, features. For example, a great deal of the Court's concrete business emerged from the tensions—which in time played a major role in the course of events leading to the outbreak of the Second World War—between Germany and Poland[18] and between Lithuania and Germany and Poland.[19] Other controversial aspects of the 1919 Peace Settlement also were brought before the Court[20] as well as some arising out of the Middle Eastern settlement with Turkey.[21] The Council of the League was even not averse to referring to the Court for advisory opinion so explosive an issue as the proposed customs union between Austria and Germany—which the Court, some seven years before Hitler brought the *Anschluss* about by force, held to be illegal. African affairs, too, occupied it—a harbinger of later events.[22] The Court, naturally, also had a certain amount of work to do in resolving other disputes, some of them quite serious, such as that relating to the sovereignty over Eastern Greenland, and occasionally to give advice on the operations of the International Labour Organization. On the other hand, it was rare for disputes arising out of sudden, and perhaps unpremeditated, incidents unrelated to a more general political background to be brought before the Court.[23] It seems that this type of quarrel may on the whole be more amenable to diplomatic settlement which will avoid raising the legal questions of principle, and acute issues of national prestige, which a reference to the Court must encounter. Many people think that the mere existence of the Court makes it easier for States to settle this type of dispute without recourse to the Court: it forces them to consider the legal aspects dispassionately, and to plan their diplomatic steps accordingly.

We may also observe, in the experience of the Permanent Court, that both the United States and the Soviet Union manifested towards the Court attitudes very similar to those which they later manifested in the period of the United Nations. Thus, the United States, itself not a member of the League, signed the Statute of the Court, but the Senate refused to consent to its ratification. On the other hand, a judge of United States nationality was always a member of the Court. The United States was not involved, either directly or indirectly, in any litigation during that period. The Soviet Union did not go quite so far even as the United States. It rejected the competence and authority of the Court in a concrete case referring directly to its own affairs;[24] it never signed the Statute of the Court, and never concerned itself to have a judge of Soviet nationality on the bench—this latter aspect was changed after 1945. The formal reason for aloofness of this character is that these Powers (except the Soviet Union from 1934) were not members of the Geneva organization: but there is reason to believe that behind the formal attitude there existed more profound considerations related to fundamental policies of the two great Powers which, after 1945, were to appear as the two most powerful nations on earth.

How, then, is the work of the Permanent Court to be assessed? One of the difficulties here is to lay down the appropriate measuring rod. The real significance of the work of an international Court cannot be based on mere statistics, or be determined merely by the formal consideration that its *ipse dixit* enjoys the formal status of being a final and binding settlement of the dispute before it. In fact much of its final and binding settlements did not survive the turmoil of the Second World War.

Let us take another look at the Court's judicial statistics, and relate them to the general developments of the political situation. We find that of the 66 cases brought before the Court, well over two thirds, 50 of them, were filed in the period 1922-32, in the heyday of the League. In the five year period 1924-8 alone, when Franco-German *rapprochement* was at its closest in the era of the Locarno agreements (1925), 24 new cases were filed, an average of nearly five per year, which itself is considerably higher than the annual average over the whole period. No new cases were filed in 1929, the year of the major financial crash. This indicates the

dependence of the idea of international litigation upon the existence
of some modicum of general pacification and stability and relaxation of international tension. After the Nazis came to power
in Germany in 1933, 16 new cases were filed in the seven years
1933-9, a sharp falling off in the Court's activities. This is not
accidental, and some disputes of that period were actually litigated
only after the Second World War.

Writing in 1944, a former judge of the Court, Manley Hudson,
doubted if the Permanent Court had fulfilled a role as a "great
bulwark of peace" (had the League of Nations?), though he recognized that some of the cases with which it dealt could have led
to serious complications had they been allowed to fester. He thought
that the Court's bolstering of the structure of peace had been ac-
complished more through the confidence it had inspired in its
methods and the encouragement which it had given to the extension of the law of pacific settlement.[25] But placing the concrete
—isolated—cases in the broader context of the general political
situation may show that what the Court, as the other organs of the
League (and often in co-operation with them) really succeeded in
doing, was for a time to keep a tense situation under some form of
control. Given other political conditions, the League would have
enjoyed greater long-term success, and the Court with it. As things
were, the major disputes with which the Court dealt were connected
with that very situation which sparked off the Second World War.
None of the skills of statesmanship and diplomacy available at the
time succeeded in avoiding that disaster, and it is too much to
expect more of the Court.

In addition to any purely political evaluation of the work of the
Court within the context of the various procedures for the settlement
of international disputes, it is generally recognized that it made a
very significant contribution to the development of international
law.[26] This is an indirect contribution to the maintenance of international peace, of no mean value, and may be set against the failure
of the League of Nations (in contrast to the success of the United
Nations)[27] in this field.

The real significance of the experience of the Permanent Court
seems to lie in a different direction. From its experimental beginnings it established the point that a permanent international judicial
organ is both feasible and necessary, even without going so far as
to be accompanied by any true compulsory jurisdiction. The real
measure of its worth is not to be found in the number of cases
decided by it (though that is by no means to be belittled) or in its
contribution to the development and clarification of the law (a
by-product of the activity of all courts in all legal systems), but in

the widely-held satisfaction at its existence. It is never seriously suggested that the Court is unnecessary, or that it has failed in its primary mission, or that its organization is fundamentally faulty, even in quarters which for various reasons are critical of some of its decisions, or of the manner in which States sometimes invoke the judicial function.[28] When the League disappeared and the United Nations took its place it was never suggested that the Court had outlived its usefulness and could well be disbanded. On the contrary: the major concern was to increase its effectiveness and to strengthen its ties with the world political organization, and if too much could not be achieved in this direction, then at least to ensure that the judicial activities could be resumed at the point they had been broken off in 1939.

The experience of the Permanent Court, its dispassionate and unhurried consideration of the issues brought before it, the high standards of personal integrity and professional competence, and worldly wisdom, of its members, the fact that the judicial pronouncements were endowed with strong moral authority in addition to their formal finality—all these constituted an intangible asset on the positive side of the balance-sheet. They provided the foundations for the reconstituted system of international adjudication after the dust of the Second World War had started to settle.

NOTES

1. Isaiah ii. 4; Micah iv. 3.

2. *De jure belli ac pacis* (1625), II, ch. xxiii § 8. English translation from Hugo Grotius, *The Law of War and Peace*, trans. Louise R. Loomis (New York, 1949), 252.

3. For the position in Ancient India, see H. Chatterjee, *International Law and Inter-State Relations in Ancient India* (Calcutta, 1958), 129. For the position in Ancient China, see Chan Nay Chow, *La doctrine du Droit international chez Confucius* (Paris, 1941), 89.

4. A. Rechid, "L'Islam et le droit des Gens", R.A.D.I., 60 (1937) (ii), 371; M. Khadduri, *War and Peace in the Law of Islam* (Baltimore, 1955), 231.

5. See C. Phillipson, *The International Law and Custom of Ancient Greece and Rome* (London, 1911); A. Raeder, *L'Arbitrage international chez les Hellènes* (Kristiania, 1912); M. Tod, *International Arbitration amongst the Greeks* (Oxford, 1913); J. Ralston, *International Arbitration from Athens to Locarno* (California, 1929); M. Taube, "Les Origines de l'arbitrage international: antiquité et moyen âge", R.A.D.I., 42 (1932) (iv), 1; G. Ténékidès, "International Law and Federal Communities in the Greece of the Cities", R.A.D.I., 90 (1956) (ii), 469.

6. E. Usteri, *Bienne-Beppet* Arbitration, in J. B. Moore (editor), *International Adjudications*, Ancient Series, II (New York, 1936).

7. See A. B. Bozeman, *Politics and Culture in International History* (Princeton, 1960), 266-7. Also J. Eppstein, *The Catholic Tradition in the Law of Nations* (London,

1935), 113 and *passim*. Yet a warning has been issued against exaggerating the role of the Church, while emphasizing its function in creating an atmosphere in which arbitration could flourish. R. Bainton, *Christian Attitudes towards War and Peace* (New York, 1960), 116-8.

8. J. B. Moore, *International Adjudications*, Modern Series, vols. 1-4 (New York, 1929-31). Vol. 5 of this Series deals with certain U.S.-Spanish and U.S.-French claims (the latter being settled, as regards individual U.S. claimants, by domestic commissions), and vol. 6 contains the proceedings of another U.S.-Great Britain Mixed Commission set up to arbitrate the title to islands in the Passamaquoddy Bay and the Bay of Fundy, between Maine and New Brunswick.

9. For text see A. G. de Lapradelle and N. Politis, *Recueil des Arbitrages internationales*, II (Paris, 1923), 713; J. B. Moore, *History and Digest of the Arbitrations to which the United States have been a party*, I (Washington, 1898), 653; British and Foreign State Papers, 62 (1871-2), 233; *U.S. Foreign Relations*, 1872, Pt. II, Papers relating to the Treaty of Washington of 1871, IV, 49 (42nd Cong. 3rd Sess., Ex. Doc. 1).

10. See J. B. Scott, *The Reports to the Hague Conferences of 1899 and 1907* (Oxford, 1917). The Tsar's initiative was not entirely disinterested. In the growing armaments race which preceded the outbreak of the First World War, Russia was lagging behind, and he was in danger of losing his own throne, and the Conferences were convened to promote peace and disarmament and to relieve international tension. In that objective they failed, but they did succeed in codifying a great deal of international law, including the law of international arbitration. See H. A. L. Fisher, *A History of Europe*, II (London, 1949), 1084; and V. Potiemkine, *Histoire de la Diplomatie*, II (Paris, 1946), 161. On the Permanent Court of Arbitration, see J. P. A. François in R.A.D.I., 87 (1955) (i), 460.

11. The codification of the rules of arbitral procedure which resulted from the Hague Conference has proved useful in practice, even for arbitration proceedings which were formally not conducted before a panel of the Permanent Court of Arbitration, and they are frequently incorporated in international arbitration treaties. A recent attempt by the International Law Commission of the United Nations to bring this branch of the law up to date was only partially successful. In 1958 the Commission submitted a set of Model Rules on Arbitral Procedure to the General Assembly. Yearbook of the International Law Commission, 1958, II, 83. By Resolution 1262 (XIII) of 14 November 1958, the General Assembly brought these articles to the attention of Member States for their consideration and use, in such cases and to such extent as they consider appropriate, in drawing up treaties of arbitration. An alternative method, quite common today, is to incorporate into arbitration treaties relevant rules from the practice of the International Court.

12. M. Hudson, *International Tribunals, Past and Future* (Washington, 1944), 7.

13. See H. Lauterpacht (editor), *Annual Digest and Reports of International Law Cases*, 16 vols. covering the period 1919-49, and his *International Law Reports*, annual since 1950, for reproductions of these awards. See also U.N., *Reports of International Arbitral Awards*, vols. 1-3 (New York, 1948-9) covering the period 1920-40, and vols. 9 ff (New York, 1959-) for awards rendered in the period 1902-20. The intervening volumes contain reports of a number of decisions of mixed claims commissions, not now otherwise easily available. For the Resolution of the Permanent Administrative Council of the Permanent Court of Arbitration of 3 March 1960, inviting new States to adhere to the First Hague Convention, see *American Journal of International Law*, 54 (1960), 933.

14. There is reason to believe that this type of constitution of an arbitration tribunal originated in Jewish private law. C. W. Jenks, *The Common Law of Mankind* (London, 1958), 99.

15. On international arbitration, see: A Mérignhac, *Traité théorique et pratique de l'arbitrage international* (Paris, 1895); J. H. Ralston, *The Law and Procedure of International Tribunals* (Stanford, 1926); J. C. Witenberg, *L'Organisation judiciaire, la procédure et la sentence internationales* (Paris, 1937); K. S. Carlston, *The Process of International Arbitration* (New York, 1946); M. Bos, *Les conditions du procès en droit international public* (Leyden, 1957); J. L. Simpson and H. Fox, *International Arbitration, Law and Practice* (London, 1959); U.N. Secretariat, *Memorandum on Arbitral Procedure*, doc. A/CN.4/35, Yearbook of the International Law Commission, 1950, II, 157; same, *Commentary on the draft Convention on Arbitral Procedure*, doc. A/CN.4/92 (New York, 1955). For general bibliography, see U.N. doc. A/CN.4/29, 20 June 1950.

Apart from the Permanent Court of Arbitration, mention must also be made, for the sake of completeness, of two other attempts to establish permanent international tribunals, both of which were unsuccessful, although their failure may have contributed to the later success of the Permanent Court of International Justice. The first was the attempt, also made at The Hague in 1907, to establish an International Prize Court to deal with claims by neutrals against belligerents arising out of the exercise of the right of prize at sea. Apart from difficulties inherent in the nature of the subject matter, the principal technical obstacle to the establishment of a permanent tribunal of this character lay in the inability to find a satisfactory procedure for electing the judges and guaranteeing their independence. The second was the Central American Court of Justice, established by the Treaty of Washington of 20 December 1907, between Costa Rica, Guatemala, Honduras, Nicaragua and El Salvador. This Court was in existence between 1908 and 1917, and dealt with a number of cases. It foundered, however, because of serious faults in its organization, including inadequate measures to assure the independence of its members, and in the definition of its jurisdiction, but above all it collapsed on the rock of political difficulties, including some which originated outside Central America.

16. These obligations were completed by Article 15 giving the Council competence for disputes which were not settled by arbitration or judicial settlement. After the adoption of the Statute of the Permanent Court of International Justice, the references to arbitration in the Covenant were changed to "arbitration or judicial settlement".

17. See *Documents presented to the Committee [of Jurists] relating to existing plans for the establishment of a Permanent Court of International Justice* (London, 1920); *Procès-Verbaux of the Proceedings of the Committee* (The Hague, 1920); *Documents concerning action taken by the Council of the League of Nations under Article 14 of the Covenant and the adoption by the Assembly of the Statute of the Permanent Court* (Geneva, 1921). See also N. Politis, *La Justice Internationale* (Paris, 1924). The leading treatise on the Permanent Court is M. Hudson, *The Permanent Court of International Justice, 1920-1942* (New York, 1943). This magisterial and definitive work—indispensable for an understanding of the Permanent Court—contains a full account of the drafting of the Covenant, the Statute and the Rules of Court, with complete references to all the documentation.

18. See the following cases: *S. S. Wimbledon*, A 1 (1923); *German Settlers in Poland*, B 6 (1923); *Acquisition of Polish Nationality*, B 7 (1923); *Polish Postal Service in Danzig*, B 11 (1925); *German Interests in Polish Upper Silesia*, A 6 (1925), A 7 (1926); *Factory at Chorzów*, A 9 (1927), A 12 (1927), A 13 (1927), A 17 (1928); *Jurisdiction of the Danzig Courts*, B 15 (1928); *Minority Schools in Upper Silesia*, A 15 (1928);

River Oder Commission, A 23 (1929); *Danzig and the International Labour Organization*, B 18 (1930); *German Minority Schools in Upper Silesia*, A/B 40 (1931); *Polish War Vessels in Danzig*, A/B 43 (1931); *Treatment of Polish Nationals in Danzig*, A/B 44 (1932); *Prince von Pless*, A/B 52 (1933), A/B 54 (1933), A/B 57 (1933), A/B 59 (1933); *Polish Agrarian Reform*, A/B 58 (1933), A/B 60 (1933); *Danzig Legislative Decrees*, A/B 65 (1935).

19. See the following cases: *Railway Traffic between Poland and Lithuania*, A/B 42 (1931); *Memel Statute*, A/B 47 (1932), A/B 49 (1932).

20. See the following cases: *Polish-Czechoslovakian Frontier (Jaworzina)*, B 8 (1923); *Monastery of Saint Naoum (Albanian Frontier)*, B 9 (1924); *Treaty of Neuilly (Art. 4)*, A 3 (1924), A 4 (1925); *European Commission of the Danube*, B 14 (1927); *Interpretation of Greco-Turkish Protocol of 1926*, B 16 (1928); *Greco-Bulgarian Communities*, B 17 (1930); *Interpretation of Greco-Bulgarian Agreement of 1927*, A/B 45 (1932); *Minority Schools in Albania*, A/B 64 (1935).

21. See the following cases: *Mavrommatis Palestine Concessions*, A 2 (1924), A 5 (1925), A 11 (1927); *Exchange of Greek and Turkish Populations*, B 10 (1925); *Frontier between Turkey and Iraq*, B 12 (1925); *Lighthouses*, A/B 62 (1934), A/B 71 (1937) (this dispute was finally settled only in 1956 by an arbitral award rendered through a Tribunal operating under the Hague Convention of 1907).

22. See the following cases: *Tunis and Morocco Nationality Decrees*, B 4 (1923); *Phosphates in Morocco*, A/B 74 (1938). For a case relating to commercial matters in the Congo, see *Oscar Chinn*, A/B 63 (1934).

23. The most significant instances of this are the *Lotus* and the *Borchgrave* cases. A 10 (1927) and A/B 72 and 73 (1937, 1938).

24. The *Eastern Carelia* case, B 5 (1923).

25. *Loc. cit.* in n. 12, 238.

26. The leading treatise on this aspect is Sir Hersch Lauterpacht, *The Development of International Law by the International Court* (London, 1958). For systematic presentation of the law as applied by the Court, see E. Hambro, *The Case Law of the International Court*, A repertoire of the judgments, advisory opinions and orders of the Permanent Court of International Justice and the International Court of Justice, I (Leyden, 1952), II (Leyden, 1960); V. Bruns (editor), *Fontes Juris Gentium*, Series A, Part I, vols. 1, 3-5, *Digest of the Decisions of the Permanent Court of International Justice and the International Court of Justice, 1922-58* (Berlin, 1931-61).

27. See e.g. Sh. Rosenne, "The International Law Commission, 1949-59", *British Year Book of International Law*, 36 (1960), 104.

28. For instance, the Socialist writers are highly critical of the law as applied by the Court, and to a large degree this criticism stems from the fact that the Marxist-Leninist concept of the role and nature of law is considerably different from that held by other political and social philosophies, and this of necessity leads to different scales of values for assessing the work of any court—including the International Court.

CHAPTER II

THE UNITED NATIONS AND THE COURT

ARTICLE 7 of the United Nations Charter establishes the principal organs of the United Nations. These include the General Assembly, the Security Council, the Economic and Social Council, the Trusteeship Council, the International Court of Justice and the Secretariat. Article 92 states that the Court shall be the principal judicial organ of the United Nations, and that it shall function in accordance with the annexed Statute, based upon the Statute of the Permanent Court, which forms an integral part of the Charter. Article 1 of the Statute repeats that the Court is established as the principal judicial organ of the United Nations, and that it shall function in accordance with the provisions of the Statute. These Articles contain—and emphasize—the general provisions setting forth the position of the Court within the Organization. The Charter also deals with the execution of the Court's decisions, and the General Assembly arranges for the payment of the Court's expenses.

The ambiguity characteristic of the relations between the League of Nations and the Permanent Court of International Justice has now been replaced by clarity. The Court is a principal organ of the United Nations and its Statute, no longer a separate international treaty, is an integral part of the Charter.

Let us briefly see how this has come about, and what are its implications.

THE WAR AND THE SAN FRANCISCO CONFERENCE (1945)

Whatever may have been the original intentions of its founders, the Permanent Court, in the course of its existence and in the light of its accumulated experience, came to discharge three distinct functions, two of them primary, and envisaged in its Statute, and the third, not originally contemplated, secondary. The outbreak of the War, of course, temporarily put an end to all these activities.

Its two primary tasks were, as mentioned in the previous chapter, to decide disputes between States, and to render advisory opinions in response to requests from the Council of the League (it could also render opinions at the request of the Assembly, but in fact the Assembly never made use of this right). The decisions were given independently of action by the League, whereas the advisory opinions represented the Permanent Court's participation in the political activities of the League, and waxed and waned in sympathy with the political fortunes of the League.

Its third function, much less known, was quite different. It was to nominate umpires, presidents of arbitral commissions and of other tribunals, and similar offices. Normally these appointments were made by the President of the Court at the request of a State, but occasionally the whole Court might be consulted, and on the first occasion, as far back as 1923, the whole Court gave its approval. This has come to be known as the "extra-judicial activity" of the Court, since it is not mentioned in the Statute, and no firm rules have been promulgated to regulate the manner of its performance. It meets several international requirements. For instance, it provides a simple way of overcoming difficulties in States' agreeing on the identity of a third arbitrator, which might lead to the frustration of an agreement for arbitration. It also forms the basis for a special arbitration procedure incorporated in certain types of agreements, especially agreements on important economic matters, in which one of the parties is not a State, and therefore cannot have access to the Court itself (which is only competent in disputes between States). International practice has shown that there is need for a form of arbitration in which the President of the Tribunal can be appointed by an independent and respected international official such as the President of the International Court. This is in order to meet the gap between the area of public law and the area of private law, and to place governments and entities which are not governments on some sort of equal basis in the procedural sense. One of the best-known transactions of this type was the Anglo-Iranian Oil Company's Concession Agreement of 1933 (which later, in 1951, came up before the new Court in international litigation proper), which had been negotiated through the good offices of the Council of the League.

The question which arose during the Second World War was whether there was still use for an international judicial organ performing all or some of these functions and, if so, was an instrument fashioned on the lines of the Statute of the Permanent Court satisfactory for these purposes.

After thorough examination both on the technical and professional level, and on the highest political level, an affirmative answer was given to those questions. There was apparently little disposition, at least among the Western Allies, to doubt the necessity for an international organ resembling the Permanent Court. The real

problem which faced them appears as one of method, but underlying the question of method were important political issues. The
problem of method was posed as whether to continue the Permanent
Court in existence with necessary changes in its Statute, or whether
to re-organize the international judicial system and make it an
integral part of the general international political organization
which would be set up after the War was won. The political problems for which this was the procedural manifestation were of two
kinds. The first, and the more important, related to the attitude
towards the future international judicial organ of those members
of the Anti-Nazi coalition, above all the Soviet Union and the
United States, which between the Wars had stood aloof from both
the League and the Permanent Court. The second, which, it seems
in retrospect, may have been given undue prominence, related to
the position of the Axis Powers which, on the contrary, having
participated in the work of the Permanent Court would, as parties
to its Statute, technically have a say in its future—this included *all*
the Axis Powers. These problems themselves were both closely
connected with the changes in the pattern of international relationships which began emerging during the War, and which were given
their first formal recognition in the differences between the major
political alignments of the United Nations in comparison with those
of the League (substitution of the Soviet Union and the United
States for Great Britain and France as the major political influences
in the Organization).

Interest in the future of the Court as a matter of immediate
political concern began to revive about the middle of 1942 when
both the British and the United States Governments on the one
hand, and the South American Governments (through the Inter-
American Juridical Committee) on the other, expressed approval
in principle for the resumption of the machinery of international
judicial activities after the War. The four leading Allied Powers,
China, the Soviet Union, the United Kingdom and the United
States, in the Moscow Declaration of 30 October 1943 on General
Security, recognized the necessity of establishing a general international organization for the maintenance of international peace
and security, though nothing was said publicly at that stage
about the Court. A little earlier, in May, the British Government took its first concrete steps, by calling together an informal inter-Allied Committee of some twelve experienced international lawyers from among those who were available in London.
These were asked to prepare an informal report which would not
be binding on their governments, but which could be of use to the
authorities in due course. The report which the Committee pres-

ented early in 1944 is the first comprehensive re-examination of
the issues connected with the Court that had taken place since the
outbreak of the War, and in the history of international adjudication it is an important document. The Committee, which did not
question the necessity for *a* Court, reached the conclusion that the
Permanent Court had on the whole worked well, and that its
Statute could be retained as the basis for the general structure of
the future Court. It did not think that the Court should be reconstituted as an integral part of any future international organization. In the Committee's view, it was preferable to retain the
Court as an independent international organism, but one always
standing at the disposal of the Organization. It also found that the
policy issues involved in the question whether to maintain the Permanent Court in existence as such, or whether to establish an entirely new Court, were outside its province.[1]

In October, 1944, matters were carried a stage further, when the
same four Governments, now called the Sponsoring Powers, con-
cretized their ideas on the future general political organization and
published them in the so-called Dumbarton Oaks Proposals for the
United Nations.[2] Included in these was definite recognition that
the International Court should be the principal judicial organ of
the Organization, that all members of the United Nations should
ipso facto be parties to the Statute of the Court, which would form
part of the Charter, and that non-members could become parties
to the Statute on conditions to be laid down by the General Assembly upon the recommendation of the Security Council. But on the
vexed question of whether to keep the Permanent Court in existence
or to create a new Court, and whether, in the latter event, the
Statute of the Permanent Court could still serve as a basis, the
Dumbarton Oaks Proposals were non-committal, though preference
was expressed for keeping to the general lines of the old Statute.

It was by now clear that further work of a technical nature was
required before the political conference, due to meet in San Francisco in April, 1945, and at which the Charter was to be finally
drafted, could profitably take the matter up. Both the Informal
Inter-Allied Committee and the Dumbarton Oaks Proposals made
it plain that comprehensive re-examination of the terms of the
Statute was needed, despite their clear preference for making as
few changes as possible. Accordingly, the four Sponsoring Powers
decided to convene a full Committee of Jurists in Washington, at
which all the United Nations could participate, to prepare the
ground for the San Francisco Conference. Forty-four States took
part in the work of this Committee, at which the Permanent Court
was also represented. It decided to retain the existing Statute,

amending it slightly, and at the end of its labours it left three major questions open: *(a)* the form in which to state the Court's mission as the principal judicial organ of the new Organization; *(b)* how to conduct the elections of the judges; and *(c)* to what extent should the jurisdiction of the Court be compulsory. Politically, this latter had now become the most significant issue, because behind it lay the more fundamental problem of whether recognition of the compulsory jurisdiction of the Court for all or certain disputes should be the condition *sine qua non* of membership in the United Nations. Such a question had not arisen, and could not arise, for the League of Nations so long as the Court was not one of its organs and the members of the League not *ipso facto* parties to its Statute.[3]

In this form the question came before the San Francisco Conference itself, where it was discussed in detail in Committee IV/1.[4] In these discussions—in which again the Permanent Court was represented by two of its Judges—it became clear that while a majority of the smaller and medium powers were in favour of making some acceptance of the compulsory jurisdiction of the Court a condition for membership in the United Nations, the major Powers, on whom the prime responsibility for maintaining the Organization would rest, and especially the Soviet Union and the United States, were not prepared to accept so far-reaching an innovation in international practice. Therefore the underlying basis on which the Permanent Court had worked, that the consent of the States concerned gives it jurisdiction to deal with a concrete case, was retained. With this out of the way there was little real difficulty in establishing the Court as a principal organ and the principal judicial organ of the United Nations, or in deciding to create in effect a new Court for this purpose. However, the relevant provisions of the Statute were drafted in such a way as to convey that this decision would not break the chain of continuity with the past and not undo the achievements attained in the field of international justice. Therefore, in some respects the new Court, called the International Court of Justice, may be regarded as the successor of the Permanent Court, even though the United Nations as a whole is not the successor of the League. The Statute emerged from this process but slightly revised, as is apparent from Article 92 of the Charter quoted above.

After the necessary administrative steps were taken by the Preparatory Commission of the United Nations, the judges of the new Court were elected in the early meetings of the Security Council and the General Assembly in February, 1946. At the same time parallel measures for the dissolution of the Permanent Court were put in hand. On 18 April, the new Court held its solemn inaugural meeting in the presence of a distinguished gathering at The Hague. On the same day, at Geneva, the League Assembly voted itself, and the Permanent Court, out of existence.

But over a year was to elapse before the first case was to be filed in the new Court, a marked contrast to what had happened when the Permanent Court was set up in 1922. What did this portend? The answer will appear from the following chapters.

PRINCIPAL ORGAN OF THE UNITED NATIONS

Apart from Articles 7 and 92 of the Charter, Article 93 gives reality to the integration of the Court in the Organization by providing, as had been proposed at Dumbarton Oaks, that all members of the United Nations are *ipso facto* parties to the Statute, to which non-members may become parties on conditions to be determined in each case by the General Assembly upon the recommendation of the Security Council. The underlying assumption is that the world political organization, already possessed of executive, deliberative and administrative organs, would be incomplete unless it possessed a fully integrated judicial organ of its own. The San Francisco records show clearly that the intention was in this way to place the Court in a position in which it could play an important role, alongside the other organs, in the new organization of nations for peace and security. The idea in making the Statute an integral part of the Charter was to secure for the Court the support of all the members. Furthermore, these provisions put an end to the anomalous situation which had existed in the structure of the League, where the international judicial community was something distinct, at least in theory, from the general political organization of the international community. This was a radical innovation made by the founders of the United Nations in 1945, and its import must not be obscured by their conservatism both in matters of form, and in the concept of the underlying basis for international litigation as it had developed during the preceding century.

What are the implications of this?

The Court, as an organ of the United Nations, operates within the framework of the general objectives which the Charter lays down for the Organization as a whole, and for its individual organs. The Court's status as a principal organ imposes on it the duty of participating in the work of the Organization on an equal footing with its other organs. This was vividly expressed by one of the judges who said that the Court, "which has been raised to the status of a principal organ, and thus more closely geared into the mechanism

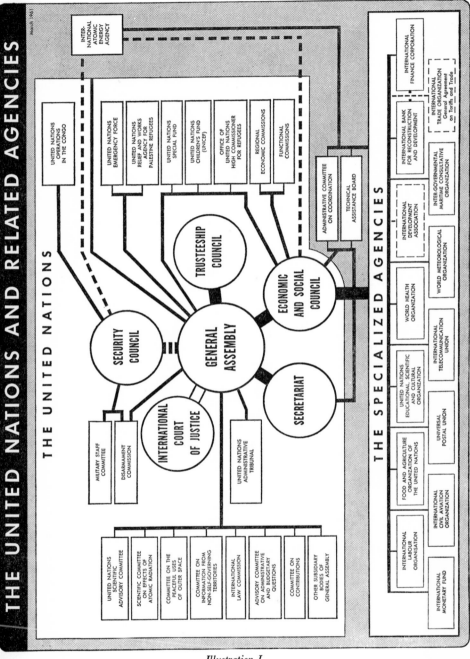

Illustration I

The United Nations and related agencies

of the U.N.O., must do its utmost to co-operate with the other organs with a view to attaining the aims and principles that have been set forth."[5] This principle of *co-operation* has been enunciated and acted upon by the Court in several different types of circumstances, but particularly as a ground for rejecting challenges to its competence to render advisory opinions. At the same time, recalling that it is not only a principal organ (Article 7) but also the principal *judicial* organ (Article 92), the Court has been insistent on maintaining one general qualification regarding this duty of co-operation. It will not co-operate with the other organs blindly, but only if it is fully satisfied that what it is being asked to do is, in the circumstances, fully compatible with its judicial character.[6] Its judicial character must be preserved at all costs. This, too, has particularly influenced its advisory competence, which, in the letter of the law, is discretionary: the Court has repeatedly stressed that in principle it should not refuse to give an opinion unless overriding considerations of judicial propriety make this imperative.[7]

The Court's status as the judicial organ also has consequences for the political organs when they have to take decisions relating to the Court. The influence of this is felt both in administrative aspects and in political aspects.

To take the first aspect, when, for instance, the Security Council has had to deal with the question of the access to the Court of States which are not members of the United Nations, the view prevailed that as the Court was a judicial organ and in consequence a non-political body, therefore the question of access to it ought not to be influenced by irrelevant political considerations.[8] To take another administrative example: When, in 1959, the General Assembly had to examine certain matters relating to the Judges' pensions, its Legal Committee insisted that full weight should be attached to the circumstance of their election and the character and requirements of the office of Judge as expressed in the Statute, and this view prevailed over a less constructive attitude of the General Assembly's Administrative and Budgetary Committee, approaching the matter exclusively from an administrative standpoint.[9]

From the point of view of substantive political activities, the fact that the political organs of the United Nations tend to make a sharp distinction between political problems and legal problems—there are some who say that at times too sharp a distinction is drawn— furnishes an explanation for the phenomenon that, unlike the League's practice, Court procedures have not been invoked by the Security Council or the General Assembly to assist them in the course of their handling of concrete political disputes. On the other hand, care has always been taken by the General Assembly, on receipt of advisory opinions, not to adopt operational decisions which could be taken to cast doubts upon the authority of the Court.

The fact that the Court is one of several principal organs means that it exists on a par with them, being neither in a position of inferiority nor in one of superiority. Consequently, it does not exist as a general "constitutional Court" of the United Nations. There is no duty on anybody to seek its opinion on the legal issues when questions of the meaning of the Charter arise. In fact, it was decided at the San Francisco Conference that each organ of the United Nations would be free itself to interpret the Charter as and when circumstances require. This does not *prevent* the Court from giving its opinion on these matters when it is asked to do so in due form. This has been applied in practice in two ways. Thus, when the President of the Security Council, the representative of the Ukraine, once explained that the Court could not be regarded as a kind of court of appeal from the decisions of the General Assembly or the Security Council, no member of the Council dissented.[10] On the other hand, the General Assembly has occasionally sought the advice of the Court on the constitutionality of action it has already decided to take, or which it is proposing to take, and has acted on the advice received.[11] Against this may be set the complicated developments in the South-West Africa situation (see p. 150 below). This case is now simultaneously on the agenda of both the General Assembly and the Court in a contentious case, and it indicates that in very special circumstances the General Assembly will not permit the fact that a case is *sub judice* in the International Court to prevent it from exercising its own responsibilities under the Charter. But this is a controversial matter, on which the last word has not yet been said.

Generally speaking it can be asserted, then, that the other organs have shown awareness that the special character of the Court imposes on them an attitude of caution towards the Court, and obliges them not to embroil it directly in issues in which the political aspects in truth predominate. Perhaps this attitude was not fully held in the early years of the United Nations, before it had become clear that judicial techniques could not advance the solution of truly political problems. However, it is now increasingly realized that, in the words of a Staff Study prepared for the United States Senate in 1955, "a judicial determination of a dispute comprised primarily of political facets may not contribute to a solution of the underlying problem. This leads to the conclusion that it is much more realistic to allow political considerations full sway."[12]

The fact that the Court is the principal judicial organ means that it is the only judicial organ directly established by the Charter,

but this does not mean that it is the only judicial organ that may
be established either by the United Nations as an organization, or
by its individual members. Article 33 of the Charter, which e-
numerates the various methods for the pacific settlement of international disputes, includes arbitration, judicial settlement, or other
peaceful means of the parties' own choice: the principle that the
parties are free to choose their own methods of peaceful settlement
is firmly enshrined. Parallel to this is Article 95 of the Charter
which spells out that nothing in the Charter shall prevent the
members from entrusting the solution of their differences to other
tribunals by virtue of agreements already in existence or which may
be concluded in the future. In fact the United Nations has been
instrumental in establishing other tribunals including, for example,
the United Nations Tribunal in Libya, the powers and functions
of which were later transferred to the Italian-Libyan Mixed Arbitration Commission. Mention here may also be made of the
United Nations Administrative Tribunal established for the express
purpose of adjudicating disputes between members of the Secretariat and the Organization, arising out of their contracts of service.

The position of the Court, as the principal judicial organ of the
United Nations, can therefore be briefly summarized. Within the
framework of this highly political organization the Court, although
an integral part of the Organization, stands in a special, and somewhat apart, position, as is indeed appropriate for a court of justice.
It is not composed of the representatives of States. It reacts to the
initiatives of States and other organs in a spirit of co-operation,
but has no power of initiating action itself. The political organs,
for their part, and the States represented on them, have on the
whole evinced care not to allow completely extraneous political
factors to influence decisions which they have been called upon to
make in relation to the Court. They have equally, on the whole,
tried not to embroil the Court in the intractable political problems
which face them daily.

In so far as prior to the San Francisco Conference some anxiety
was expressed lest too close an association of the Court with the
Organization might impair its standing and its ability to perform
its judicial functions dispassionately, it can fairly be said that
nothing has occurred since to justify apprehensions of that nature.
This does not mean, however, that world political trends, themselves reflected in the United Nations, have left the Court unaffected, but that is another matter.

THE COURT AND THE SPECIALIZED AGENCIES

The United Nations does not exist alone in the world of the organized international community. It stands in the centre of a complicated system of international organizations, established by inter-governmental agreement and having wide international responsibilities in economic, social, cultural, educational, health and related fields. The Charter makes it possible for these organizations to be brought into formal relationship with the United Nations by means of agreements, called "Relationship Agreements", to be approved by the General Assembly. These are called Specialized Agencies, and they form part of the United Nations family. They today include the International Labour Organization (I.L.O.), the Food and Agriculture Organization (F.A.O.), the United Nations Educational, Scientific and Cultural Organization (UNESCO), the International Civil Aviation Organization (I.C.A.O.), the World Health Organization (W.H.O.), the International Bank for Reconstruction and Development (I.B.R.D.), the International Monetary Fund (I.M.F.), the International Finance Corporation (I.F.C.), the Universal Postal Union (U.P.U.), the International Telecommunication Union (I.T.U.), the World Meteorological Organization (W.M.O.), the Intergovernmental Maritime Consultative Organization (I.M.C.O.), the International Development Association (I.D.A.) and, for some purposes, the International Atomic Energy Agency (I.A.E.A.). Most members of the United Nations are members of most of these Specialized Agencies which, while being autonomous and independent organizations, are at the same time subject to certain overriding controls of the United Nations itself. One of the matters which the United Nations controls, through the General Assembly, is their relations with the Court.

The International Court, as the principal judicial organ of the United Nations, also serves these organizations in a similar capacity. The ties between the Court and the Specialized Agencies are regulated in the Relationship Agreements.[13] The contacts between the Court and these Agencies are spread over three dimensions.

Firstly, most of the constitutions of the Specialized Agencies, unlike the Charter of the United Nations itself, contain a provision to the effect that disputes between members arising out of the application or interpretation of the Constitution may be referred to the Court. This, in fact, is a normal compromissory clause, and provides the basis for contentious litigation. No instance of this has occurred yet.

Secondly, Article 34 of the Statute of the Court empowers the Court to request public international organizations (whether or not Specialized Agencies in the technical sense), to furnish it with information relevant to cases before it. The Relationship Agreements contain undertakings by the Specialized Agencies to furnish information so requested.[14] The Court has occasionally made use of this facility, not limiting its approaches only to Specialized Agencies, and of course the Organizations approached have all furnished replies. These include the International Labour Organization and the Organization of American States.

Thirdly, Article 96 (2) of the Charter, which deals with the right to request advisory opinions, empowers the General Assembly to authorize the Specialized Agencies to request advisory opinions on legal questions arising within the scope of their activities. All the Specialized Agencies, with the exception of the Universal Postal Union (which has an internal system for settling legal disputes), are now authorized to request advisory opinions, the Relationship Agreements specifying which organs of the Specialized Agencies may initiate the request. This authorization does not extend to questions concerning the mutual relationships of the United Nations and the Specialized Agencies, an aspect left to the exclusive competence of the Economic and Social Council in exercise of its general role of supervisor and co-ordinator of the Specialized Agencies: moreover, whenever any Specialized Agency decides to request an advisory opinion, it has to inform the Economic and Social Council of its action.

Contrary to early expectations, this has not led to any marked increase in the judicial business of the Court. Only two Specialized Agencies have availed themselves of their right to request advisory opinions, UNESCO and the International Maritime Consultative Organization.[15] As can be expected, in dealing with these request the Court has followed the same principles that it enunciated in relation to the United Nations itself: in particular it has reasserted its duty to co-operate in the activities of the organizations concerned while preserving the strictly judicial character of its own actions.

It is therefore appropriate to regard the Court not merely as the principal judicial organ of the United Nations but as the principal judicial organ of the Specialized Agencies, indeed of the whole United Nations structure.

EXECUTION OF THE COURT'S DECISIONS

As has been seen in the previous chapter, the international arbitral procedure of the nineteenth century came as a matter of course to include in every arbitration agreement an implied obligation that the decisions of the arbitral tribunal would be executed in good faith. This is also a fundamental principle of the law governing international litigation before the International Court. When the international community was not organized on the political level, no ready-made machinery existed, or indeed could exist, for compelling a recalcitrant party to comply with the terms of an award which it did not like. But when the League of Nations was established, opportunity was taken to insert in Article 13 of the Covenant a stipulation to the effect that in the event of failure to carry out a decision of the Permanent Court, the Council should be empowered to propose what steps should be taken to give effect to it. Instances of this were very rare, and in fact the problem of the execution and enforcement of the decisions of the Permanent Court did not appear to be a serious one. Since the jurisdiction of the Court was based on the consent of the parties, it may be assumed that they consent in advance to carry out the judgment.

These ideas have been taken over into the Charter of the United Nations.

The basic principle, that the decison of the Court is binding, final and without appeal, is enunciated in Article 59 of the Statute, and that is because it relates to the functioning of the Court as such. This is supplemented by two important provisions which, having broader political implications, are contained in the Charter.

The first is found in the first paragraph of Article 94, which lays down shortly and simply: "Each Member of the United Nations undertakes to comply with the decision of the International Court of Justice in any case to which it is a party". States which are not members of the United Nations but which become parties to the Statute of the Court, and States which are not parties to the Statute of the Court but which are parties to litigation before the Court, have to give a corresponding undertaking before they are admitted to the Court.

The second appears in paragraph two of that Article: "If any party to a case fails to perform the obligations incumbent upon it under a judgment rendered by the Court, the other party may have recourse to the Security Council, which may, if it deems necessary, make recommendations or decide upon measures to be taken to give effect to the judgment." The underlying implication of this provision is that if failure to comply with a decision of the Court creates a new political problem, the Security Council is given wide powers to deal with the resultant situation. This type of situation would not be unlike that which a few years ago confronted the Federal authorities in Little Rock.

Although the damages awarded to the United Kingdom against

Albania in the *Corfu Channel* case (£ 843,947) have not been paid over—the only instance, so far as is known, of complete failure to comply with a judgment of the Court—the competence of the Security Council has not yet ever been invoked in order to secure compliance with a judgment. On the other hand it was invoked, in 1951, by the United Kingdom in an attempt to secure compliance by Iran with the interim measures of protection (the international term for interim injunction) indicated by the Court, in the early stages of the Anglo-Iranian dispute, in order to preserve the object of the litigation pending its outcome. However, the Security Council showed little enthusiasm for this procedure, which led to no concrete result.[16] In fact, the efficacy of this provision depends upon the general ability of the Security Council to carry out its responsibilities for the maintenance of international peace. That, in turn, depends upon the unanimity of the five Permanent Members. Their inability to reach agreement on major political issues is the fundamental reason for the failure of the Security Council to face up to the challenge which was presented to it by the United Kingdom in 1951.

<h2 style="text-align:center">THE COURT'S FINANCES</h2>

The expenses of the Court are borne by the United Nations in such manner as the General Assembly decides.[17] These expenses include, besides the normal running costs of the institution, the salaries of its members and staff, and their pensions.

The estimate of expenditure is included in the annual budget approved each year by the General Assembly (by a majority of two thirds), after detailed scrutiny by the Advisory Committee on Administrative and Budgetary Questions, and the Fifth (Administrative and Budgetary) Committee of the General Assembly. Frequently a member of the Registry Staff is in attendance in order to furnish any necessary explanations. The Court's accounts are also submitted to external audit in accordance with the normal United Nations financial and accounting procedures, and ultimately approved by the General Assembly.

The members of the Court are each entitled to an annual salary of $25,000. On top of this, the President receives a special annual allowance of $6,000, and the Vice-President when acting as President $37.50 *per diem* up to a maximum of $3,750 *per annum*. For judges *ad hoc* a special allowance of $45 *per diem* is paid. In addition, travel and subsistence allowances are payable in accordance with the appropriate regulations.[18] The Registrar receives a salary equivalent to that of an Under-Secretary in the United Nations Secretariat, and the members of the Registry staff are graded according to the grades in force in the Secretariat.

The Judges' retirement pensions, which were revised in 1960, provide for a pension which, for a judge who has served for a term of nine years, is fixed at $10,000 and which increases by a fixed rate for longer service up to a maximum not exceeding two-thirds of his annual salary. For judges who have served for less than nine years the pension is reduced.[19] The pensions of the Registrar and the Registry Staff are payable out of the United Nations Joint Staff Pension Fund.

Income attributable to the Court includes contributions to its expenses by States not members of the United Nations, income arising from the application of Staff Assessment under the United Nations Tax Equalization Scheme, applicable to the Registry staff, and introduced in 1949 to take the place of national income taxes in cases where United Nations salaries are tax free, income arising from sale of publications and other miscellaneous sources. States which are parties to the Statute but which are not members of the United Nations are assessed by the United Nations procedures (through the Committee on Contributions and the General Assembly), and pay a fixed percentage of the Court's annual expenses. States which are not parties to the Statute, but which are involved in contentious litigation before the Court, are assessed by the Court which applies the same principles, but on a *pro rata* basis for the Court's expenses in the period during which the case was before it.

The present arrangements for financing the Court are an improvement on those used for financing the Permanent Court, when difficulties arose in collecting the contributions due from States which, being parties to the Statute, were not members of the League.

In the period 1946-1960 the total audited expenses of the United Nations were given as $709,374,998.00, of which those incurred on behalf of the Court (the only organ of the United Nations which is accounted for separately in the Financial Reports) amounted to $9,051,309.00 or about 1.3%. In the same period the income attributable to the Court is placed at $371,520.00 (for details, see Table I on p. 47).

NOTES

1. For the Report of the Informal Inter-Allied Committee, see British Parliamentary Paper, Cmd. 6531 (1944). It was also republished in *American Journal of International Law*, 39 (1945), Supplement section of documents, 1.

2. For the Dumbarton Oaks proposals (which take their name from the estate in Washington, D.C., in which the Conference was held at which they were

finally drafted), see Documents of the United Nations Conference on International Organization (abbreviated U.N.C.I.O.), vol. 3.

3. For the records of the Washington Committee of Jurists, which was in session between 9-20 April 1945, see U.N.C.I.O., vol. 14. A selection of documents illustrating the work of this Committee is contained in *The International Court of Justice, Selected Documents relating to the Drafting of the Statute* (Washington, 1946), Department of State, Publication 2491, Conference Series 84.

4. For the records of Committee IV/1 see U.N.C.I.O., vol. 13. And see *The United Nations Conference on International Organization,* selected documents (Washington, 1946), Department of State, Publication 2490, Conference Series 83. For a comprehensive index to the proceedings of the San Francisco Conference, see U.N.C.I.O., vol. 21.

5. Judge Azevedo, Rep. 1950, at 82.

6. For judicial discussion of this inter-action between Article 7 and Article 92 of the Charter, see particularly in the *Interpretation of the Peace Treaties* case. Rep. 1950, 65 at 71-2.

7. Ibid. Repeated in the *Genocide Convention* case, Rep. 1951, 15 at 19.

8. See discussion in the 76th meeting of the Security Council on 15 October 1946. Off. Rec. 1st yr. 2nd series, No. 19, 466 ff.

9. Doc. A/C.6/L.454, G.A. O.R. 14th session, annexes, agenda item 63.

10. 338th meeting, 15 July 1948.

11. Instances are the *South-West Africa Voting Procedure,* Rep. 1955, 67; the *Grant of Hearings to Oral Petitioners on South-West Africa,* Rep. 1956, 23; and the *Constitution of the Maritime Safety Committee of I.M.C.O.* case, Rep. 1960, 150. Nevertheless, the conception of requiring the Court as a matter of course to adjudicate upon the constitutionality of action by the General Assembly or the Security Council is not widely held. It would probably not be suitable for the expeditious conduct of international affairs nor is it likely to assist in preserving the independence of the Court.

12. Review of the United Nations Charter. Staff Studies prepared for the use of the Subcommittee on the United Nations Charter of the Committee on Foreign Relations. 83rd Congress, 2nd Session, Senate Document No. 164 (Washington, 1955), 223 at 236.

13. The texts of most of the Relationship Agreements can be found in *Agreements between the United Nations and the Specialized Agencies,* doc. ST/SG/1 (New York, 1952).

14. This undertaking does not appear in the Relationship Agreements with the international financial organizations, or in that with the Universal Postal Union.

15. *Judgments of the Administrative Tribunal of the I.L.O. upon complaints made against UNESCO* case, Rep. 1956, 77; *Constitution of the Maritime Safety Committee of I.M.C.O.* case.

16. S.C. O.R. 6th yr., 559th-563rd and 565th meetings, 1-19 October 1951.

17. Statute, Article 33.

18. Statute, Article 32. And see General Assembly Resolution 1738 (XVI) of 20 December 1961. These salaries and allowances are free of all taxation. In December, 1961, the General Assembly decided to increase the previous emolumenst by 25%.

19. General Assembly Resolution 1562 (XV) of 18 December 1960.

TABLE I

THE COURT'S FINANCES

Year	Court's Annual Audited Expenses	Court's Annual Income	U.N's Annual Audited Expenses
	$	$	$
1946	423,983		19,330,287
1947	525,554		27,290,241
1948	596,658		38,387,531
1949	588,512	1,950	42,575,368
1950	590,544	29,282	43,746,264
1951	596,540	34,217	48,628,383
1952	627,116	32,206	50,270,153
1953	585,537	27,022	49,292,552
1954	557,656	27,865	48,510,009
1955	594,463	24,638	50,089,808
1956	582,041	27,106	50,508,095
1957	642,948	36,145	53,172,964
1958	674,966	41,723	60,848,555
1959	732,584	42,146	61,460,607
1960	732,207	47,220	65,264,181
TOTAL	9,051,309	371,520	709,374,998

Sources: Columns one and three are taken from the Annual Financial Reports and Accounts and Reports of the Board of Auditors Submitted to the General Assembly, and published in its Official Records. Column two is taken from the Court's Yearbooks.

Note. From 1950 the Court's income includes amounts attributed to it through operation of Staff Assessment under the Tax Equalization Scheme.

CHAPTER III

THE JUDGES

In the previous chapters we have attempted to describe the growth of the idea of international adjudication and the place of the International Court as an institution among the organs existing for the settlement of international disputes by peaceful means. Let us now turn to the Court itself. Who are the men in whose hands is confided the power to decide international legal disputes? How do they reach their position?

The Court consists of fifteen judges, each of a different nationality, elected independently by the Security Council and the General Assembly. They serve for a term of nine years (commencing from 6 February following their election) and are eligible for re-election. One third of their number retires each three years. Occasional vacancies in their ranks, caused for example by the death or resignation of a Judge, are filled in the same way, a person elected at an occasional election taking office immediately and serving only for the unexpired portion of his predecessor's term. The process by which these elections are conducted is complex, and unavoidably so.

THE JUDGES' QUALIFICATIONS

All political societies face a delicate problem when they come to determine how their judges are appointed. The international society is no exception. The natural aspiration of those having power to appoint judges in whom they have confidence, persons sympathetic to their political and social aims and ideals, is not always reconciled with equally natural desires for an independent judiciary (though it must not be assumed that there is an unbridgeable gulf between the two); and conflicts between those having political power and the judiciary are always painful episodes. In Western legal systems this type of problem is largely overcome by a tradition of good faith coupled with a delicately balanced system of checks and counter-checks in which the representative political institutions (the Parliaments) usually have a say. But ultimately, in most countries, the responsibility for the appointment of the judges rests with the executive branch of the government. The difficulty in the international field is that international political life is conducted on an entirely different basis, and there is no executive as such responsible to an electorate for the proper conduct of its affairs. In the last resort the choice of the international judge is, as is the choice of a domestic judge, a political operation, in which the attempt has been made to impose some limitations on the free play of political aspirations. But in international affairs the nature of that political operation is fundamentally different from what it is in the domestic arena.

These differences are reflected in the provisions of the Court's Statute regarding the qualifications of the judges.

These qualifications are of two distinct kinds—those of a personal character and those of a more general character.

The requirements of a personal character are set forth in Article 2, by which the Court shall be composed of a body of independent judges elected regardless of their nationality from among persons of high moral character, who possess the qualifications required in their respective countries for appointment to the highest judicial offices, or are jurisconsults of recognized competence in international law.

There is no international machinery for ascertaining that the candidates possess these qualifications in fact, although, as we shall see, certain safeguards have been inserted into the Statute and others have been developed in international practice in order to maintain the high standards of professional competence required of the judges. This aspect is left to the good sense of the individual States. Most of them have an interest in seeing that the Court is composed of highly qualified persons and that the reputation of the Court as a whole should remain high. That interest does not only derive from the possibility, however slight it may be as a matter of political reality (keeping in mind that the Court can only decide cases when the parties consent that it should, as will be described in the next chapter), that they themselves may become involved in litigation before the Court, whether as plaintiffs or as defendants. It is also connected with the natural desire of all States that authoritative pronouncements on questions of international law should be made by as "strong" a Court as it is possible to create.

REGIONAL DISTRIBUTION OF SEATS

The more general requirement appears in Article 9 of the Statute, by which, at every election, the electors are directed to bear in mind not only that the persons to be elected should individually possess the qualifications required, but also that "in the body as a whole the representation of the main forms of civilization and of the principal legal systems of the world should be assured." That requirement introduces the political factor into the composition of the Court.

That formula itself is a refined version of the cruder principle of "equitable geographical distribution" which the Charter lays down as the governing principle for the allocation of elective seats in most of the organs of the United Nations. The formula has been in common use since 1920 for the international legal organs, and is found, for example, also in the Statute of the International Law Commission. Both these formulas rather assume that the world is neatly divided into a number of clearly defined regions and forms of civilization (the division itself being both comprehensive and static), each of which has competent organs capable of negotiating with its partners. But the realities of the international situation are quite different, and the assumption has little justification. In practice, two sets of problems beset the elections of the judges. The first concerns the manner in which the places on the Court will be allocated *to* the main forms of civilization and the principal legal systems of the world; and the second concerns the manner in which, after the primary allocation has been made, the positions will be shared *within* the main forms of civilization and the principal legal systems of the world. This latter aspect obliquely introduces the factor of the nationality of the individual candidates.

These problems are resolved partly by a series of "understandings" which have either been negotiated diplomatically or which have emerged *de facto* in the United Nations: but in the last resort, if real contest ensues, the answer can only be given through a trial of political strength in the electing organs. These understandings are essential both for the successful functioning of the Court, and for the smooth conduct of the elections. The membership of the Court must reflect the international community as it is, and not in an idealized form.

The first of these understandings apparently is that each one of the five permanent members of the Security Council—China, France, the Soviet Union, the United Kingdom and the United States of America—may always have a judge of its nationality on the Court.[1] This is the modern form of the answer to the demand of the Great Powers for presence on any permanent international judicial organ—one aspect which the Hague Conference of 1907 was unable to solve in the absence of an organized international political community, and which was only solved, along approxi-

TABLE II

DISTRIBUTION OF SEATS BY CONTINENTS

	1922	1931	1946	1952	1955	1958	1961
Africa			1	1	1	1	1
America (N.)	1	1	2	2	2	1	1
America (S.)	2	3	4	4	4	4	4
Asia	2	2	1	2	2	2	2
Australasia						1	1
Europe	10	9	7	6	6	6	6
	15	15	15	15	15	15	15

mately similar lines, by the League of Nations. The first serious challenge to this principle was in 1956, when a Japanese candidate offered stiff competition to one of Chinese nationality, but ultimately the traditional arrangement prevailed.

The existence of this tradition means that in fact only ten seats are available for distribution among the rest of the world. When the United Nations was first established, it had 51 members: today there are 110 members together with three other States which are parties to the Statute without being members of the United Nations. Competition for the remaining places on the Court has therefore become progressively keener.

Little in the way of overt understanding regarding the distribution of these ten seats is apparent, and it is likely that such understandings as may once have existed are unable to withstand the new pressures which built up after the first large-scale admission of new members in 1955, and the second large-scale admission of new members in 1960. Following those events, the relative strength of the different groupings inside the United Nations has altered radically. It is possible to see in the results of the initial election of 1946 a reflection of an inter-regional understanding. Adopting the customary United Nations nomenclature, that election gave the following regional distribution: Afro-Asia, 1; Western Europe, 2; Eastern Europe, 2; Latin America, 4; British Commonwealth (British territories), 1. The distribution lasted until 1951 when, after a bitter fight (in which one of the most experienced members of the Court was not re-elected), Western Europe lost one of its seats to the Afro-Asian group. That distribution lasted until 1957, when Western Europe was able to regain its seat at the expense of the East European seat held by a judge of Yugoslavian nationality. These changes are further illustrated by Tables II-V which show respectively the distribution of seats by continents (since 1922), by regional groups (since 1946), by reference to the principal legal

TABLE III

DISTRIBUTION OF SEATS BY REGIONAL GROUPS

(*Excluding Permanent Members of Security Council*)

	1946	1952	1955	1958	1961
Afro-Asia	1	2	2	2	2
W. Europe	2	1	1	2	2
E. Europe	2	2	2	1	1
Lat. America	4	4	4	4	4
Br. Com.	1	1	1	1	1
	10	10	10	10	10

systems of the world (since 1922)—that is this author's subjective attempt to depict the legal systems represented on the Court—and by nationality of the judges (since 1922). Full particulars of the composition of the Permanent Court and of the present Court are given in Appendix 3.

Competition is also keen within the groups, and the absence of internal regional cohesion may lead to a change in inter-regional distribution (as occurred in 1951 and 1957). Here less is known about the understandings, except that the Latin American group will apparently strive to ensure that at least one member of the Court comes from Central America. The fluctuation in intra-regional distribution is well illustrated by the history of West European representation on the Court since 1946—a history which is typical also for other regions. The original West European seats were held by two judges, both from the northern part of the Continent (Belgium and Norway). The Belgian seat was lost in 1951, and when the lost seat was regained in 1957 it went to Greece, thus giving a more balanced distribution. In 1960, an Italian candidate put up stern competition and won, thereby taking the seat from Scandinavia. The West European legal systems now represented on the Court are the French, the Italian and the Greek. This gives an unbalanced reflection of the legal culture of Europe.

Apprehension is frequently expressed that unless care is taken, the general criterion of Article 9 will clash with the personal qualifications required by Article 2, leading to a lowering of the standards required for the Court as a whole. On the other hand there is equal danger in exaggerating the possibility of discrepancy. Having regard for the primary purposes for which the Court exists, it seems to follow that the emphasis may rightly be placed on Article 9. Taking that as the point of departure, obviously it is most desirable that the individual judges should be reasonably competent in the theory and practice of international law (an expression which is

TABLE IV

REPRESENTATION OF PRINCIPAL LEGAL SYSTEMS

	1922	1931	1946*	1952**	1955***	1958	1961
Common Law	2	2	3	4	4	4	3
Roman Law							
(W. Europe)	5	5	3	2	2	3	3
(S. America)	2	3	4	4	4	4	4
(E. Europe)		1					
(Balkans)	2	1	1	1	1	1	1
Germanic Law	2	1					
Islamic Law			1	1	2	2	1
Communist Law			2	2	2	2	2
Asian Law	2	2	1	2	2	2	2

Notes:

* Note the decentralization of the British Common Law after the Statute of Westminster of 1931.

** In 1951 an Indian judge was elected. He may be said to represent the Common law, and Asian law.

*** In 1954 a Pakistani judge was elected, representing the Common law, Asian law and Islamic law.

broad enough to include both persons who have had practical experience of international law in the course of a diplomatic career and those whose qualifications are for the most part academic or whose experience is more secluded). However, in order to ensure a properly balanced Court for the purposes of Article 9, it is permissible to depart from that test provided in that event that the persons elected are qualified to hold the highest judicial offices in their own countries. In fact there are usually found amongst the members of the Court at any given moment judges who are highly qualified and experienced international lawyers as such, judges who have had considerable diplomatic experience at a high level of responsibility (including one or two former Foreign Ministers), and judges whose main experience has been in domestic judicial and administrative activities. It is not necessary that every judge be highly familiar with the whole of contemporary international law, but out of a Court of fifteen judges there should be no difficulty in finding a sufficient number of judges who can speak with authority on all the problems which arise. The practical exercise of the judicial function undoubtedly requires a high level of statesmanship and practical wisdom in addition to knowledge of the law, and this mixture of talents is generally speaking adequate and meets the international requirements.

Yet the question is being asked with increasing insistence whether the prevalent distribution of seats is fully satisfactory, and it can be

TABLE V

NATIONALITY OF JUDGES

Country	Period P.C.I.J.	I.C.J.
Argentina		1955-—
Australia		1958-—
Austria	1931-36 (Deputy-Judge)	
Belgium	1931-45	1946-52
Brazil	1922-30	1946-55
Canada		1946-58
Chile		1946-55
China	1922-30 (Deputy-Judge) 1931-45	1946-—
Colombia	1931-42	
Cuba	1922-46	
Denmark	1922-30	
Egypt (later United Arab Republic)		1946-—
Finland	1931-36 (Deputy-Judge) 1938-45	
France	1922-45	1946-—
Germany	1931-35	
Greece		1958-—
India		1952-53 1961-—
Italy	1922-45	1961-—
Japan	1922-45	1961-—
Mexico		1946-52 1955-—

Country	Period P.C.I.J.	I.C.J.
Netherlands	1922-45	
Norway	1922-30 (Deputy-Judge)	1946-61
Pakistan		1954-61
Panama		1959-—
Peru		1961-—
Poland	1931-40	1946-—
Portugal	1931-36 (Deputy-Judge)	
Rumania	1922-30 (Deputy-Judge) 1931-45	
Salvador	1931-45	1946-59
Spain	1922-45	
Sweden	1936-37	
Switzerland	1922-30	
United Arab Republic (see Egypt)		
U.S.S.R.		1946-—
United Kingdom	1922-45	1946-—
United States	1922-45	1946-—
Uruguay		1952-61
Yugoslavia	1922-36 (Deputy-Judge)	1946-58

surmised that with the emergence of a numerically strong group of African Powers in the United Nations, this question will become more acute in the future. There does exist apprehension lest the prevalence of political factors (too powerful to be ignored) may make it difficult to maintain the high standards of professional qualifications required. As a solution to this problem, the suggestion is frequently heard that a slight increase in the size of the Court from the present fifteen members ought to be contemplated. It is not believed that this would make the Court too unwieldy, and although to effect such an increase would require a formal amendment of the Statute (Article 3), an amendment which could only be achieved by the procedure laid down for the amendment of the Charter itself, it is to be hoped that proposals of this nature will receive the constructive attention they deserve in the near future.[2]

The rather complicated system by which candidates are nominated and elected is designed to ensure that the double test laid down by the Statute is applied in practice. In this connexion, it is obvious that the primary responsibility for attaining the desired standards rests with those who *nominate* candidates, especially when they have reasonable prospects of seeing their nominees elected. For the electors can only perform *their* task in the light of the objective situation placed before them. Their role is limited to choosing from among the candidates presented.

NOMINATING CANDIDATES

In an attempt to ensure that the candidates will possess the desired personal qualifications, the Statute adopts the principle not of direct nomination by the governments desirous of putting candidates forward, but of indirect nomination, by existing or specially constituted "National Groups" in each country. The original idea, when the Statute was first drafted in 1922, was that the national groups of four persons chosen by a country as its members on the panel of the Permanent Court of Arbitration (see p. 16 above) would nominate candidates for the Permanent Court of International Justice. Where a country was not a party to the Hague Convention, it was supposed to constitute a national group along the same lines. As a further check on the candidates' qualifications, the Statute recommended each of these groups to consult with its highest court of justice, its legal faculties and schools of law, and its national academies and national sections of international academies devoted to the study of law.

When the Statute was revised in 1945, there was a strong move to alter these provisions, on the grounds that in fact the system had not worked as intended, and that the same results would be attained by direct nomination by governments, especially if they would undertake a series of consultations such as were enjoined on the national groups. But in the end it was decided to retain the previous system. However, out of the present total of 113 parties to the Statute (including the non-members of the United Nations), it is understood that no more than 60 are parties to the Hague Convention of 1907. This means that in fact the nominations are in very many instances made by specially constituted nominating colleges.

At least three months before the date of the election, the Secretary-General of the United Nations communicates with the national groups (through the Foreign Minister of each country), and invites them to undertake the nominations. Each national group may nominate not more than four persons, of whom not more than two may be of their own nationality; and in no case may the number of candidates nominated by a group be more than double the number of seats to be filled.

On receipt of the nominations, the names, in alphabetical order, are presented to the General Assembly and the Security Council, by whom the actual elections are conducted. Only the persons on these lists are eligible for election, save in the case of a complete deadlock between the Security Council and the General Assembly. In addition to the list, the Secretary-General customarily circulates biographical details of the candidates. This is a useful practice which enables the electors to make their choice in full knowledge of the qualifications of the persons chosen.

Although there may, at times, be an element of artificiality in the nominating process, especially since, in the present circumstances, a ready-made national group does not exist for many members of the United Nations, the decision of 1945 to retain the existing system was wise. The International Court is the only principal organ of the United Nations which is composed of individuals not directly representing States. While it is true that a person is elected judge not only on the basis of his personal qualifications but also having some regard to his nationality, the present nominating system, if conscientiously applied, does offer the best possibility of ensuring that the candidates will be duly qualified.[3]

THE ELECTIONS

As stated, the judges are elected for a period of nine years. For the Permanent Court, all the judges were elected simultaneously for each nine-year period, and elections accordingly took place in 1921 and 1930, those due to be held in 1939 being postponed on account of the War. In 1945 a fundamental change was introduced, when it was decided that five of the judges would retire each third year, the initial choice of three, six and nine year terms being made by lot. As a consequence, the whole bench of fifteen judges was elected in February, 1946, and since then partial elections of five judges a time have been held in the sessions of the General Assembly of 1948, 1951, 1954, 1957 and 1960. The proposal for this change was made by the Washington Committee of Jurists, which felt that the previous system presented serious drawbacks principally on the ground that while it preserved continuity *during* the nine-year period, it did not maintain it *beyond* the nine-year period. It was thought that the new system would therefore overcome that deficiency, while allowing for reasonable change in the personnel of the

Court each three years.[4] On the other hand, the San Francisco
Conference rejected proposals to alter the system of elections, by
entrusting them to the General Assembly alone. Accordingly, the
League system has been retained, and judges are elected by the
General Assembly and the Security Council, which proceed "in-
dependently of each other".

To be elected, a candidate has to receive an absolute majority
of votes in each of these two organs. In the General Assembly,
States parties to the Statute which are not members of the United
Nations (there are today three States in that category) participate on
a footing of equality. In the Security Council, no distinction is made
between the permanent and the non-permanent members (i.e. the
so-called "veto" does not apply).[5] But although the permanent
members do not now have any privileged position, they are able to
ensure the election of candidates of their own nationality—something which, as has been emphasized, is essential for the successful
functioning of the Court—though it is doubtful if they can today
do much more than that. Nor does it appear that the non-permanent
members of the Security Council (they are six in number) secure
any particular advantage for themselves through their double votes,
although they may be able to influence the outcome should a contest develop between two regions over a single seat. Experience has
shown that on the whole, apart from the candidates of the nationality of the permanent members, the General Assembly is able to
have its way in the end.

The Statute also contains elaborate provisions to overcome a
deadlock between the two organs, but there has been no need to
apply them yet. The prolonged phases through which an election
may go before it is clear that deadlock is really developing are
usually sufficient to allow the normal processes of diplomacy to
bring about a solution.

How are the elections conducted? As stated, the two organs proceed independently of each other. This means that the results of
the voting are not communicated until both organs have completed
their meetings, and only then is a comparison made between the
two sets of results. It does not mean that the individual States do
not know the results in one or other organ. The two sets of elections
are carried out by secret ballot in separate meetings, but the results
are announced after each ballot. The meetings of each organ
continue until the *exact* number of candidates to fill the vacant
places has received the required majority, and balloting will be
continued in each meeting until that result is attained. As soon as
the two lists are complete, they are formally communicated to the
other organ, and candidates whose names appear on both lists are

formally declared elected. One meeting may therefore have an indefinite number of ballots. If places remain to be filled after the
first meetings, the process continues for a second and a third meeting
of each organ, and again each of the meetings continues for as
many ballots as may be necessary. As the process of counting the
ballots in the General Assembly naturally takes a long time, the
meeting itself may be adjourned for as much as twenty-four hours,
and although that is a matter of the personal convenience of the
delegations, it is at the same time useful in permitting further consultations between delegations for the eventuality that no candidate
will receive the necessary majority. Only after three meetings have
been held in this way, with still not all the places filled by both the
Security Council and the General Assembly, will the machinery
for resolving the deadlock be put into operation. This machinery
consists of a joint conference of three members of each of the
Security Council and the General Assembly for the purpose of
choosing by absolute majority one name for each seat still vacant,
for submission to the Security Council and the General Assembly
for their acceptance. If the joint conference is unanimous it may
choose a person whose name does not appear on the original list
of candidates. As a final safeguard, if the joint conference is unsuccessful, the judges already elected are empowered, within a
period to be fixed by the Security Council, to fill the vacant seats by
selection from among the candidates who have obtained votes
either in the Security Council or in the General Assembly, the
eldest judge (and not the President) having a casting vote in the
event of a tie.[6]

An occasional vacancy created by the death or resignation of a
judge is filled by the same process. Such elections take place during
the next session of the General Assembly following the creation of
the vacancy, the person elected taking office immediately.[7] Occasional elections have been held in 1951, 1953, 1954, 1957, 1959
and 1960, and even if a triennial election is due at the same time,
they are kept distinct, both as regards the nomination and as regards
the election.

It goes without saying that the whole process of election is accompanied throughout by a considerable amount of diplomatic
negotiation which frequently commences even before the nominating phase. Sometimes an individual who wants to become a
judge will himself start by canvassing his chances on his own
account: the results of that phase will enable him to open negotiations with his own national group. Sometimes a government will
initiate its diplomatic overtures well in advance—as much as a
year or two. It is not unknown for a candidature to go forward to

election without real chance of immediate success, simply to provide a jumping-off point for sustained diplomatic effort leading to a renewal of the candidature at a later date with better prospects. The reaction to these early steps is important for the nomination phase, for it enables all concerned (including the candidate himself) to assess the probabilities. After the list of candidates is published, and especially after the session of the General Assembly begins, the diplomatic contacts become much more intense, and there is little doubt that at times a delegation is instructed to vote for a given candidate in return for promises of support on another matter of close concern to it, whether its own candidature in another election or a matter of substantive concern. It is difficult to see why such bargains should be deprecated (except out of an exaggerated regard for legal purism), because both the General Assembly and the Security Council are purely political bodies and it is not expected of them, or of the States of which they are composed, to exclude political considerations when they come to perform the very important function of electing the judges. These diplomatic contacts are also valuable in maintaining the desired professional standards of the Court. Through them, influential governments are able to indicate discreetly their view that a given candidate is or is not qualified for the duties, and there is reason to believe that this too is a factor which influences the final outcome of the elections.

CASE STUDY—THE ELECTIONS OF 1960

The operation of the whole process may be demonstrated by the elections of 1960, when both an occasional vacancy caused by the death of the United Kingdom judge, and five vacancies caused by the normal retirement of five serving judges, had to be filled.

The United Kingdom judge died on 8 May 1960, and on 31 May the Security Council decided, in accordance with normal practice, that the election to fill the vacancy would be held during the fifteenth session of the General Assembly. Five candidates were nominated (three of them of United Kingdom nationality, but two of these intimated that they did not wish to be considered for election). At the 915th meeting of the General Assembly and the 909th meeting of the Security Council, held on the afternoon of 16 November 1960, the remaining candidate of United Kingdom nationality was elected virtually unanimously. (Normally, the occasional elections are practically uncontested, but instances have occurred when the contest was severe.)

Immediately after disposing of the occasional election, the two organs proceeded to the regular election. The five retiring judges were of Norwegian, Pakistani, U.S.S.R., U.S.A. and Uruguayan nationality, and four of them were candidates for re-election. Twenty-six candidates were nominated, and it is interesting to see their distribution by regions. For the two seats being vacated by nationals of permanent members of the Security Council, two U.S. nationals (including the sitting judge) and three Soviet nationals (also including the sitting judge) were nominated by various national groups, but three of these (including the two sitting judges) withdrew their nominations, leaving one candidate from each of these two Powers, and their election was virtually uncontested. For the remaining three places, held respectively by Western Europe, Latin America and the Afro-Asian group, the candidates were divided as follows: Afro-Asia (one of whom withdrew), 5; Western Europe, 8; Eastern Europe, 1; Latin America, 6; Miscellaneous (Switzerland), 1. It will be noticed that for each of the three groups represented by the retiring judges, *intra*-regional competition was keen.

At the 915th meeting the General Assembly proceeded to hold its first ballot, at which two candidates, the American and the Soviet, received the necessary majority. After a procedural discussion a second ballot was held, at which the Japanese candidate only received the necessary majority and, it being already late, the meeting was suspended for twenty-four hours. In the meantime, the Security Council had continued its 909th meeting and on the first ballot had given the necessary majority to the American, Soviet, Italian, Paraguayan and Japanese candidates. At the end of the day it too suspended its meeting for twenty-four hours.

When the meetings were resumed the next afternoon, the General Assembly held its third ballot, at which no candidate received the necessary majority. At the fourth ballot it gave the majority to the Peruvian candidate, and at the fifth to the Italian candidate. As a result, four of the five places had been filled by the two organs, but the Latin American vacancy remained unfilled. The meetings were then both terminated and the two organs immediately reconvened in new meetings for the purpose of filling the remaining vacancy. At the 910th meeting of the Security Council, which began late in the afternoon on 17 November, the Peruvian candidate received the necessary majority on the first ballot. The General Assembly also held one ballot at its 916th meeting, which convened at the same time, and the same person received the majority. In that way the election was completed.

We have mentioned that this election was characterized by keen *intra*-regional competition. How did this find expression? The main competitive pressures were felt in the Latin American group, between Peru and Paraguay, and in the Afro-Asian group, between India, Pakistan and Japan, but the fact that the General Assembly required five ballots to elect a West European candidate also indicates the difficulties which existed there. The procedural discussion in the 915th meeting of the General Assembly was initiated by India in an attempt to improve the chances of the Indian candidate, after the first ballot had shown how the wind was blowing.[8] But it is believed that the unexpected point of order which was raised by India caused some resentment which found immediate expression in the second ballot at which the Japanese candidate was elected, thus putting an end to Indian (and Pakistani) hopes. As for the Latin American candidate, although the Paraguayan candidate started with more support from the Latin American group than his Peruvian rival, it seems that his candidature did not attract sufficient support outside Latin America, possibly because it was felt that his professional standing was not quite sufficient. When it became apparent that he would not obtain a majority in the General Assembly, the Security Council withdrew its support for him and transferred it to the Peruvian candidate. It was the easier for the Security Council to do this, as the rivalry was a purely internal one and did not affect the inter-regional distribution of seats on the Court.

THE INDEPENDENCE OF THE JUDGES

The Statute does not content itself with the general provision of Article 2 that the judges shall be "independent", but proceeds to clothe it with other provisions to give it reality.

The underlying principle is that in the exercise of their judicial functions, judges are to act independently of any instructions received from their governments. This principle is incorporated in the solemn declaration, required to be made in public by every judge before he takes up his functions, in the following terms: "I solemnly declare that I will perform my duties and exercise my powers as judge honourably, faithfully, impartially and conscientiously."[9] No member of the Court may exercise any political or administrative function, or engage in any other occupation of a professional nature, any doubt being settled by the Court.[10] This means that any member of the Court who, immediately prior to his election, was in the service of a government or international organization has to resign his office on his election, and it is also believed that if he possesses financial holdings which could lead to a conflict of interest, he should divest himself of those holdings.[11] No member of the Court may act for one of the parties in any case before the Court, and if, before he became a member, he had previously advised one of the parties, or had served as a member of a national or international court or commission of enquiry or in any other capacity in connection with the case, he has to stand down and refrain from participating in the decision of that case by the Court. Again, any doubt is to be settled by the Court.[12]

Judges are granted security of tenure during their term of office (but have no right to re-election), and are offered attractive financial terms and pension rights. A judge can only be dismissed if, in the unanimous opinion of the other members, he has ceased to fulfil the required functions.[13] In principle, each judge is supposed to participate in each case unless he is on leave[14] or is prevented by sickness; but if the President considers that for some special reason one of the members should not sit in a particular case, or if one of the members himself reaches that conclusion, he may be excused from participation.[15]

These provisions seem to have worked reasonably well in practice, and no instance is known, whether from the history of the Permanent Court or in that of the present Court, in which doubt has been cast on the independence of the Court as a whole, or of any one of its members.

THE PRESIDENT

The Court elects its President and Vice-President, who each hold office for three years.[16] The President is responsible for directing the work of the Court, as well as for its proper administration. He also performs important diplomatic and representative functions, both *vis-à-vis* the host government (the Netherlands) and in relation to others, and if necessary he will represent the Court in the meetings of the General Assembly. When the Court is not sitting, he has extensive powers to make orders for the procedure of pending cases. He directs the Court's deliberations, and he is *ex officio* a member of the Drafting Committee which prepares the final texts of the Court's decisions, whether or not he concurs in the decision (see p. 117 below).

It is obligatory for the President to reside at The Hague (no such obligation is imposed on the other judges), and when he is away the Vice-President has to be continuously available. The President, together with the Registrar, signs all formal orders, judgments and advisory opinions: this is for purposes of authentication and does not commit the signatories to their contents.[17]

In return for their onerous duties, the President and the Vice-President (when he is acting as President) receive a special non-pensionable allowance (see p. 44 above).[18]

The President and Vice-President take precedence over all the other judges. After them, judges elected at the same time take precedence according to seniority of age, those re-elected retaining their original precedence. In public sessions of the Court, the Vice-President sits to the President's right, and the other judges take their seats to his left and right in order of precedence. In the closed deliberations of the Court, the judges vote in inverse order of precedence, as is usual in judicial bodies.[19]

If the President is the national of one of the parties to a contentious case before the Court, he has to abstain from acting as President for that case, and will hand over his duties to the Vice-President or, if he is unable to act, to the next senior judge who is not disqualified.[20]

Very frequently the "extra-judicial activities" of the Court (see p. 32 above) are confided to the President, and in carrying them out he will observe the same principles.

JUDGES *AD HOC*

What happens when one party to a case has a judge of its nationality on the Court, but not the other? Several solutions are possible: the nationality of the judges could be ignored on the ground that they do not "represent" States; or the "national judge" (or judges) could be asked to stand down; or, when only one party has a national judge, the other party could be entitled to appoint a judge of its own for the occasion. The answer given by the draftsmen of the Statute is a combination of the first and third solutions.

Firstly, a judge is not disqualified from sitting in a case merely because he is a national of one of the parties. The Statute lays this down specifically.[21]

Secondly, whenever in any litigation the bench does not include a judge having the nationality of one or both of the parties, then those parties may each choose a judge, who shall take part in the decision on terms of complete equality with his colleagues. Such judges are known as judges *ad hoc*, and a judge *ad hoc* may be appointed not only to equalize the situation when the bench already includes a judge of the nationality of one of the parties, but also when it includes no judge having the nationality of *either* of the parties.

These provisions have given rise to controversy, principally on the grounds that they distort the "international character" of the international magistrature and that they conflict with the principle that no man should be judge in his own cause.[22] From the theoretical point of view this is undoubtedly true. But as we have seen, the notion of "national arbitrators" is deeply rooted in the practice of international arbitration, and indeed the facility to appoint them is probably a *sine qua non* for the success of the whole idea. The important thing for ensuring third-party judgment is not that national arbitrators or judges should disappear, but that the balance in the tribunal should be held by neutral judges. This is the conception which has been incorporated in the Statute, for in practice the decision is not likely to be influenced by the views of the judges having the nationality of the parties who, in the nature of things, tend to cancel each other out. The justification for the presence especially of judges *ad hoc* is to be placed on more general and psychological grounds connected with the nature of international relations and the special function performed in that context by international litigation: it is not to be sought in any strained concepts of legal theory, with which, indeed, it may conflict.

What is the role of these judges *ad hoc*? It is sometimes said that they perform a useful function in supplying "local knowledge and a national point of view",[23] and objection is then taken that if the parties cannot do that in their pleadings, so much the worse. But clearly, it is not their function to continue the pleadings in the Council Chamber. Rather their task would seem to be more to participate in the formulation of the judgment than to influence the actual decision (except, perhaps, when the division in the Court is very close). It has to be remembered that a State is not only interested in the operative part of a judgment: and even when the decision goes against it the wording of the reasons of the judgment may be of no less significance for it. Once the pleadings are closed, the parties have no further opportunity of bringing their points of view to bear on the Court, and it rests with the judge or judges *ad hoc* not to continue to plead their countries' cases (that would be virtually impossible), but to represent their countries' interests in the actual wording of the decision. If their role could, then, be more accurately designated as that of assessors, the grant to them of the status of judge represents a concession to diplomatic susceptibilities.

In most cases in which they have been appointed, judges *ad hoc* have voted in favour of their countries' point of view and have appended a dissenting opinion of their own if the majority decided against it. Indeed, so prevalent is this that one may be tempted to speculate whether a judge *ad hoc* is not expected to act in this way, and whether it is not in the long-term interests of the Court as an

ELECTION OF FIVE MEMBERS OF THE INTERNATIONAL COURT OF JUSTICE

ELECTION DE CINQ MEMBRES DE LA COUR INTERNATIONALE DE JUSTICE

ELECCION DE CINCO MIEMBROS DE LA CORTE INTERNACIONAL DE JUSTICIA

BALLOT PAPER   BULLETIN DE VOTE   CEDULA DE VOTACION

     Representatives are requested to place an (X) to the left of the name of the candidates for whom they wish to vote.

     Les représentants sont priés de mettre une croix (X) a gauche du nom des candidats pour lesquels ils désirent voter.

     Se ruega a los señores representantes poner una cruz (X) a la izquierda del nombre de los candidatos por quienes desean votar.

☐ ARMAND-UGON, Enrique C. (Uruguay)

☐ BARROS JARPA, Ernesto (Chile)

☐ BARTOS, Milan (Yugoslavia)

☐ BUSTAMANTE Y RIVERO, José Luis (Peru)

☐ CASTRÉN, Erik (Finland)

☐ FERNANDES, Raúl (Brazil)

☐ FLOR, Manuel Elicio (Ecuador)

☐ GUGGENHEIM, Paul (Switzerland)

☐ HACKWORTH, Green H. (United States of America)

☐ JESSUP, Philip C. (United States of America)

☐ KAECKENBEECK, Georges (Belgium)

☐ KLAESTAD, Helge (Norway)

☐ KOJEVNIKOV, Feodor I. (Union of Soviet Socialist Republics)

☐ KORETSKY, Vladimir M. (Union of Soviet Socialist Republics)

☐ MATINE-DAFTARY, Ahmad (Iran)

☐ MORELLI, Gaetano (Italy)

☐ NISOT, Joseph (Belgium)

☐ PAL, Radhabinod (India)

☐ PETRÉN, Sture (Sweden)

☐ PRODJODIKORO, Wirjono (Indonesia)

☐ SAPENA PASTOR, Raúl (Paraguay)

☐ SØRENSEN, Max (Denmark)

☐ TANAKA, Kotaro (Japan)

☐ TROLLE, Jørgen (Denmark)

☐ TUNKIN, Grigory I. (Union of Soviet Socialist Republics)

☐ ZAFRULLA KHAN, Sir Muhammad (Pakistan)

Illustration II—Reproduction of an actual Ballot Paper

institution that he should do so. The reason is that having regard to the fragile foundations of international adjudication, the presence of a judge *ad hoc* on the bench, and the inclusion of his dissenting opinion in the text of the judgment itself, lends reality to the dictum that justice must not only be done but that it must be seen to be done. It makes it easier for a government to decide to entrust its affairs to the International Court.

Although judges *ad hoc* display a clear tendency to find in favour of their countries, this is by no means so marked in the case of national judges, and there have been some notable instances of national judges finding against their own countries even in cases of major importance. The best known is Lord McNair's rejection of the British Government's contentions in the *Anglo-Iranian Oil Co.* case, but this is far from being a unique instance. On the other hand, there has been no case of a national judge or a judge *ad hoc* dissenting from a majority decision in his country's favour.

Judges *ad hoc* have to possess all the personal qualifications required of the titular judges, and any doubt is to be settled by the decision of the Court. They also have to make the same solemn declaration. On the other hand, they are *appointed*, and are not subject to any form of international election. They need not be nationals of the State appointing them, and indeed instances have occurred in which one or both judges *ad hoc* themselves came from "neutral" countries. They sit supernumerary to the titular judges taking part in the case, which means that the bench may include up to seventeen judges. They take precedence after the titular judges.

The failure or unwillingness of a State to exercise its right to choose a judge *ad hoc* does not obstruct the Court in trying a case. States sometimes agree between themselves that no judges *ad hoc* will be appointed.

CHAMBERS OF THE COURT

The Court normally sits in its full composition subject to leave of absence, sickness, etc., but in no circumstances may the number of titular Judges taking part in a case fall below nine.[24] The number of judges who participate in a case is not unduly large considering the nature of the issues that come before the Court, though it is larger than is customary for the supreme courts of the common law countries.

The Statute also makes it possible for Chambers of the Court to be constituted. Two kinds of Chambers are envisaged.

It is obligatory for the Court to form annually a Chamber for Summary Procedure consisting of five judges. The object here is to maintain in existence a small court specially attuned to the speedy despatch of business, and a special summary procedure is also laid down in the Rules of Court.[25] However, States show no disposition to avail themselves of this facility. In fact, in the combined existence of the Permanent Court and the present Court, only one case has been referred to the Chamber for Summary Procedure.

Apart from this statutory Chamber, the Court is empowered from time to time to form one or more chambers for dealing with particular categories of cases; for example, labour cases and cases relating to transit and communications, or for any other case for which the formation of a chamber may be requested by the parties. The minimum number of judges to constitute a chamber of this type is three.[26] There is no instance of the invocation of this procedure, and indeed it is probable now that this type of case is more suitable for settlement through the expert machineries of the various Specialized Agencies (including their special types of arbitral tribunals in which technical experts are also given a place).

THE REGISTRAR AND THE REGISTRY

The Court has its own officials who are recruited specially and who are technically not part of the United Nations Secretariat. The Statute confers on the Court power to appoint its Registrar and such other officers as may be necessary.

The Registrar, who is elected by secret ballot and by an absolute majority of votes from among candidates proposed by members of the Court, serves for a period of seven years and is eligible for re-election provided that his candidature is again proposed by a member of the Court. A Deputy-Registrar is appointed in the same way. The other officers of the Court are appointed by the Court on the proposal of the Registrar.

The Registry Staff consists of not more than 30 officials, who form a highly trained cadre which can be supplemented whenever necessary by temporary assistance. Their duties have been officially classified under four heads, which in fact overlap: judicial, diplomatic, administrative and linguistic. They are specified in greater detail in the Court's Instructions for the Registry. Apart from the Registrar and Deputy-Registrar, the other officers are accorded the usual diplomatic titles.[27]

DIPLOMATIC PRIVILEGES

The members of the Court and the Registrar, when engaged on the business of the Court, enjoy full diplomatic privileges and immunities. In addition, the agents, counsel and advocates of the parties before the Court, and the Court's officials, enjoy the privileges and immunities necessary to the independent exercise of their functions. The details are regulated in an exchange of notes between the President of the Court and the Minister for Foreign Affairs of the Netherlands of 26 June 1946, which was approved, and slightly supplemented (with the consent of the Netherlands) by the General Assembly in its Resolution 90 (I) of 11 December 1946.

NOTES

1. As regards the other principal collegiate organs of the United Nations, this is specifically written into Article 86 of the Charter dealing with the composition of the Trusteeship Council. On the other hand, no such formal stipulation appears in Article 61, dealing with the composition of the Economic and Social Council, but in fact it has always been applied there until the elections held in 1960.

2. See the cautious resolution adopted by the Institute of International Law on 26 April 1954 on the basis of the important report by Prof. Max Huber, former President of the Permanent Court of International Justice. *Annuaire de l'Institut de Droit International*, 45 (1954), t.1, 407, t.2, 60-107, 296. The question of the increase in the size of the Court has been placed on the agenda of the General Assembly in 1956, 1957 and 1958, but no decisions were adopted. For the procedure of amending the Statute, see Statute, Article 69, and Charter, Articles 108 and 109.

3. See Statute, Articles 4-7. Very few details are in fact available of the manner in which the nominating process is carried out. In the nature of things this is done discreetly. An instance is reported in which the Supreme Court of the Argentine was consulted in 1946 concerning the qualification of a candidate whom the Argentinian National Group proposed nominating. R.R. Araya, *El Derecho Internacional interpretado por la Corte Suprema de la Nación (1836-1956)* (Rosario, 1958), 71. For the consultations of the United States National Group in 1960, with the Chief Justice of the United States, the Presidents of the American Society of International Law and of various Bar Associations, and the Deans of a number of Law Schools, see R.R. Baxter, "The Procedures employed in connection with the United States Nominations for the International Court in 1960", *American Journal of International Law*, 55 (1961), 445.

The question of the personal qualifications of the individual members arises for some other organs of the United Nations, notably the functional commissions of the Economic and Social Council. Here a different principle is followed, whereby, although States are elected to these Commissions, the actual representative is designated by the Government concerned after consultation with the Secretary-General, and is subject to confirmation by the Council. J. G. Hadwen and J. Kaufmann, *How United Nations Decisions are Made* (Leyden, 1960), 18. Such a system would not be appropriate for the International Court.

4. It is not too clear on what the assumption was based. Of the members of the Court serving in 1939, who continued in office until the dissolution of the Permanent Court in 1946, five had been first elected prior to the general elections of 1930, and a further two had previously been deputy-judges (a post which was abolished in 1936). Three judges were continuously members of the Court from its establishment to its dissolution. They served two full terms of nine years plus the further six War years. Of the fifteen judges elected to the present Court in 1946, only three remained on the Court after the election of 1960. It seems that the present system of triennial partial elections has in fact increased the rate of turn-over among the judges. This, in turn, is believed by many observers to have had an unsettling effect on the Court, and obstructed the creation of its "esprit de corps".

5. A majority of six is therefore sufficient in the Security Council, the only instance of voting in that organ by which a decision can be reached by a simple majority. For all other decisions, whether or not the "veto" applies, the minimum number of votes required is seven out of the membership of eleven. The relevant rules are now interpreted as requiring an absolute majority in the General

Assembly, i.e. one half plus one of the total number of votes entitled to be cast. This is a change from the practice in the League Assembly where a simple majority, i.e. one half plus one of the votes actually cast, was required. The reasons for this change are not entirely clear. Cf. A. W. Rudzinski, "Election Procedure in the United Nations", *American Journal of International Law*, 53 (1959), 81. It was decisive for the election of Sir Zafrulla Khan in 1954. For the participation of non-members, parties to the Statute, in the General Assembly, see Resolution 264 (III) of 8 October 1948.

6. Statute, Articles 8-12. And see Rules 151 and 152 of the Rules of Procedure of the General Assembly (A/4700) and Rules 40 and 61 of the Provisional Rules of Procedure of the Security Council (S/96/Rev. 4). These Rules incorporate the current interpretation of the word "meeting", to the effect that it continues until as many candidates as are required for all the seats to be filled have obtained in one or more ballots an absolute majority of votes.

7. Statute, Articles 14, 15.

8. It is interesting to observe the full results of the voting in this election. In the General Assembly, the required majority was 52. In the first meeting, the results were as follows: first ballot (101 valid ballots); Messrs. Jessup (U.S.A.), 77; Koretsky (U.S.S.R.), 62; Tanaka (Japan), 51; Bustamente y Rivero (Peru), 42; Zafrulla Khan (Pakistan), 42; Morelli (Italy), 41; Klaestad (Norway), 37; Sapena Pastor (Paraguay), 37; Pal (India), 31; Armand-Ugon (Uruguay), 14; Nisot (Belgium), 11; Guggenheim (Switzerland), 10; Bartoš (Yugoslavia), 7; Kojevnikov (U.S.S.R.), 6; Petrén (Sweden), 5; Tunkin (U.S.S.R.), 3; Matine-Daftary (Iran), 3; Barros (Chile), 3; Hackworth (U.S.A.), 3; Castrén (Finland), 3; Flor (Ecuador), 1; Prodjodikoro (Indonesia), 1. Second ballot (100 valid ballots): Tanaka, 56; Bustamente y Rivero, 48; Morelli, 43; Zafrulla Khan, 34; Klaestad, 33; Sapena Pastor, 31; Pal, 28; Bartoš, 3; Guggenheim, 2; Armand-Ugon, 2; Matine-Daftary, 2; Nisot, 1; Petrén, 1; Prodjodikoro, 1. Third ballot (94 valid ballots): Bustamente y Rivero, 46; Morelli, 40; Klaestad, 28; Sapena Pastor, 28; Zafrulla Khan, 17; Pal, 13; Guggenheim, 5; Flor, 1; Armand-Ugon, 1; Matine-Daftary, 1; Nisot, 1; Prodjodikoro, 1; Petrén, 1; Sørensen (Denmark), 1. Fourth Ballot (98 valid ballots): Bustamente y Rivero, 53; Morelli, 45; Sapena Pastor, 29; Klaestad, 27; Zafrulla Khan, 16; Pal, 11; Guggenheim, 4; Nisot, 3; Sørensen, 1; Flor, 1; Prodjodikoro, 1. Fifth ballot (97 valid ballots): Morelli, 56; Klaestad, 24; Pal, 8; Zafrulla Khan, 5; Sapena Pastor, 3; Matine-Daftary, 1. Second meeting, first ballot (89 valid ballots): Bustamente y Rivero, 66; Sapena Pastor, 13; Zafrulla Khan, 4; Pal, 3; Klaestad, 2; Guggenheim, 1. Four of the candidates who obtained votes in the General Assembly, Messrs. Hackworth, Kojevnikov, Tunkin and Prodjodikoro, had withdrawn their candidature before the voting commenced. In the Security Council, the required majority was 6. The result of the first ballot of the first meeting (11 valid ballots) was: Messrs. Jessup, 11; Koretsky, 9; Morelli, 7; Sapena Pastor, 6; Tanaka, 6; Bustamente y Rivero, 5; Klaestad, 4; Pal, 3; Armand-Ugon, 2; Zafrulla Khan, 2. The result of the first ballot of the second meeting was: Bustamente y Rivero, 10; Sapena Pastor, 1. The point of order raised by India between the first and second ballots of the first meeting of the General Assembly was sustained on a roll-call vote by a majority of 47 to 27, with 25 abstentions.

9. Statute, Article 20. Rules of Court, Article 5.   10. Statute, Article 16.

11. See correspondence between the Prime Minister of Australia and a member of the Commonwealth Parliament, published in the Australian press of 12 September 1958.

12. Statute, Article 17.   13. Statute, Article 18. Rules of Court, Article 6.

14. Statute, Article 23. Rules of Court, Articles 26, 27.

15. Statute, Article 24. The Statute does not contain anything corresponding to the continental system of *récusation*, i.e. a direct appeal by a party against the participation of a judge on ground of relationship, or known personal bias towards one or other of the parties. However, this provision does, it is believed, enable discreet action to be taken in that direction should one of the parties feel it necessary.

16. Statute, Article 21. Rules of Court, Article 9.

17. Statute, Article 21. Rules of Court, Articles 9-12.

18. Statute, Article 32, paragraphs 2 and 3.

19. Rules of Court, Articles 2, 30.   20. Rules of Court, Articles 11-13.

21. Article 31.   22. *Nemo judex in causa sua.*

23. This was the view of the Informal Inter-Allied Committee of 1944, in support of its recommendation that the institution of judge *ad hoc* be retained.

24. Statute, Article 25.

25. Statute, Article 29. Rules of Court, Article 24.

26. Statute, Article 26.

27. See I.C.J. Yearbook, 1946-7, 55-87, for a description of the organization of the Registry, the Staff Regulations and the Instructions for the Registry.

HOW THE COURT WORKS

Considering the arguments of the parties, appraising the evidence produced by them, establishing the facts and declaring the law applicable to them—the definition by the Court of how a judicial organ works, in an advisory opinion of 13 July 1954.

CHAPTER IV

JURISDICTION

By "jurisdiction" we mean the power or authority of the Court to render a binding decision on the snbstance, or merits, of a case placed before it. The International Court receives this power only from the consent of the States concerned that it should so act. Neither the Charter of the United Nations, nor any general rule of contemporary international law, imposes on States the obligation to refer their legal disputes to the Court. The San Francisco Conference rejected all proposals to make some compulsory jurisdiction over certain defined types of disputes a condition for membership in the world Organization.

Although the San Francisco Conference did not accept the principle of compulsory adjudication as a condition for membership in the international organization, it did accept the *political* principle that as a general rule legal disputes should be referred by the parties to the Court, in accordance with the provisions of its Statute. This appears in Article3 6, paragraph 3, of the *Charter*. On the other hand, the general principle that the Court's jurisdiction depends on the consent of the parties is equally clearly enunciated in Article 36, paragraph 1, of the *Statute*: "The jurisdiction of the Court comprises all cases which the parties refer to it and all matters specially provided for in the Charter of the United Nations or in treaties or conventions in force."

The fact that the Court obtains jurisdiction to decide a concrete case only from the consent of the States concerned means, that the decision to have recourse to the Court is, in all cases, a deliberate political decision.

The Permanent Court once defined in clear terms the role of the Court in the settlement of international disputes by peaceful means: ". . . the judicial settlement of international disputes, with a view to which the Court has been established, is simply an alternative to the direct and friendly settlement of such disputes between the Parties; . . . consequently it is for the Court to facilitate, so far as is compatible with its Statute, such direct and friendly settlement."[1] Article 33 of the United Nations Charter contains a general obligation on the members to seek a pacific solution of their disputes and enumerates a number of methods of achieving that aim, the choice of which is left to the parties themselves. They include judicial settlement, and the present Court has warned against hampering the free play of that provision by, for instance, drawing strict legal conclusions from actions and positions taken by parties with a view to resolving their disputes.[2] Such an attitude is not to be regarded as expressive of undue modesty on the part of the Court: it is rather a fair assessment of the place in diplomatic techniques of the judicial settlement of international disputes, and it serves notice that the Court will not make excessive claims for its particular brand of pacific settlement, while at the same time adhering firmly to the duties imposed upon it by its Statute.

But to say that the jurisdiction of the Court depends upon the consent of the States concerned, can, through an excess of brevity, be misleading. There are a number of ways in which States can give their consent, and some of these are undoubtedly moving in the direction of true compulsory jurisdiction, and as a result of this probably most States have accepted the jurisdiction of the Court in one way or another, even if for only very limited types of dispute. The Court has facilitated the development of this process. Some of these ways will now be described more fully (while avoiding technicalities), because it is only through the advances in the techniques of conferring jurisdiction on the Court that the practice of international adjudication can make any headway at all.

A COURT FOR STATES

The first thing to be stressed is that only States may be parties in cases before the Court.[3] This excludes as parties to litigation both intergovernmental organizations, on the one hand, and individuals on the other. This is a matter of deliberate choice. The Court has been established to decide disputes between States, and not for other purposes. What this means is that the Court's procedures can only be set in motion by governments in exercise of the responsibilities entrusted to them. It does not mean that the interests of an individual can never be the subject of international litigation: to the contrary. But before the Court can deal with such a case the individual's government has to take it up and make of it an international claim in accordance with international law (espouse the claim in the exercise of its right of diplomatic protection of its citizens, to use the technical expression). When that happens, the litigation is conducted exclusively between the two governments concerned, and the individual has no *locus standi* in the Court itself.

Both the Permanent Court and the present Court have seen several instances of this.[4]

The fact that only States may be parties in litigation excludes the possibility that the United Nations, Specialized Agencies, and other international organizations may be parties in litigation, whether with other international organizations or with States. This rule originated in the idea that only States possess international personality, and the San Francisco Conference refused to change the traditional basis. However, it inserted a provision into the Statute not only entitling the Court to request relevant information from international organizations, but also entitling those organizations to submit information to the Court on their own initiative.[5] Since that idea itself is not an accurate description of contemporary international law, the perpetuation of the traditional concept of international litigation is criticized. This criticism has gained in strength since 1949, when the International Court itself explained that the United Nations itself possesses international personality, and was entitled and able to advance international claims on the diplomatic plane against States, whether or not members of the Organization.[6]

As far as disputes between organizations are concerned, this is now partly covered by the authorization conferred on the Economic and Social Council to request advisory opinions on legal questions concerning the mutual relationship of the Specialized Agencies and the United Nations. This is, however, little more than a residual power, as in fact close co-ordination between these different organizations is maintained through existing United Nations machineries, both on the Secretariat level and on the political level, and the possibility of conflict between them is in fact remote. (Legal disputes of such a nature as to justify recourse to the Court are also politically unlikely, seeing that for the most part the membership of the United Nations and of most of the Specialized Agencies is the same.)

As for disputes between an international organization and an individual State, if the legal question is of sufficient general interest, there is no reason why it should not be made the subject of a request for an advisory opinion.

All States, whether or not they are members of the United Nations, may be parties in litigation with other States. The Court is established as a World Court. States which are not members of the United Nations may become parties to the Statute of the Court, on conditions of complete equality with the members of the United Nations, if they accept the conditions laid down by the General Assembly on the recommendation of the Security Council. Four States have done this—Switzerland, Liechtenstein, San Marino and

Japan (before becoming a member of the United Nations in 1956).
States which are not parties to the Statute may also be parties in
litigation if they accept the conditions laid down by the Security
Council in its Resolution of 15 October 1946. In brief, the effect
of this resolution is to place such States in a position of equality, as
far as concerns the obligations deriving from recourse to the Court
including the obligation imposed by the Charter as regards the
carrying out of the Court's decision, with the States parties to the
Statute.[7] Now that the United Nations is to all intents a truly
universal organization, the question of access to the Court by States
not parties to the Statute has lost much of the practical importance
it once might have had.

The fact that a State—whether or not a member of the United
Nations—is a party to the Statute means that it is *qualified* to be
party in litigation. It does not mean that it has agreed to confer
jurisdiction on the Court. To confer jurisdiction is a separate act
altogether, which has to be directed specifically towards a defined,
or ascertainable State, in respect of a defined, or ascertainable type
of, dispute.

HOW JURISDICTION IS CONFERRED

There are two basic ways, and many variations, by which jurisdiction to decide contentious cases is conferred on the Court or, to
put it more conveniently, by which a title of jurisdiction may be
created. These are depicted in Illustration No. III. The first is by
specific agreement between two or more States. The second is by
unilateral declaration emanating from a State and deposited with
the Secretary-General of the United Nations, accepting the jurisdiction of the Court for defined types of legal disputes, in accordance
with a special procedure contained in the Statute. This is sometimes
called the compulsory jurisdiction—a phrase which is misleading to
the extent that it causes the voluntary nature of the acceptance of
the jurisdiction to be overlooked.

There are no formal requirements for an international agreement
conferring jurisdiction on the Court, and the Court has deliberately
kept this aspect elastic as part of its general policy of facilitating
recourse to the judicial organ. The important thing is that the Court
should be satisfied that the parties are in agreement that it should
decide the case, and not how that agreement is expressed. In fact
this question will only arise if one of the parties should challenge
the jurisdiction of the Court on the ground that no such agreement
exists, a process for which a special procedure is established.

At least four systems of conferring jurisdiction on the Court by way of international agreement can be distinguished.

Firstly, two or more States may conclude a special agreement *(compromis)* referring to the Court a defined issue (see p. 101 below). This is similar in substance to the early type of a special agreement to submit a dispute to arbitration, but is now usually considerably simplified in form owing to the existence of the elaborate provisions of the Statute and Rules of Court governing all the procedural aspects. Although the special agreement was a relatively common method of conferring jurisdiction on the Permanent Court (no less than 11 cases were so brought before it), it seems to be falling out of use now, and only three cases have been decided by the present Court on this basis.[8]

Modern diplomatic requirements have introduced a refinement into the special agreement which also should be noticed. This consists in a formal agreement between two States that a dispute exists and that it should be settled by the Court, without, however, defining the precise point in dispute, and leaving it to one or other of the parties to concretize it unilaterally. This manner of conferring jurisdiction originated in Latin America. Its value is that through the agreement to invoke Court procedures, the later unilateral reference to the Court cannot be castigated as an inimical act. On the other hand, by not defining accurately the substance of the dispute, it may prevent the Court from reaching a conclusive decision, as in the *Asylum* case (p. 146 below). Two cases have come before the Court in this way.[9] This development in diplomatic techniques—which could be combined with the power of the Security Council to recommend judicial settlement—was only made possible by the fact that a permanent international judicial organ is in existence: it is inconceivable for *ad hoc* arbitration.

A second method of conferring jurisdiction on the Court is by a compromissory clause in a multilateral treaty according to which any disputes arising out of the application or interpretation of the treaty may be referred by any of the parties to the Court. This, too, originated in nineteenth century arbitral practice. Here the scope of the disputes that may be referred to the Court is defined in advance by reference to the treaty, while the number of States who can be potential litigants is limited to the actual parties to the treaty.

In the practice of the League of Nations, and in the early practice of the United Nations, a compromissory clause of this nature was included almost as a matter of course in most multilateral conventions of general character drawn up under the auspices of the international organization, and there must by now be hundreds of these agreements still in force. However, in recent years a change of sentiment is to be noticed. According to a view which is being advanced with insistence by the Soviet Union, the inclusion of procedural rules for the settlement of disputes in treaties dealing with substantive matters could jeopardize the efficacy of the substantive provisions by making it difficult for States to accept the obligations of the Convention. This clash of principle came to a head in the Geneva Conference on the Law of the Sea of 1958, and the solution which was then adopted consisted in placing the provisions conferring jurisdiction on the Court in a separate protocol which States are free to accept or reject at will.[10] This development may be regretted, it being a retreat from the more advanced position reached by the League of Nations. However, there is little doubt that it accurately reflects contemporary international realities, including the fact that an important group of States, headed by the Soviet Union but not confined to its Allies, are not willing to agree in advance to submit undefined disputes to judicial settlement.

Despite the large number of treaties containing compromissory clauses of this nature, they have not proved to be a fruitful source of business for the Court, and in fact it seems that this type of dispute is on the whole well suited to the normal diplomatic processes of adjustment. However, these in turn may be able to operate more efficiently when the Court exists in reserve, so to speak, should all other methods fail. Only three cases have come before the present Court on the basis of this type of title of jurisdiction—all of them relating to African affairs.[11]

The third manner in which jurisdiction can be conferred is through a bilateral treaty, which may be a bilateral treaty on some specific topic containing a general compromissory clause of the type mentioned, or one in which the arbitration or judicial settlement of disputes is the very substance of the agreement (such as a Treaty of Friendship, and the like). Here the scope of the litigation is limited to the two parties to the treaty and materially, by the terms of the treaty. This too is a system which originated in nineteenth century arbitration practice. It was greatly encouraged by the League of Nations and the Permanent Court, and has continued to be popular in the present time, and there are undoubtedly hundreds of these clauses in existence conferring jurisdiction on the Court. But here, again, this has not turned out to be a fruitful source of judicial business, probably because most of these treaties are in force between pairs of States which are likely to be able to settle their disputes amicably and through normal diplomatic processes, and the real value of the Court is as an instance of last resort when the diplomatic processes are unsuccessful.[12] It is indeed

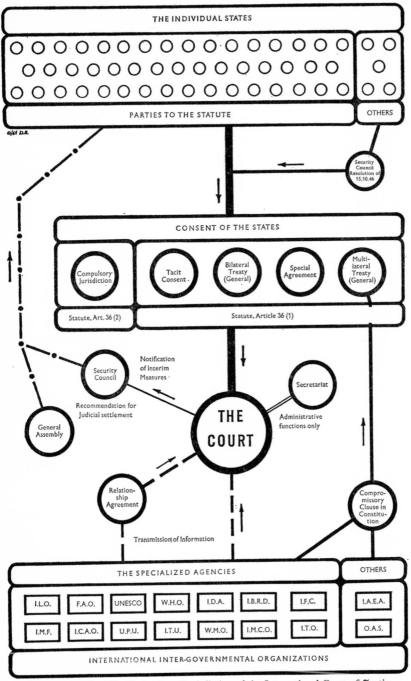

Illustration III—The Contentious Jurisdiction of the International Court of Justice

significant that a number of cases which originated in this way have
been ultimately settled out of court and the judicial proceedings
discontinued.[13]

Finally, and this is a particularity of judicial procedure proper
(it being almost impossible for *ad hoc* arbitration procedure), the
International Court recognizes that as it is concerned with the
substance of the agreement that it should exercise jurisdiction, and
not with the form in which it is expressed, the consent may be given
informally even after the proceedings have been started. The
commonest example of this is when the defendant pleads to the
case on the merits while formally refusing to recognize the title
of jurisdiction invoked by the plaintiff State. Once the issues on
the merits have been joined, the defendant State cannot be heard
to deny the jurisdiction of the Court. This kind of tacit agreement
is a useful system for perfecting the jurisdiction of the Court when,
for any reason, the case in the course of the pleadings extends
beyond the strict letter of the title of jurisdiction.

This form of conferring jurisdiction achieved some prominence
in 1948 as a result of the manner in which the Court held that it
had jurisdiction in the *Corfu Channel* case, and during the fifties a
number of attempts were made to bring cases before the Court by
means of a unilateral invitation to the defendant to confer jurisdiction on the Court, contained in an application instituting proceedings. Most of these cases were instituted by the United States
in connection with various claims against the Soviet Union and its
Allies arising out of incidents involving American military aircraft,
but two cases were also instituted by the United Kingdom against
Argentina and Chile relating to the disputed sovereignty over the
Falkland Islands.[14] In none of these cases did the defendant State
accept the invitation, and in the absence of any jurisdiction whatsoever, the Court ordered the cases to be removed from the list. The
fact that these attempts were made, and that the practice of the
Court permits them, is nevertheless significant and demonstrates
new possibilities in opening up ways of access to the Court.

JURISDICTION BY UNILATERAL DECLARATION
(THE COMPULSORY JURISDICTION)

The most noteworthy advance in the techniques of conferring jurisdiction on the Court introduced by the Statute of the Permanent
Court, and maintained by the Statute of the present Court, is the
possibility which it contained of conferring jurisdiction over legal
disputes, as defined in the Statute, by means of a unilateral dec-

laration. This is today frequently called the compulsory jurisdiction or the sytem of the optional clause (it being optional for States to make such a declaration), and it is embodied in Article 36, paragraph 2, of the Statute as follows:

"The states parties to the present Statute may at any time declare that they recognize as compulsory *ipso facto* and without special agreement, in relation to any other state accepting the same obligation, the jurisdiction of the Court in all legal disputes concerning:

a. the interpretation of a treaty;
b. any question of international law;
c. the existence of any fact which, if established, would constitute a breach of an international obligation;
d. the nature or extent of the reparation to be made for the breach of an international obligation."

Such declarations may be made unconditionally or subject to reservations which are not incompatible with the purposes of the optional clause. Reciprocity is inherent in the system, and where two declarations are in different terms, jurisdiction exists only to the extent they coincide. They may be limited or unlimited in time. No questions of form are prescribed, but as a matter of procedure they have to be deposited with the Secretary-General of the United Nations, and take effect immediately.

It will be noted that the description of "legal dispute" for which jurisdiction can be conferred in this way is virtually identical with that which appeared in Article 13 of the Covenant of the League of Nations (see p. 21 above).

The introduction of this type of jurisdiction in 1922 was a great innovation in international practice, and time was required before diplomatic techniques could adjust themselves to it. It was not until about 1930 that the Great Powers of the League of Nations finally decided to translate the abstract principle into the language of reality by themselves making declarations under the optional clause, but they did so only in a half-hearted way by recognizing the jurisdiction subject to many reservations and safeguards, the effect of which was to reduce its scope within limits somewhat narrower than seem to have been originally contemplated. This led a great number of other States to follow in their footsteps, and it has been estimated that at its height, in 1934, there were in force 42 declarations accepting the compulsory jurisdiction of the Permanent Court, this being the equivalent of 861 bipartite agreements.[15] In eleven of the cases of which the Permanent Court was seised such a declaration was invoked as the title of jurisdiction, ten of them occurring after 1930. Clearly this was a method of conferring jurisdiction on the Court of growing importance, and it was taken over, virtually unchanged (save in some technical details) when the Statute was revised in 1945.

The kinds of reservations and exclusions which are made in these declarations fall into a number of common patterns, and most of them are reasonable. They include, for instance, reservations limiting the jurisdiction to disputes arising after a given date, to disputes for which a solution is not reached through diplomatic means or for which the parties have not agreed on some other method of settlement, excluding disputes relating to events occurring in time of war, and so on. Occasionally individual States have inserted special conditions appropriate to their particular international situation.[16]

A common form of reservation excludes disputes which come within the domestic jurisdiction of States. This is not strictly necessary, as if the subject of the dispute comes within the domestic jurisdiction of States it cannot be a legal dispute governed by international law and therefore in the nature of things cannot come within the scope of the compulsory jurisdiction. The League Covenant excluded from the competence of the League disputes arising out of a matter which "by international law is solely within the domestic jurisdiction" of a party,[17] and in this form it was taken over into the compulsory jurisdiction. However, in the equivalent provision of the United Nations Charter the words "by international law" have been omitted (although they appeared in the original Dumbarton Oaks Proposals).[18] This has led some countries, headed by the United States of America (on the insistence of the Senate), to exclude from their acceptances of the compulsory jurisdiction of the present Court disputes with regard to matters essentially within their domestic jurisdiction *as determined by themselves*.[19] Such a subjective reservation largely vitiates the acceptance of the compulsory jurisdiction because, as in the case of the early arbitration treaties which were illusory to the extent that they conferred a power of unilateral determination concerning the justiciability of a dispute after it had arisen (see p. 18 above), it deprives the Court of the power of determining whether it has jurisdiction, although that power is expressly conferred on it by the Statute. For that reason the view is now widely held that a reservation in these terms is incompatible with the purposes and objects of the compulsory jurisdiction, and that effect cannot be given to it.[20]

The fact that the United States has accepted the compulsory jurisdiction in this extremely restricted manner, and that the Soviet Union has not accepted it at all (a striking parallelism with the attitude of the former Great Powers in the period 1922-29), is probably responsible for the fact that acceptance of the compulsory jurisdiction is today confined to a relatively small number of States. Out of the international judicial community of 113 members, the compulsory jurisdiction is accepted by only 38 of them.[21] Never in the joint history of the Permanent Court or the present Court has the percentage of members of the organized international community having accepted the compulsory jurisdiction been so low. This is a regrettable fact which runs in series with the attitude of a number of powerful and influential States which are only prepared to recognize the jurisdiction of the Court by express agreement relating to a defined dispute.

Despite this unfavourable political atmosphere, the compulsory jurisdiction is probably the most important source of judicial business for the Court today. Indeed, of the 49 cases brought before the Court since 1946, the compulsory jurisdiction was invoked as the title of jurisdiction in 12 of them, including the politically most important cases which the Court has decided (*Fisheries*, *Anglo-Iranian Oil Co.*, and *Right of Passage*).

The significance of the compulsory jurisdiction ought not to be measured solely by the number of States which have accepted it, or by the number of instances in which it has been invoked (although the increase in the frequency of its invocation is a factor to be noted). The chief importance of the system is psychological. It is a useful instrument for disseminating the idea that judicial settlement of international disputes is both possible and desirable. If States are agreed, on the political level, to have recourse to the Court, the fact that they have both accepted the compulsory jurisdiction may make it unnecessary for them to take any further steps in order to bring their dispute before the Court thus, from the political point of view, greatly facilitating recourse to the Court. There is reason to believe that something like this occurred in the diplomatic phase of the Fisheries dispute between the United Kingdom and Norway, which was decided by the Court in 1951. On the other hand, if the political agreement is not present, the defendant State may well challenge the jurisdiction of the Court, which will then proceed to decide, on the basis of law, whether the dispute comes within its acceptance of the compulsory jurisdiction so as to oblige it to recognize the jurisdiction in the concrete case. Experience has shown that the Court will display the maximum of prudence and judicial caution in dealing with that type of situation, and not allow the existence of the system of the compulsory jurisdiction to be abused in such a way as to compel a State to submit to the jurisdiction when it is clearly not obliged to do so.

CONTINUITY OF JURISDICTION BETWEEN THE
PERMANENT COURT AND THE PRESENT COURT

Most of these different systems of conferring jurisdiction became established for the Permanent Court, and when it was decided, at San Francisco, to liquidate that Court and establish a new Court in its stead, the question arose of the future of the various treaties and agreements in force conferring jurisdiction on the Permanent Court, and of the various declarations recognizing its compulsory jurisdiction. It was decided to make every effort to keep these instruments in force, at least as between the States parties to the new Statute, in order to maintain continuity in the domain of international justice and to prevent the reorganization from adversely affecting the achievements in this sphere.

To that end, two stipulations were inserted into the new Statute. The first provides that declarations accepting the compulsory jurisdiction of the Permanent Court which were still in force should be deemed, as between the parties to the new Statute, to be acceptances of the compulsory jurisdiction of the new Court for the period which they still had to run and in accordance with their terms.[22] The second states that whenever a treaty or convention in force provided for reference of a matter to the Permanent Court, the matter should, as between the parties to the new Statute, be referred to the new Court.[23] The Court has given an unexpectedly narrow interpretation to the first of these provisions, by holding that it only applies to the original members of the United Nations and not to members admitted subsequently, unless these had given some other indication that they were willing to recognize the Court's compulsory jurisdiction.[24] If a similar interpretation is given to the second of these provisions (which from the numerical point of view is the more important), the effect may be to curtail the jurisdiction of the present Court more than a superficial reading of these two provisions would suggest.[25]

INTERIM MEASURES OF PROTECTION

A special provision appears in the Statute giving the Court power to indicate, if it considers that circumstances so require, any provisional measures which ought to be taken to preserve the respective rights of either party; and as this is likely to be a matter having political implications, the Court is under the duty of giving notice of the measures which it suggests not only to the parties, but also to the Security Council.[26] This power enables the Court to take steps roughly equivalent to the interim injunction which domestic courts are frequently empowered to issue pending the final determination. A request for an indication of such measures may be made at any time in the course of the proceedings, and the Court will normally only accede to the request if there is the possibility that the object of the litigation will be prejudiced by the action of the defendant State—for example if there is a danger that economic assets which are the object of the claim may be lost. An order indicating measures of protection will remain in force so long as the Court is dealing with the case, unless previously revoked.

The present Court has twice been asked to indicate interim measures. In the first case—*Anglo-Iranian Oil Co.*—it acceded to the request but the Security Council was unable to take any action to effectuate the measures indicated.[27] In the second case, the Court found that there was no urgency, and therefore declined to accede to the request.[28]

As this power is exceptional, the Court is strict in insisting upon the observance of the proper procedure. It will not give general instructions to the parties to abstain from any measure capable of exercising a prejudicial effect on the subject-matter of the case or which might bring about an aggravation or extension of the dispute, unless the power to indicate interim measures is expressly invoked. In this connection it has to be recalled that the Court as such does not have the direct responsibility for the maintenance of international peace. That responsibility is expressly confided in the Security Council by Article 24 of the Charter.[29] On the other hand, the Court is entitled to rely on the general good faith of the parties not to exacerbate a dispute with which it is dealing.

DISPUTES OVER JURISDICTION
(PRELIMINARY OBJECTIONS)

A State against which legal proceedings are instituted is not obliged to accept the title of jurisdiction invoked by the plaintiff State, and if it considers that it has good reason, it may challenge the jurisdiction of the Court to determine the merits. For this purpose a special procedure—the preliminary objection procedure—exists. The State making use of this right is, however, obliged to accept the decision of the Court on the question of jurisdiction. This follows from the obligation imposed by the Charter on all parties to the Statute to comply with the decision of the Court (see p. 43 above), and it is possible to say that as regards the decision on jurisdiction to determine the merits, true compulsory jurisdiction does exist.

It has been seen (p. 18 above) that already nineteenth century arbitral procedure had reached the position that disputes over the jurisdiction of an arbitral tribunal should normally be settled by the tribunal itself and not be referred back to the parties, unless the arbitration agreement provided otherwise. When the Statute of the Permanent Court was drawn up specific power was inserted enabling the Court to decide on all disputes concerning its jurisdiction, and this has been taken over into the present Statute unchanged.[30] This being a specific power conferred on the Court, any submission to the jurisdiction which purports to override it would probably be held to be inconsistent with the Statute, and effect would not be given to it.

The insertion of this provision in the Statute, coupled with the permanence and universal quality of the international judicial organ, was an innovation, and a few years were required before it could be fully assimilated into both diplomatic and judicial practice. The main features of the preliminary objection procedure are that if a party—in very exceptional circumstances the *plaintiff* State may challenge the jurisdiction[31]—wishes to contest the Court's jurisdiction to determine the merits, it must do so *before* it pleads to the merits. If it decides to take that step, the proceedings on the merits will be suspended until the question of jurisdiction is decided. The question of jurisdiction is pleaded in complete independence of the main proceedings (indeed normally the parties' roles are reversed, the defendant on the merits appearing as the plaintiff on the objection),[32] in the form of a case within the case. Furthermore, these proceedings are interlocutory, and as such are not finally decisive of the merits of the action. The Court has three possibilities open to it. It can decide that the objection is well-founded, in which case the proceedings will come to an end; or it can decide that the objection is unfounded, in which case the proceedings on the merits will be resumed; or it can postpone its decision and join the objection to the merits. When it does this the main proceedings will be resumed, but in its judgment the Court will first have to dispose of the objection before it can go on to decide the merits. If it then accepts the objection, it will not give a decision on the merits. This course is usually adopted if the facts on which the objection depends are closely associated with the facts on which the merits depend, so that the Court could not give a decision on the objection which would not prejudice the position of the parties on the merits.

Broadly speaking, preliminary objections fall into three categories. One type argues that the title of jurisdiction invoked by the plaintiff State simply does not exist, for instance that it is a treaty, or a declaration accepting the compulsory jurisdiction, which has lapsed or is for some reason or other void. Clearly, this kind of obiection is the remotest from the merits with which, indeed, it has no direct connection. A second category of objection does not contest the existence of the title of jurisdiction as such, but argues that the concrete dispute does not come within the scope of the jurisdiction conferred on the Court. For instance, if jurisdiction is accepted only as regards disputes arising after a certain date, the argument that the dispute arose before that date would be raised as a preliminary objection. Judicial examination of this type of objection may be closely connected with the merits and the Court's decision on it is frequently, though not invariably, postponed.

The third category is not really an objection to the jurisdiction at all, but it is normally treated procedurally in the same way. Accepting the jurisdiction of the Court, it argues that the suit is inadmissible, usually on the ground that some rule of general international law has not been complied with—for instance the substantive conditions of the law for the exercise of the right of diplomatic protection.

Preliminary objections are a prominent feature of the work of the Court. In the Permanent Court, objections were raised in 13 cases, being upheld in three, rejected in eight (one of which was subsequently discontinued), and in two cases the main proceedings were broken off before the Court gave its decision on the objection. Since 1946, objections have become more frequent. Up to the end of 1962, preliminary objections had been raised in 16 cases (of which, incidentally, nine had been instituted in reliance on the compulsory jurisdiction), with the following results. In five cases they were dismissed; in five (four of them compulsory jurisdiction cases) upheld; in two cases the main proceedings were discontinued before the Court decided on the objection; in one the plaintiff State recognized the objection as being well-founded and discontinued the main proceedings; and in one, where the objection was purely technical, it was withdrawn and the proceedings on the merits resumed. One of the cases in which the Court found it was without jurisdiction was of major political significance—the *Anglo-Iranian* case—and this has thrown the problem of preliminary objections into sharp relief. Two cases are now pending.

Coupled with the growing frequency with which the Court's jurisdiction is challenged is another factor, namely, that nowadays it is rare for the jurisdiction to be challenged on a single, simple, ground. Instead, multiple objections, falling into all the categories previously mentioned, are put forward. Of the 15 cases in which preliminary objections have been raised since 1946, only four raised a single objection. Cases have occurred in which as many as six distinct objections, some of them further subdivided, have been advanced. When this happens, and especially when the objections relate both to the jurisdiction and to the admissibility, the nominally interlocutory proceedings are liable to assume a somewhat different character, for the pleadings on the objections are then bound to encroach upon the merits, even if only obliquely. It would be an over-simplification to regard a judgment declining jurisdiction given in those circumstances as being necessarily a merely technical matter, or to assume that because of the objections the Court has been prevented from making an effective contribution to the settlement of the dispute. It may be that the issues which were discussed and decided by the Court in the preliminary and to some extent procedural form of a preliminary objection were in fact issues which exacerbated the political situation and made the settlement of the dispute more difficult. Many people, for instance, regard the decision in the *Anglo-Iranian* case as being a more valuable contribution to the final settlement of that dispute than a decision dismissing the objections and resuming the case on the merits would have been; and it is believed that there have been other instances in which the formal decision of the Court declining jurisdiction has in fact assisted the parties in reaching an agreed solution of their difficulties.

Impatience is often expressed at the prevalence of the practice of raising preliminary objections and at the apparent frequency with which the Court has accepted them. But such impatience is misplaced. A State—as any private litigant—is fully entitled without abusing the due process of law to adopt any tactics allowed by the law to prevent judgment being given against it. Every State is entitled to intimate, through the preliminary objection procedure, that it is not willing for a concrete dispute to be decided by the Court—its subjective willingness being something quite different from its objective legal obligation to submit to the jurisdiction, on which the Court will pronounce itself in the decision on the objection. Every State has the right that the existence of that obligation be judicially determined before it takes issue with the plaintiff on the merits. And so long as the international community is not prepared to accept the principle of compulsory jurisdiction as such, the Court is certainly justified in the prudence and circumspection with which it deals with questions of its own jurisdiction, and in its refusal to attribute to States intentions which they themselves have not clearly formed.

In addition to the parties' right to ask for a decision on the question of jurisdiction, the Court has an inherent power to raise on its own initiative the question whether it has jurisdiction to do what the parties are asking it to do. This power is sparingly used in contentious cases, and when the parties are in agreement about submitting a case to the Court, it is more likely that what the Court itself might raise is not so much a question of jurisdiction in the formal sense, as whether it would be proper for the Court, as a Court of international justice, to give the decision requested. There were some instances of this in the Permanent Court, but none have occurred since 1946, although individual judges have occasionally recalled the existence of this power, and indeed duty, of the Court to satisfy itself that it can do what it is being asked to do.

ADVISORY JURISDICTION

The principle underlying the advisory jurisdiction is that qualified international organs are entitled to ask the Court for an opinion on legal questions, that opinion itself not constituting *per se* a "decision" with which anyone is legally bound to comply. In a number of national legal systems the Executive has power to request the Supreme Court to render an advisory opinion of this nature: though other legal systems tend to look askance on the idea of a Court rendering advisory opinions, on the ground that it distorts the true function of a Court of law, which is to render binding decisions on disputes (for instance, in 1793 the United States Supreme Court refused to give an advisory opinion to President Washington).[33] The introduction of this idea into the Covenant of the League of Nations was thus a controversial innovation.

After considerable hesitation and experimentation, the main lines of the international advisory practice were clarified by the middle thirties. Its features include the following: *(a)* the right to request advisory opinions should be retained by organs of international organizations, which would be expected to weigh the interests of the organization as a whole before making the request; *(b)* although the advisory jurisdiction opened up new ways of access to the Court, its existence should not be taken to authorize the surreptitious introduction of compulsory jurisdiction to decide concrete disputes between States by devious means; *(c)* the Court, in the exercise of its discretion to render advisory opinions, would remain faithful to its character as a Court of justice, and as the supreme international tribunal, incorporating into its advisory practice such of the basic principles of its contentious jurisdiction as were appropriate; *(d)* subject to this, the *procedure* for dealing with advisory matters would be assimilated as far as possible to that for dealing with contentious matters. Indeed, the main difference, from the procedural point of view, between the two classes of case is that in advisory matters there are technically no "parties" and no binding "decision": the role of individual States in advisory cases is essentially that of supplying "information"—an *amicus curiae* function so to speak.

Since the organs authorized by the Covenant to request advisory opinions were the Council and the Assembly of the League alone, on which only States were represented, it follows that the advisory competence did not constitute any departure from the basic nature of the Court, as a tribunal established by and for States. Only States, collaborating in the duly qualified organs, could initiate an advisory case. The difference between access to the contentious jurisdiction, and access to the advisory jurisdiction, is that in the first type of case a State could go to the Court on its own responsibility, while for the second it required the concurrence of other States, expressed in the form of a resolution requesting the Court to give the opinion. Suggestions are sometimes heard that certain individuals, for instance the Secretary-General, might be empowered to request an advisory opinion, but these have not been acceded to. It is also sometimes suggested that individual States, or at least pairs of States, might be authorized to request advisory opinions. This, too, has been rejected, for to accept it would surely mean to make possible the substitution of the advisory jurisdiction for the contentious—a real distortion of the true function of the Court.

The San Francisco Conference approved the patterns of advisory jurisdiction as they had developed previously, and contented itself merely with a few technical and drafting changes which have, however, had the effect of accentuating the differentiation between the advisory and contentious competences.

Accordingly, the Charter grants the Security Council and the General Assembly the right to request an advisory opinion on "any legal question". It further extended the right to request advisory opinions to other organs of the United Nations and Specialized Agencies which, so long as they are so authorized by the General Assembly, may request advisory opinions on legal questions arising within the scope of their activities.[34] At the same time the Statute confirms that the Court "may give"—i.e. has a discretionary power —an advisory opinion on any legal question at the request of any duly authorized body.[35] All the principal organs of the United Nations (excluding the Secretary-General), and the Specialized

Agencies are now authorized to request advisory opinions (as explained on p. 42 above): in addition the Interim Committee of the United Nations, and the Committee for Review of Administrative Tribunal Judgments, have been so authorized. (See Illustration IV. And see Appendix 5 for the particulars of the authorizations given.)

The real changes brought about at San Francisco and which influence the advisory jurisdiction as it has developed since 1946 are of a political character. They relate to the manner in which the United Nations organs operate, in comparison with the League's organs. In the League, unanimity, or virtual unanimity, was the rule for the adoption of substantive decisions, and a simple majority was required for the adoption of procedural decisions. The Council never decided clearly whether a decision to request an advisory opinion was substantive or procedural, but in an early advisory opinion the Permanent Court explained that the votes of the parties should not be taken into account in ascertaining whether there is unanimity,[36] and that was the practice commonly adopted both by the Council and by the Assembly. It does not seem that the Permanent Court ever gave an advisory opinion against the *opposition* of one of the parties: however, in one case it exercised its discretion not to give an advisory opinion when a State directly concerned, which had not been invited to participate in the discussion in the Council, categorically refused to take part in the examination of the question by the Court. The Court found that to answer the question would be substantially equivalent to deciding the dispute between the parties, and in the absence of the necessary consent held that it should not do so. It also pointed out that the case involved an enquiry into the facts, for which the collaboration of the two parties was essential.[37]

But in the United Nations, the unanimity rule has been completely abandoned. In the General Assembly the most that is required is a two-thirds majority, and in the Security Council a majority of seven out of eleven is sufficient (subject to the right of "veto"). This has meant that the decision to request the advisory opinion can—and indeed has—been taken in the teeth of strong opposition.

In the early fifties, the General Assembly several times decided to request advisory opinions on matters directly connected with the Cold War—the cases on *Admission into the United Nations*, on the *Interpretation of the Peace Treaties with Bulgaria, Hungary and Rumania.* These decisions were reached despite strong opposition of the Soviet Union. Although the Court decided that it should answer the questions thus put to it, these attempts to invoke Court procedures in the sensitive political areas of Soviet-U.S. relations were no more

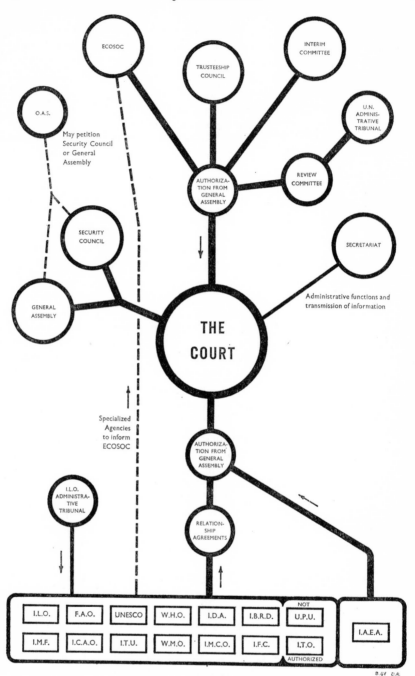

Illustration IV—The Advisory Competence of the International Court of Justice

successful than corresponding attempts to invoke contentious procedures, and they have not been repeated. On the other hand, the
advisory procedure has been useful in obtaining authoritative answers
on legal questions of general international concern, such as the
capacity of the United Nations to bring international claims in
respect of damages it has suffered, the effect of objections to reservations to multilateral conventions, and the binding character of
awards rendered by the Administrative Tribunals. These cases could
not have come before the Court but for the advisory jurisdiction.

The combination of the two factors—that a request for an advisory opinion may be adopted despite the opposition of the States
directly concerned, and that the advisory opinion itself is not formally "binding"—has become an element of great importance in
the dispute between the Union of South Africa and the United
Nations over the question of South-West Africa. The General
Assembly, after having taken the opinion of the Court in 1950 on the
international status of the Territory, has repeatedly insisted that
South African policies should conform to the advisory opinion, but
the Union has equally repeatedly refused. In an attempt to find a
way out of this stalemate, which was partly caused by ambiguity
over the precise legal obligations of South Africa, the General
Assembly encouraged States to seek a decision in a contentious
case, a result which could reduce some of the ambiguity at present
felt. That case, which is now pending, raises a number of complicated and delicate issues. These concern both the mutual relations
of the Court and the General Assembly, and those between the
contentious and the advisory jurisdiction. What is significant, however, is that in a case with heavy political implications, but which
does not directly raise Cold War issues, the General Assembly has
not shown itself averse to invoking the advisory procedures, and
indeed to putting "teeth" into them.

Since 1946, twelve requests for advisory opinions have been made,
ten by the General Assembly, one by the Governing Body of
UNESCO, and one by the Assembly of the Intergovernmental
Maritime Consultative Organization. In each case the requesting
organ has subsequently adopted policies corresponding to the legal
position as advised by the Court. Moreover, apart from the policies
of the organizations as such, most States have individually com-
ported themselves in accordance with the legal position indicated
in the advisory opinion, although this is not invariable. The possibility of requesting an opinion has been broached on a number
of other occasions in the Security Council, the Economic and Social
Council and in the Trusteeship Council, but has either not been
put to the vote or the draft resolution has not been adopted. Most

of these proposals have related to major political issues or concrete disputes, and in the absence of unequivocal agreement of the parties to refer the matter to the Court, it is probably to the general advantage that the Court was not embroiled in them.

While in most respects current practice in regard to the advisory procedure is in direct continuation from that initiated by the League, in one respect the United Nations has broken new ground. That is in the employment of the advisory procedure as part of the machinery for judicial review of the decisions of the Administrative Tribunals. This was first introduced by the International Labour Organization when it inherited the Administrative Tribunal of the League of Nations. That Tribunal was established in 1927 to deal with disputes between the members of the Secretariat and the Organization arising out of the contracts of service. In 1946, when the Statute of the Tribunal was revised and the Tribunal converted into the I.L.O. Administrative Tribunal, a provision was inserted empowering the Governing Body, if it wished to challenge a decision of the Tribunal confirming its jurisdiction, or if it considered that a decision was vitiated by a fundamental fault in the procedure followed, to submit the question of the validity of the decision to the International Court for an advisory opinion. No similar provision appeared in the Statute of the United Nations Administrative Tribunal which was established in 1949. Difficulties subsequently arose and in 1955 it was decided to institute a form of review, along similar lines to that of the International Labour Organization. For this purpose a Special Committee, to which a member State, the Secretary-General or a person in respect of whom a judgment has been rendered by the Tribunal, have access, was created, and authorized to request advisory opinions. That Committee, which is composed exclusively of the representatives of States, is empowered to decide whether there is any substantial basis for an application to request an advisory opinion.

These provisions do not have the effect of setting up the Court as a court of appeal from the decisions of the Administrative Tribunals. That means that it is not empowered to rehear the case. Its task is more limited, namely to review the procedure or the decision of the Tribunal and to give an opinion on the legal issues which thereby present themselves.[38]

Only one case of this nature has come before the Court. Its significance is that the Court did not regard it as incompatible with its judicial function to give such an advisory opinion, and that the Court showed that its procedure was sufficiently flexible to enable the contentions of the individuals concerned to be brought before it (see p. 159 below).

NOTES

1. *Free Zones case*, A 22 (1929), 13.

2. *Nottebohm* case (second phase), Rep. 1955, 19.

3. This is specifically laid down in Article 34 (1) of the Statute.

4. For instance in the present Court, see the following cases: *Ambatielos, Anglo-Iranian Oil Co., Nottebohm, Interhandel*. They, and the other cases mentioned here and decided since 1946, are described more fully in Chapter VI. The fact that the individual has no *locus standi* means that neither he, nor his legal representative, is entitled to address the Court. They are, of course, entitled to be present in the Court-room, as members of the general public, and usually are.

5. Statute, Article 34 (2). No instance of this has yet occurred.

6. *Reparation for Injuries Suffered* case.

7. Statute, Article 35 (2).

8. *Corfu Channel* (in a later stage), *Minquiers and Ecrehos*, and *Frontier Lands* cases.

9. *Asylum* and *Honduras-Nicaragua Frontier* cases. The *Monetary Gold* case may be seen as a variation on this theme, in very special circumstances.

10. See U.N. Conference on the Law of the Sea (1958), O.R. II, 7, 33 for the discussion which brought out all the underlying political issues. For the text of the Optional Protocol of Signature concerning the Compulsory Settlement of Disputes (doc. A/CONF.13/L.57) see ibid., 145. A similar solution was adopted in the United Nations Conference on Diplomatic Intercourse and Immunities (Vienna, 1961). See the Optional Protocol in doc. A/CONF.20/12.

11. *French Nationals in Egypt* case; *South-West Africa* case (Ethiopia and Liberia v. South Africa) relating to the League of Nations Mandate over South-West Africa; and the *Northern Cameroons* case relating to the Trusteeship Agreement over the British Cameroons.

12. Instances of this type of title of jurisdiction being invoked include the *Haya de la Torre* and *Ambatielos* cases.

13. These include the following cases: *Électricité de Beyrouth; Barcelona Traction, Light and Power Co.*; and *Compagnie du Port, des Quais et des Entrepôts de Beyrouth and Société Radio Orient*.

14. See the various *Aerial Incident* cases (other than the case concerning the *Aerial Incident of 27 July 1955*) and the *Antarctica* cases.

15. M. Hudson, *The Permanent Court of International Justice, 1920-1942* (New York, 1943), 473.

16. See in general, Herbert W. Briggs, "Reservations to the Acceptance of the Compulsory Jurisdiction of the International Court of Justice", R.A.D.I., 93 (1958) (i), 223.

17. Covenant of the League of Nations, Article 15 (8).

18. Charter of the United Nations, Article 2 (7).

19. Such reservations have been made at one time or another by France, India, Liberia, Mexico, Pakistan, South Africa and, as stated, by the United States, and in a different form by the United Kingdom. Since 1957, those by France, India, Pakistan and the United Kingdom have been withdrawn. The Executive Branch of the United States Government has also attempted to obtain the advice and consent of the Senate to the withdrawal of this reservation from the United States acceptance, but without success. For some reason or other, the issue raises emotional reactions in the United States.

20. In the Court this view has been advanced with vigour by the late Sir Hersch Lauterpacht, as well as by other judges, especially in the *Norwegian Loans* and *Interhandel* cases, and there is little doubt that the recent withdrawals of this type of reservation have been prompted by that criticism. For an account of Lauterpacht's attitude, see Sh. Rosenne, "Sir Hersch Lauterpacht's Concept of the Task of the International Judge", *American Journal of International Law*, 55 (1961), 825, especially at 844 ff.

21. According to the Secretary-General of the United Nations, on 31 December 1960 the following States had deposited declarations accepting the compulsory jurisdiction: Australia, Belgium, Cambodia, China, Denmark, Finland, France, Honduras, India, Israel, Japan, Liberia, Liechtenstein, Mexico, Netherlands, Norway, Pakistan, Phillippines, Portugal, Sudan, Sweden, Switzerland, Thailand, Turkey, Union of South Africa, United Arab Republic (Egypt), United Kingdom, United States of America. In addition, declarations by the following States made in relation to the Permanent Court of International Justice are believed to be in force: Canada, Colombia, Dominican Republic, El Salvador, Haiti, Luxembourg, New Zealand, Nicaragua, Panama, Uruguay. See doc. ST/LEG/3, Status of Multilateral Conventions in respect of which the Secretary-General acts as Depositary, pp. I—9-29. The declaration of the United Arab Republic is that dated 18 July 1957 regarding the operation of the Suez Canal, and is not a general acceptance of the compulsory jurisdiction, as are the others.

22. Statute, Article 36 (5).

23. Statute, Article 37.

24. This seems to be the combined effect of the *Aerial Incident of 27 July 1955* and *Temple of Preah Vihear* cases.

25. Owing to important differences in the wording of these two provisions, reflecting the different sets of circumstances with which they respectively deal, it does not follow that the interpretation given to Article 36 (5) in the concrete situation of the *Aerial Incident* case would be automatically applicable to the interpretation of Article 37 in entirely different conditions.

26. Statute, Article 41. And see Article 61 of the Rules of Court.

27. See p. 44 above. For the order indicating the measures, see Rep. 1951, 89.

28. *Interhandel* case, Rep. 1957, 105.

29. Cf. *Right of Passage* case, Rep. 1957, 152. And see p. 115 below.

30. Statute, Article 36 (6). Rules of Court, Article 62.

31. See *Monetary Gold* case.

32. This follows the principle of Roman law—*reus excipiendo actor est*—according to which by opposing an exception to the plaintiff's claim the defendant acts as plaintiff.

33. F. Frankfurter, "A Note on Advisory Opinions", *Harvard Law Review*, 37 (1924), 1002.

34. Charter, Article 96.

35. Statute, Articles 65-68. Rules of Court, Articles 82-85.

36. *Frontier between Turkey and Iraq* case, B 12 (1925). And cf. the separate opinion of Sir Hersch Lauterpacht in the *South-West Africa* (voting procedure) case. Rep. 1955, 67 at 98.

37. *Eastern Carelia* case, B 5 (1923).

38. By virtue of Article 14 of the Statute of the U.N. Administrative Tribunal, the competence of the Tribunal has been extended also to I.C.A.O. In addition,

that Tribunal has competence to deal with applications alleging non-observance of the Regulations of the U.N. Joint Staff Pension Fund as regards I.L.O., UNESCO, F.A.O., I.C.A.O., and W.H.O. As for the I.L.O. Administrative Tribunal, its competence has been extended to include the staff of W.H.O., UNESCO, I.T.U., W.M.O., F.A.O., the Secretariat of GATT, the European Organization for Nuclear Research (not a specialized agency) and the International Atomic Energy Agency.

CHAPTER V

HOW A CASE IS TRIED

PROCEDURE in the International Court is governed for the most part by the Rules of Procedure, and in some details by the Statute itself. But these procedural requirements are little more than a framework to guide those responsible for the conduct of a case. It would not be appropriate for an International Court to attempt to regulate its procedure in the precise and detailed fashion which is necessary for domestic tribunals. For the International Court has few litigants, actual or potential, not millions; and it derives its power from those litigants themselves, and not from any superior sovereign authority. Moreover, subject to the general control exercised by the Court, the parties are free to suggest procedural modifications to suit their particular circumstances, although instances of this are rare.

There are three characteristic features of the Court's procedure. The first is the sharp division of a case into two distinct phases of the written pleadings and the oral pleadings. Although the Court might permit variations in the *quantity* of pleadings in each of these two phases, it insists on the maintenance of the two phases themselves. Secondly, the Court very rarely gives any directions as to how it wants the case pleaded, or what it wants the pleadings to discuss. The reasons are deep (see p. 112 below). The third is the complete secrecy which attends the deliberations of the Court itself. No word of these ever reaches the public. So strictly is this rule kept that no judge is ever obliged to indicate how he voted, though he is free to do so, by means of a separate or a dissenting opinion, should he desire (see p. 120 below).

Illustration V depicts the normal stages through which a case goes from the institution of the proceedings to the final judgment. It is proposed now to demonstrate how a case is tried by reference to an actual case—the *Right of Passage* case—which occupied the Court from the end of 1955 until the middle of 1960, and in one form or another raised most of the kinds of problems which are encountered in international litigation.

THE *RIGHT OF PASSAGE* CASE: BACKGROUND

In the Indian Peninsula are situated three districts of Goa, Daman and Diu, which are Portuguese territory. Daman also includes two enclaved parcels, Dadra and Nagar-Aveli, entirely surrounded by Indian territory. It was in respect of communications between these enclaves and Daman and between each other that the question of a right of passage in favour of Portugal through Indian territory arose. Commencing in 1950, India has been trying to annex all those districts, in pursuance of its policy of expelling the last vestiges of European colonialism from the Peninsula. In 1954, an internal insurrection overthrew Portuguese authority in Dadra and the enclaves, and in the light of the tension produced by those events in the neighbouring Indian territory, the Indian Government then suspended all passage over its territory to and between them. That suspension has remained in force, and it has prevented Portugal from restoring its authority. At that point the legal dispute between the two countries crystallized.

In 1954 Portugal was not a member of the United Nations and not a party to the Statute of the Court. The only way in which it could then have brought its dispute with India before the Court was by making an appropriate agreement with India. Portugal's application to become a member of the United Nations was first submitted in 1946, but the Security Council and the General Assembly only completed their action on that request on 14 December 1955. Portugal at no time requested to become a party to the Statute without being a member of the United Nations.

India had accepted the compulsory jurisdiction of the Permanent Court by a declaration of 28 February 1940 which excluded from the jurisdiction disputes with regard to questions which by international law fall exclusively within the jurisdiction of India; and the acceptance was limited to disputes arising after 5 February 1930—the date upon which India had first accepted the compulsory jurisdiction—with regard to situations or facts subsequent to that date (this was a common form of reservation). That declaration had remained in force in accordance with the arrangements contained in the present Statute for preserving continuity in the administration of international justice (see p. 84 above). On 19 December 1955, five days after becoming a party to the Statute, Portugal deposited with the Secretary-General of the United Nations a declaration accepting the compulsory jurisdiction of the present Court. That declaration contained the following condition, which was subsequently to play an important role in the *Right of Passage* case:

"3. The Portuguese Government reserves the right to exclude from the scope of the present declaration, at any time during its

Illustration V—How a case is tried

validity, any given category or categories of disputes by notifying the Secretary-General . . . and with effect from the moment of such notification."

Three days later, on 22 December 1955, the Portuguese Minister at The Hague filed with the Registrar an application instituting proceedings against India.

THE INSTITUTION OF THE PROCEEDINGS

Cases may be begun in two ways, by special agreement or by application. The choice is a matter for the States concerned, the Statute not stating when one or other method shall be employed.

A special agreement both confers jurisdiction on the Court and defines the question which the Court is requested to decide. For example, the special agreement of 29 December 1950 between France and the United Kingdom stated:

"The Court is requested to determine whether the sovereignty over the islets and rocks (in so far as they are capable of appropriation) of the Minquiers and Ecrehos groups belongs respectively to the United Kingdom or the French Republic."

In such cases, the Court's judgment will normally consist of a formal answer to the precise question.

But when the case is introduced unilaterally, by application, the situation is different. The application has to include certain obligatory contents, such as an indication of the two parties and the subject of the dispute. It must also specify as far as possible the provision on which the applicant founds the jurisdiction of the Court, state the precise nature of the claim, and give a succinct statement of the facts and grounds on which the claim is based, these being further developed in later pleadings.[1]

Accordingly, the Portuguese application defines the subject of the dispute as concerning "the right of Portuguese officials and nationals, as well as foreigners authorized by Portugal, to cross India on their way between the Portuguese territory of Daman and the Portuguese enclaved territories of Dadra and Nagar-Aveli, and between each of the two last-mentioned territories." It was stated that Portugal, to whom the right unquestionably belongs, has claimed and continues to claim it, and that India has opposed and continues to oppose its exercise. That was the dispute submitted by Portugal to the verdict of the Court.

This is followed by a succinct statement of the facts and a summary of the law applicable. The jurisdiction of the Court was specified as founded on the compulsory jurisdiction, and the Court was formally petitioned to recognize and declare the Portuguese right of transit and the violation by India of its international obligations arising out of the right, and to adjudge that India must put an immediate end to the *de facto* situation by allowing Portugal to exercise its right of passage.

The application was in the English language. It stated that the Minister had been appointed Agent for the purposes of the case by the Portuguese Government, and that his address for service was the Portuguese Legation in The Hague.

OFFICIAL LANGUAGES

The official languages of the Court are French and English. The parties may agree to use one or the other language exclusively, in which case the judgment too shall be delivered in that language. In the absence of agreement, each party is free to use whatever official language it prefers. The Court may also authorize a language other than English or French to be used by a party, but in that case an English or French translation has to be attached. If a party conducts its oral pleadings in a language other than English or French, it must make its own arrangements for the translation into one of the official languages.[2]

In the present case, there was no agreement between the parties regarding language. The Portuguese written pleadings were in French (other than the application) and those of India in English. In the oral pleadings, the Portuguese used exclusively French but the Indian delegation used both languages. The authoritative text of each of the eight orders and the two judgments given in this case was English.

REPRESENTATION OF THE PARTIES

The person in whose hands is entrusted the formal representation of a party in international litigation is called the Agent. He, of course, may be assisted in the pleadings by counsel and advocates, and other experts who may be required.[3]

The status of Agent is roughly equivalent to that of a head of a special diplomatic mission, and he must be authorized to bind his country. As far as the Court is concerned, it is assumed that a man who is appointed Agent is fully authorized to represent his country, and frequently full powers are conveyed to the Court (although this is not an absolute requirement). In that capacity, he has to sign every important document relating to the case, and he has to confirm every important and binding statement made in his government's name in the course of the proceedings.

There are no formal qualifications for the position of Agent. States exhibit two tendencies, either to appoint a high-ranking member of their diplomatic service (for example, their Ambassador or Minister at The Hague), or the Legal Adviser (or one of his subordinates) of the Ministry for Foreign Affairs, but this is not invariable, and occasionally a practising lawyer is appointed.

An application should be signed by the Agent, and if he is not the accredited diplomatic representative of his country at The Hague, that diplomatic representative has to authenticate the signature on the application. The defendant government has to appoint its agent when acknowledging receipt of the application, or as soon as possible thereafter.

In the present case, Portugal appointed its Minister at The Hague as Agent together with the Director of the Faculty of Law in the University of Lisbon. India appointed its Attorney-General as Agent, and the Legal Adviser of its Ministry of External Affairs as Assistant Agent.

Similarly, there are no formal qualifications for counsel and advocates. These are frequently chosen from experienced members of the national bar, but in addition there has grown up over the years a small group of international lawyers, drawn mainly from the legal professions of England, France, Belgium and Switzerland, who have specialized in pleading cases in the International Court. Both parties availed themselves of the services of such men in the present case. Thus, in addition to the Agents, there pleaded for Portugal in one or other phases Professor Bourquin of Geneva (who had pleaded in many cases before the International Court) and Professor Pierre Lalive, also of Geneva; and the Indian Agent was assisted by Sir Frank Soskice, former Attorney-General of England, Maître Henri Rolin of Brussels (who had commenced his career at the international bar in the Permanent Court), Professor Guggenheim of Geneva (who, in addition to having pleaded in several cases, had also once served as judge *ad hoc*), and Professor Waldock of Oxford, who had also pleaded in a number of other cases. Two strong teams were to be ranged against each other.

STEPS FOLLOWING THE INSTITUTION OF PROCEEDINGS

As soon as the application was handed to the Registrar, he had to carry out a number of statutory duties.

Firstly, after assigning the case a number and opening a folio in the Court's general list (this case was No. 32), he must forthwith communicate the application to all concerned. This includes first of all the respondent Government, and secondly the members of the Court.[4] Standing arrangements exist for the direct transmission of communications from the Court to Governments—for India the channel is direct communication to the Minister of External Affairs in New Delhi. However, after Agents have been appointed, they are the sole channel of communication for all matters connected with the case, at an address for service selected by them in The Hague.[5]

Secondly, all members of the United Nations have to be notified of the institution of the proceedings, through the Secretary-General, and all other States entitled to appear before the Court. For this purpose the application (or special agreement) is translated into the other official language, printed, and certified copies are sent off. The object of this communication is to serve general notice to all governments of the institution of the proceedings, and what they are about, so as to enable them to consider whether they wish to intervene in the case. Also for more general political reasons, it is important that governments should have exact knowledge of cases pending in the Court.

The Statute grants two possibilities of intervention. Whenever a State considers that it has an interest of a legal nature which may be affected by the decision, it may submit to the Court a request for permission to intervene at any time up to the opening of the oral proceedings. The application for permission to intervene is given the same wide circulation as the original application instituting proceedings. The Court decides by judgment whether to admit the application, and if so arrangements are made for the intervening State to file appropriate pleadings. There has been no instance of States availing themselves of this right.[6] By another provision, whenever the construction of a convention to which States other than those concerned in the case are parties is in question, those States are to be notified forthwith: they have the right to intervene, and if they do so the construction given by the judgment will be equally binding on the intervening States.[7] One instance of this occurred in the Permanent Court and one in the present Court. The same principle is applied, by analogy, to determine what States are to be invited by the Court to submit information in advisory cases.

No requests for intervention, of either kind, were submitted in the *Right of Passage* case.

After these communications have been made, and the two Agents

Inaugural meeting 1946

Photo: De Spaarnestad, Haarlem

A signed and sealed Judgment

Photo: United Nations

Photo: Ed. van Wijk NFK ,The Hague

Regular Session of the Court 1960

Ambassador Eban (Israel) deposits declaration accepting compulsory jurisdiction

The Registry Staff at work

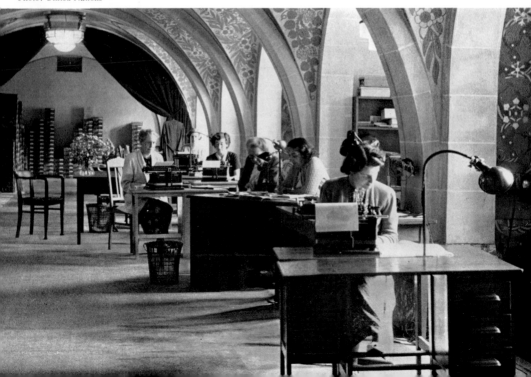

duly appointed, the next step is for the President to ascertain their intentions regarding the future conduct of the case. He does this either by correspondence or he may summon the Agents to a meeting with him. (The Agents need not always attend personally. Depending on the circumstances, their place may be taken by the diplomatic representative at The Hague.) After informing himself on this aspect, the President is in a position to make the necessary procedural orders.

In the present matter, the first order was made on 13 March 1956: it fixed the time-limits for the first stage of the written pleadings—15 June for the Memorial and 15 December for the Counter-Memorial.

Parties are normally granted equal time for their various pleadings, but this does not fully apply to the first round of written pleadings, because it is fair to assume that, except perhaps in cases of great urgency, before a Government decides to institute proceedings, it has carefully considered the case it wishes to present and has at least the outlines of the Memorial prepared. Indeed, since there is a close relation between the application and the Memorial, it is difficult to see how an application could be properly drafted if this were not the case.

THE WRITTEN PLEADINGS

No precise rules are laid down for the form of written pleadings except that they have to be printed, and this is a matter in which States are usually guided by their own national traditions and their sense of good taste. The fact that the pleadings are all ultimately published and remain on permanent record should influence the presentation of a case in the pleadings.

On the other hand, the Court's practice regulates to some extent the contents of the pleadings. Thus the Memorial, as the first written pleading of the plaintiff State is called, is supposed to contain a statement of all the relevant facts, a statement of law, and submissions; and copies of all relevant documents should be annexed. The Counter-Memorial, the first written pleading of the defendant government on the merits of the case, should contain more—an admission or denial of the facts stated in the Memorial; additional facts, if any; observations concerning the statement of law in the Memorial; a statement of law in answer thereto; and submissions. Again all relevant documents should be annexed. A preliminary objection should set out the facts and the law on which the objection is based, and the submissions, relevant documents also being annexed. The second round of written pleadings on the merits consists of a Reply and a Rejoinder, by the plaintiff and the defendant respectively (these pleadings are not usual in preliminary objection cases and in other formal interlocutory phases). No rules regulate their contents, and their purpose is essentially to amplify the case as presented in the Memorial and Counter-Memorial.[8] It frequently occurs that the issues are not all fully brought out until the Counter-Memorial is filed, for instance when that document contains a counter-claim. Even if it does not, it is only when the argument and submissions of the Memorial and those of the Counter-Memorial are compared that it is possible to see what the case is really about, for only then does its presentation cease to be unilateral. That is why the Reply and the Rejoinder are important stages of pleading in the International Court.

The original of every written pleading is signed by the Agent and filed in the Registry together with a number of copies, now usually fixed at one hundred. The Registrar delivers one certified copy and a sufficient number of plain copies to the other party and circulates the document to the members of the Court and other interested persons, including governments who have been authorized to receive them. He also prepares an unofficial translation of the pleading into the other official language. Unlike the procedure in international arbitration, the parties do not communicate their pleadings directly to one another. In cases of urgency, the Court will accept a pleading sent to it by modern methods of communication such as the telegraph if it is received before the expiration of the time-limit, and then the original signed text may be filed later in the normal course. This procedure is naturally rare.

Nowadays, pleadings are normally filed by the parties consecutively, as in domestic litigation, but in cases introduced by special agreement it is possible for the parties to file their written pleadings simultaneously. This used to be the common practice in international arbitration, and its justification is the equality of States and the absence, in true arbitration, of the idea that the parties are in the formal relationship of plaintiff and defendant, or applicant and respondent. But experience has shown that this is an inconvenient mode of pleading, and modern special agreements usually specify the order in which the pleadings shall be filed.

The written pleadings are not normally made generally available until after the termination of the case. This is in order to avoid exposing them to public, and perhaps polemical, discussion which, it is considered, would not be conducive to the good administration of international justice. However, any government may apply to the Court and ask for the pleadings to be made available to it, and this will normally be granted after enquiry of the Agents. Exceptionally, and if both parties consent, the Court may authorize the pleadings to be made generally available before the termination of the case, and in that event a set will be placed in the Library of the Peace Palace at The Hague.[9]

Now let us come back to our case. Portugal filed its Memorial by the date fixed. It is a relatively short document expanding the case as set forth in the application. It consists of 25 pages of text together with 54 annexes and two maps, 92 pages in all. Its submissions are slightly different from the claim as originally included in the application. The Court is asked:

"(1) To judge and declare:
(a) that Portugal has a right of passage through the territory of India in order to ensure communications between its territory of Daman and its enclaved territories of Dadra and Nagar-Aveli;
(b) that this right comprises the transit of persons and goods, as well as the passage of representatives of the authorities and of armed forces necessary to ensure the full exercise of Portuguese sovereignty in the territories in question.
(2) To adjudge and declare:
(a) that the Government of India must respect that right;
(b) that it must therefore abstain from any act capable of hampering or impeding its exercise;
(c) that neither may it allow such acts to be carried out on its territory.
(3) To adjudge and declare that the Government of India has acted and continues to act contrary to the obligations recalled above.
(4) To call upon the Government of India to put an end to this unlawful state of affairs."

With the filing of this document, the initiative passed to India. What choices were open to it?

First, it could let the case go by default, an unlikely event. Second, having now seen the applicant's case, it could decide to take issue on the merits and file its Counter-Memorial. Third, it could challenge the jurisdiction of the Court by raising one or more preliminary objections. India had six months in which to make up its mind. It decided on the latter course, but ran into difficulties in preparing its pleading. On 10 November 1956 the Indian Agent requested a six months extension of time to which Portugal was opposed, while trusting in the discretion of the Court to make the extension as short as required by the interests of justice. After a conference with the Agents the Court extended the time-limit by four months, expiring on 15 April 1957, by order of 27 November 1956.

Within the new time-limit India filed a pleading 78 pages long, together with 431 pages of annexes. In this, six preliminary objections were raised. The case now took on a new turn.

THE PRELIMINARY OBJECTIONS

The first objection argued to the effect that the Portuguese declaration accepting the compulsory objection was invalid on the ground that the third condition was incompatible with the Statute, the consequence being that India was under no obligation to recognize the jurisdiction *vis-à-vis* Portugal. This raised highly technical issues related to the manner in which the compulsory jurisdiction works. The second and fourth objections were connected with that argument, but they attacked the Portuguese action in bringing the case on the basis of a surprise move, before India had had any opportunity of seeing the Portuguese declaration and of availing itself of the possibility of amending its own declaration. This was an attack on Portuguese good faith, for it contained the implication that the terms of the Portuguese declaration, and particularly its third condition, were in fact tailored to suit Portugal's immediate ends in her dispute with India and were not a genuine acceptance of the jurisdiction of the Court. These three objections belong to that general category which argues that the title of jurisdiction invoked by the plaintiff State simply does not exist, and that the manner in which the case was instituted was invalid. They belong, therefore, to the remotest class of objection.

The third objection argued that diplomatic negotiations had not been exhausted before the application was filed, and that because of that no legal dispute existed between the parties. The fifth objection argued that the dispute related to a matter within India's domestic jurisdiction and therefore was excluded from the acceptance of the jurisdiction contained in the Indian declaration of 28 February 1940. The sixth objection argued that the dispute, if it existed, arose before 5 February 1930 and concerned facts or a situation antecedent to that date, and therefore did not come within the jurisdiction accepted by India, which was limited to disputes arising after that date. These three objections, which were intimately connected with the actual dispute brought before the Court, therefore belonged to the general category of objections which argue that the concrete dispute does not come within the scope of the jurisdiction conferred on the Court: and the third objection is of a

THE PRELIMINARY OBJECTIONS

type that in some circumstances can be regarded as an objection to the admissibility, although it was not so treated in the present case.

The effect of this document was to suspend the proceedings on the merits. These were put aside for the time being. At one time a preliminary objection was regarded as a new case which was notified to all concerned in the usual manner. But later the Court decided that it was to be regarded as an incident in the procedure: at most a general notification is made that the preliminary objections have been filed and that the proceedings on the merits are suspended, leaving it to interested governments to take steps to ascertain if they have any reason to think of intervening (in fact there is no instance of any attempt at intervention in the preliminary objection phase). Accordingly, on 16 April 1957 an order was made recording the suspension of the main proceedings, and fixing 15 June as the time-limit within which Portugal could present its written observations and submissions on the objections. These are normally the only written pleadings in a preliminary objection phase: it is an assumption that by the time preliminary objections have been filed the plaintiff government has had sufficient opportunity to foresee the possible objections (or at least most of them), and is ready to meet the challenge. For this reason, too, the Court usually likes to dispose of the objections after a short time-limit for the written pleading. However, the Indian objections in this case were undoubtedly long, and the case, although preliminary, correspondingly heavy, and early in May the Portuguese Agent was compelled to ask for an extension of the time-limit. India made no objection and on 18 May the time-limit was extended for two months to 15 August.

On that date Portugal filed its pleading on the question of jurisdiction. The pleading itself was 77 pages in length, to which were appended 168 pages of annexes. The submission was short: that not one of the preliminary objections was justified, and therefore that they should all be rejected and the proceedings on the merits resumed.

On 15 August 1957, with the filing of the last written pleading, the case on the question of jurisdiction reached the technical stage of being "ready for hearing".[10]

THE CASE READY FOR HEARING

There are two consequences of a case becoming ready for hearing. The first is that it is entered into the list for oral proceedings. If more than one case is ready for hearing on the same date, the order in which they will be heard is fixed either by agreement between the various parties, or by reference to their places on the Court's general list. When this phase of the *Right of Passage* case became ready for hearing, no other pending case was in the same position. However, while the hearings were taking place Switzerland filed a request for interim measures of protection in another case in which it was concerned. Such a request has absolute priority over all other cases.[11] That application was filed on 3 October. The hearings thereon took place on the 12th, and the order was made on 24 October 1957, immediately after the hearings in our case.

The Court decided to commence the hearings in the present case immediately after its summer vacation.[12]

The second consequence of a case being ready for hearing is that no further documents may be filed except with the consent of the other party or by leave of the Court, which will usually give its decision after hearing argument by the parties.[13] The Court does not like the belated submission of documents if this is avoidable, yet it is flexible and undogmatic on this aspect, treating each case on its merits. Government archives are rarely so efficiently run that all the documents in its files—especially if the case has long historical antecedents—are always easily available for the lawyers working on a case, and it often happens that new documents are discovered after a case is ready for hearing. Parties, too, usually are not too formal on these questions: it would be wholly exceptional for the result of international litigation to be dependent upon a single document not produced in good time, and as there is a general obligation on the parties to co-operate with the Court in ascertaining the true facts, a formalistic attitude is rarely likely to be helpful.

THE HEARING

In the hearings on the preliminary objection, India appeared as "plaintiff" and Portugal as "defendant". It therefore fell to India to open these oral proceedings.

Unlike the written pleadings, the oral pleadings are in principle held in public, though in exceptional circumstances (which have not yet occurred in the present Court) the public may be excluded.[14] They take place in the dignified setting of the Great Hall of Justice in the Peace Palace at The Hague. The members of the Court and the Registrar wear their judicial robes: the Agents (if they are members of the legal profession), counsel and advocates their professional or academic robes. In front of the Court sit the official recorders, interpreters and other members of the staff on duty.

Immediately opposite the President is the speaker's rostrum, to the left of which sits the plaintiff's Agent and his delegation, and to the right the defendant's Agent and his delegation.

At the hour appointed for the opening of the meeting the Huissier (Court Usher), after ascertaining that all is ready (and especially that the representatives of the parties are present), gives the traditional cry *La Cour*. All rise. The judges proceed with measured steps to their seats. At a sign from the President they are seated, and the others follow. The atmosphere is subdued and forensic. The Great Hall of Justice is bigger than many court-rooms, but discreetly placed microphones easily carry the voices to all corners. The remarks of the President and his colleagues are translated immediately: speeches, which are usually delivered from full notes if not from prepared texts, are broken off every ten minutes or so for translation. The Court's practice is to employ consecutive, and not simultaneous, interpretation.

It is the oral pleadings which have the most direct impact. The written pleadings lay the foundation—of fact and of law—on which good oral pleading can be based. One cannot fail to be struck by the close attention with which they are followed: for they have great psychological value and act as the focusing point for the work of the Court. While, clearly, there is no room for histrionic advocacy appropriate for a jury trial, the effect of intonation, of candour, of inflexion, of command of language and a cultivated presentation of the case, of mastery of complicated issues, and, where appropriate, a touch of humour, of drama, a well-timed quotation —all this is concealed in the lifeless printed versions of the oral all, it is at the oral hearings that the two parties first meet face to pleadings which are subsequently circulated and published. Above face. Their cases emerge from the remote tranquility of Counsel's chambers and clash head-on in the hands of highly skilled lawyers, each of whom knows the strength, and the weakness, of his own and of his opponent's cases. The pleading is strenuous.

The Court is careful to preserve the good "atmosphere" which is essential for the proper and dispassionate consideration of the case. The style of pleading is courteous—indeed the Court is one of the few international organs in which old-style diplomatic courtesies have survived. The good custom has recently been introduced by which the President offers a formal dinner to the two Agents at which all the members of the Court and the staff of the Registry, and of the two delegations (together with their ladies) are present. This usually happens early in the case and is important for creating those intangible mutual contacts between the parties and the Court which assist in the smooth conduct of the litigation.

The normal order for addressing the Court is that first the oral argument of the plaintiff State is presented, then that of the defendant State. This is followed by the oral reply of the plaintiff and the oral rejoinder of the defendant. The Agent usually opens the pleading, and if he is not going to address the Court himself will introduce his advocates and counsel. In the course of the oral pleadings, usually during the first statements, the Agent will present his "final submissions".

Witnesses as to fact are not normally heard in the International Court: in the one case in which evidence was taken from witnesses —the *Corfu Channel* case—they testified after the first round of statements, but the Court has retained a general right to determine for each case when the evidence shall be taken.[15]

In the preliminary objection phase of the *Right of Passage* case the hearings commenced on 23 September 1957 and terminated on 11 October, occupying fourteen meetings of the Court. Five persons presented the Indian case, and three that of Portugal, and the printed record covers some 263 pages.[16]

Members of the Court have the right to put questions to the parties and ask them for explanations[17] but this right is rarely exercised. In all the fourteen days of the hearings under discussion, there is no record of any interruption by any member of the Court. This is very unlike the procedure in the Common Law Courts, where the judges frequently interrupt Counsel, but it is common in the Continental Courts. The International Court is sometimes criticized for its apparent inactivity in the course of the written and oral pleadings, but such criticism is generally misplaced, and fails to appreciate the delicate position of the international judge deciding a dispute between sovereign States. The pleading is frequently an act of State, permanently on public record, and its representatives may have their own reasons for pleading a case in one way or another. Their case stands or falls on the ground of their own choice, and it would not be proper for an international Court to interfere more than is absolutely necessary for the orderly conduct of the trial.

FINAL SUBMISSIONS

It has been mentioned that certain written pleadings—including all those which have been filed in our case up to now—have to contain "submissions". In the course of the oral pleadings, usually during the two opening statements, the parties present what are commonly called their "final submissions".[18] So important are these that it is obligatory for the Court's judgment to set forth the parties' submissions.

A submission is an extremely concise statement of what each party wants from the Court. Each submission indicates what that party considers should be the language of the operative part of the judgment (as opposed to the pleading, which explains the party's view on the relevant reasons of fact and of law in support of its submission). It shows what the party is asking the Court to decide concretely. When a case is introduced by application, the decision of the Court is given on the final submissions, but when it is introduced by special agreement that, as we have seen, defines what it is that the Court has to decide. The final submissions, therefore, are the ultimate concretization of the dispute and as such have to be regarded as an act of State. The outcome of the case will depend on their formulation, and the interpretation of the final submissions may in turn depend upon a comparison of them with the earlier submissions in the case.

For this reason, and to assist the clarity of the discussion, the Court has, in the course of its judicial experience, come to require certain attributes of the final submissions. They should be worded in the form of a positive statement: if they are worded negatively, or interrogatively, they may not provide a satisfactory basis for the decision, and the Court may not be able to give effect to them. As a statement of what a party thinks the decision should be, they should also not contain a series of arguments or propositions in support. That is the function of the pleadings. However, it is today fairly common for States to commence their submission by a series of preambles, "Whereases . . ."—in which the whole case is epitomized with the maximum of succinctness, a practice which is sometimes deprecated as not being consonant with the proper function of a submission, but which may be justified if the diplomatic role of the judicial settlement of international disputes is kept in mind. For its part, however, the Court will ignore the irrelevant parts of submissions—as it did in our case.

Furthermore, the submissions should stand in direct relation to the original statement of the claim as it appeared in the application (or preliminary objection). They do not have to be identical with it, and through the normal processes of pleading modifications, sometimes far-reaching, will appear in the shape of the case through the successive developments in the pleadings. The Court will watch this carefully, in order to guard against a change in the character of the case which might affect the basis of its jurisdiction, and in order to make sure that, by reason of such change, circumstances have not arisen in which notice should be given to third States to alert them to the possibility that they may have to apply for permission to intervene. As between the parties, however, the principle that consent to the jurisdiction can be given tacitly means that when they file submissions they are taken to accept any possible irregularities in the jurisdiction which might exist up to that stage. Submissions which "match" will normally confer jurisdiction on the Court.

Having regard to their importance, the final submissions which are read during the oral proceedings have to be filed in Court in writing, signed by the Agent. They may be further modified up to the last moment, and the party against whom they are filed is always given the opportunity of commenting on them (as an act of courtesy the Agents usually communicate their final submissions directly to the other party in the course of oral proceedings, although the formal communication is, of course, made by the Registry).

The final submissions in our case were complicated. The direction which the case took was fixed by India. On the first four objections, and on the sixth, the submission was for the Court to declare that it was without jurisdiction broadly speaking on the grounds set forth in the preliminary objections themselves. But the submission on the fifth objection was further subdivided into five parts. Three of these were closely based on the arguments of the parties in law and in fact, whereas two raised general questions of principle, including the novel argument that in effect the Portuguese had not disclosed an arguable cause of action under international law, and therefore India had no case to answer. (This was partly based on the shortness of the Portuguese Memorial.) In reply to this, Portugal's final submissions asked for the first, second, third, and fourth objections to be dismissed. On the fifth it asked either for the objection to be dismissed or for it to be joined to the merits, and the same was at first submitted as regards the sixth. Portugal went further and, claiming that the Indian argument that there was no case to answer was in fact a new objection filed out of time, objected that it was inadmissible and should be dismissed. Finally, Portugal added a new claim that the Court should recall to the parties the universally admitted principle that they should facilitate the accomplishment of the Court's task by abstaining from any measure capable of exercising a prejudicial effect in regard to the execution of its decision or which might bring about either an aggravation or an extension of the dispute. As a result of this, the original six preliminary objections had now expanded into eight distinct issues, and this gave India the right to make modifications in its final submissions. On the "no case to answer" argument, India took to the offensive and filed a new final submission calling for the rejection of the Portuguese claim. On the last issue, India was quick to point out that if Portugal wanted an interim injunction it should proceed accordingly, and it therefore asked for the submission to be rejected.

This in turn gave rise to a further reaction on the part of Portugal which modified its previous submission on the sixth objection, and now asked for its outright dismissal.

This affords a good illustration of how the direct encounter of the parties before the Court affects the issues which the Court is to decide.

INTERIM MEASURES OF PROTECTION

As we have seen (p. 84 above), a request for interim measures of protection can be filed at any time during the proceedings. That request is a formal document which initiates interlocutory proceedings of a summary character, and the decision of the Court is only given after argument. It is the Court's practice to communicate such requests in the same way that applications instituting proceedings are communicated, and the Court's decision is usually couched in the form of an order.

Nothing like this procedure was followed by Portugal in the present case. In fact the Portuguese Government expressly disclaimed any intention of invoking the provisions of the Statute concerning the indication of interim measures of protection. In those circumstances the Court did not think that it should comply with the Portuguese request.

CLOSURE OF ORAL PROCEEDINGS

After, subject to the control of the Court, the parties have completed their presentation of the case, the President formally declares the hearing closed. He may do this at the termination of the last hearing devoted to the case, or he may wait a few days, depending on the circumstances. Once the oral hearings are closed, no further evidence or pleading may be submitted by either party (unless the Court calls for it), and the Court withdraws to consider the judgment.[19] The parties can now relax, and the initiative passes to the Court.

THE BENCH

The Court met for this phase of the case under the Presidency of Judge Hackworth, of the United States of America. All the titular judges participated in the hearing. As neither of the parties had a judge of its nationality on the bench, they both exercised their right to choose a judge *ad hoc*. India chose the Hon. Mahomad Ali Currim Chagla, who was then Chief Justice of Bombay and who later became his country's ambassador in Washington, and Portugal Senhor Manuel Fernandes, Director-General at the Ministry of Justice and a member of the International Relations Section of the Upper House. At the beginning of the meeting on 23 September the two judges *ad hoc* made the solemn declaration required of all judges, Mr. Chagla having precedence (by virtue of age).

For this phase of the case the Bench consisted of seventeen judges.

THE COURT'S DELIBERATION

The following are the basic rules governing the manner in which the Court deliberates. The judgment has to state the reasons on which it is based.[20] All questions are decided by a majority of the judges present, the President* having a casting vote in the event of a tie.[21] If the judgment does not represent in whole or in part the unanimous opinion of the judges, any judge is entitled to deliver a separate opinion.[22] The Court sits in private for its deliberations, only the judges and assessors (if any) taking part, but the Registrar or his substitute is present. The President (or the Acting President) is generally responsible for the conduct of the deliberations. Each judge should state his opinion together with the reasons on which it is based, and if any judge so desires the question to be voted upon has to be drawn up in precise terms. The decision is based on the conclusions concurred in after final discussion by a majority of the judges, who vote in inverse order of precedence. No detailed minutes are prepared of these private meetings. Such minutes as there are are confidential and record only the subject of the debates, the votes taken, the names of those voting for or against, and statements made expressly for the record.[23] On that basis the contents of a judgment have been laid down. They must include a statement whether delivered by the Court or a Chamber, the date of delivery, the names of the judges participating (in the final vote), the names of the parties and their agents and representatives, a summary of the proceedings, the submissions, a statement of the facts, the reasons in point of law, the operative provisions of the judgment, any decision in regard to costs, the number of judges constituting the majority, and an indication of the authoritative text. Any judge may attach his individual opinion to the judgment, or a bare statement of his dissent.[24]

* The term President here includes the judge acting as President for a given case (see p. 63 above).

Within that framework, the Permanent Court had tried several ways before it was able to reach its final decision on the best method of formulating its judgments. This was ultimately consolidated in its Resolution regarding the Court's judicial practice, first adopted on 20 May 1931 and revised on 17 March 1936. The present Court, on 6 May 1946, "took note" of that Resolution and decided to adopt "provisionally" the same method of deliberation.[25]

According to that Resolution, the earliest general consideration of the case by all the judges takes place between the termination of the written proceedings and before the commencement of the hearing, when they meet in private to exchange views in order to see if, on examination of the written pleadings, there are any points on which it would be necessary to ask for supplementary verbal explanations. In fact, this is rarely done, except perhaps in an informal way, and the Court has, for reasons already explained, shown a marked diffidence towards interfering in the manner in which the parties conduct the oral pleadings. Apart from this preliminary examination, the Court's deliberations start in earnest only after the oral pleadings are over.

The first step is to allow the judges a suitable period of time, not too long, to study the case as it now presents itself. After that, the first collective deliberation is held. The purpose of this is to bring out the questions to be solved, and to initiate the discussion of them individually. It is the responsibility of the President to ensure that all questions called to notice by himself or by the other judges are discussed, and that each judge makes known his impressions regarding them. Following this deliberation, each judge formulates his personal view in the form of a note, but at this stage he is not committed to a definite opinion. On the basis of these notes the President prepares a plan of discussion, provisionally determining the order and the terms of the questions on which the Court must give its opinion. This plan is submitted to the Court, but its adoption commits neither the Court's freedom to modify it subsequently, nor the right of the judges at any stage to call upon the Court to express its opinion on any question in any form in which they consider desirable. Finally the questions, after discussion on them is exhausted, are put to the vote and decided.

The Court is now in a position to set about drafting its judgment. On the basis of the majority of the votes cast at that final deliberation, the Court appoints a drafting Committee, consisting of the President *ex officio* (regardless of how he voted) and two judges chosen by secret ballot and by an absolute majority of votes, to prepare the draft. The Committee circulates its draft to all the judges, who are entitled to submit amendments. On that basis the final text is prepared and submitted to the Court, and after approval finally translated into the other official language and prepared for delivery. Separate or dissenting opinions are circulated among the judges between the first and second readings of the Court's decision and, in matters of form at least, are subject to a certain measure of control and guidance from the drafting Committee (a matter of importance for the judges *ad hoc* who, of course, lack the concrete experience of this manner of deliberation).

When all is ready, the parties are notified of the date of the public meeting at which the judgment will be delivered.[26] At the public meeting the judgment is read in its authentic text, a translation also being read of its operative clause, and signed and sealed copies of it are handed to the Agents (a further signed and sealed copy is retained in the archives of the Court).[27] A copy of every judgment is also sent officially by the Registrar to every member of the United Nations and to every State entitled to appear before the Court.[28] The text is immediately made available to the Press.

The judgments, advisory opinions and orders are published consecutively throughout each year. At the end of the year they are collated, indexed and bound, and form a series of *Reports* similar to domestic series of Law Reports. Apart from official distribution to governments, these texts (as the other publications of the Court) are also placed on sale to the general public.[29]

THE JUDGMENT OF 26 NOVEMBER 1957

The deliberations in this phase of the *Right of Passage* case lasted from 11 October to 26 November 1957, when the judgment was delivered. In a document of 31 pages (18 devoted to the formal parts), the Court rejected the first objection by fourteen votes to three, rejected the second objection by the same vote, rejected the third by sixteen votes to one and the fourth by fifteen votes to two. The fifth, however, it decided to join to the merits by a vote of thirteen to four, and it reached the same decision on the sixth by fifteen votes to two. A declaration of dissent was made by Judge Kojevnikov, and dissenting opinions were appended by Vice-President Badawi, Judge Klaestad (with which Judge *ad hoc* Fernandes concurred) and by Judge *ad hoc* Chagla. The document as a whole is 59 pages long. In consequence, the proceedings on the merits were resumed, and new time-limits fixed.

At first sight, this was an impressive victory for Portugal. Four of the objections had been rejected by very substantial majorities, while two had been postponed. Portugal had overcome the first hurdle and was now assured that the case would be fully ventilated on its merits.

But let us see what effect this judgment had on the case. As stated, the first, second and fourth objections had related exclusively to the title of jurisdiction and the manner in which the proceedings had been instituted in reliance on it, and discussion of those issues in the pleadings and in the judgment had no direct connection with the merits of the case. Psychologically, however, these objections had undoubtedly put Portugal's good faith in issue, although this is nowhere overtly expressed in the judgment.

It was otherwise with the discussion of the other objections. The dismissal of the third preliminary objection, which argued that the filing of the application was premature because the diplomatic negotiations had not been exhausted and therefore the existence of the dispute was not sufficiently disclosed, knocked away one of the props of India's case, but this was partly compensated by the manner in which the Court dealt with the fifth objection. Here it adopted the purely formal position that the facts and their interpretation were disputed between the parties so that it could not pronounce on that objection at that stage without prejudging the merits. For that reason it found it unnecessary to examine the other questions which had arisen in regard to that objection, including the whole question of whether Portugal had produced a reasonably arguable case. This for Portugal was no light matter to have still open. Even more significant was the Court's reasoning on the sixth objection. Although in form this type of objection—that the dispute relates to situations and facts occurring before a certain date—appears highly technical, its impact on any case is in fact extremely strong, because it compels the Court to examine the dispute in all its *minutiae* so that it can establish precisely of what elements it is composed in order to relate it to the date which governs the jurisdiction of the Court in the concrete case. In so far as the date is accidental[30] this is really an artificial process, because historically the dispute developed without any direct connexion with that date, but in practice it is of considerable psychological importance. The Court had given notice that in due course it would investigate these questions closely, but decided to postpone that process for the moment on account of divergences of fact between the parties. The adjournment of these two objections enabled India to stress in all the subsequent stages that it was still contesting the jurisdiction of the Court.

What had India gained by this procedure? In the first place, by interrupting the normal course of the pleadings, it had forced its adversary to show its cards earlier than obviously was intended, as appears by comparing Portugal's Memorial with its observations on the preliminary objections. The pleadings on the third, fifth and sixth objections in particular had drawn attention to a number of weaknesses in Portugal's case as a whole, and in fact made serious dents in it. India was able to exploit this in the later phases of the case.

Secondly, India had gained time—in fact something like a year if not more. A defendant nearly always wants to gain time. India was in no hurry for the Court to reach its final decision, for the case was taking place against a general political background which was changing to India's advantage. Furthermore, triennial elections were due to take place at the end of 1957, and the composition of the Court was likely to change. The effect of this was, of course, unknown in advance: but it could not be excluded that the changes would be beneficial to India, for at best it would mean that the final decision would be given by a Court different in its composition from that which Portugal had in mind when it decided to commence the proceedings.

Thirdly, the treatment of the sixth objection had raised the fundamental question of what was the precise dispute which the Court was to decide. It is tactically useful to have this kind of issue pending throughout this type of case.

THE SEPARATE AND DISSENTING OPINIONS

An opinion given by a judge who supports the view of the majority is called a separate opinion, and one given by a judge who disagrees with the view of the majority is called a dissenting opinion—a formal distinction which refers primarily to the attitude adopted by the individual judge on the final vote and the operative clauses of the judgment. The term "individual opinion" covers both types of opinion.

The system for the preparation and promulgation of judgments is a combination of the Continental system, which prefers a single judgment given in the name of the Court as a whole, without any indication of dissentient views, and the Common Law system in which each judge is entitled to express his own opinion and state the reasons for it. (Something like the Continental system is followed by the Judicial Committee of the Privy Council in London.) The judgment of the International Court is collective and anonymous: at the same time each judge is entitled, but not obliged, to express his own views, by means of a separate or a dissenting opinion. Usually it is possible, by a simple process of arithmetic, to work out who were the judges comprising the majority (but even then it is not possible to know who actually drafted the Court's judgment), but this is not always so. A case recently occurred in which the Court reached its decision by nine votes to five, but as only two dissenting opinions were appended there is no possibility of knowing who were the nine and who were the other three members of the five.

Many people think that the right of each judge to append his own opinion is essential for the effective working of the Court. A former President of the Permanent Court of International Justice, Dr. Max Huber, stated in 1929 that this right was "a guarantee against any subconscious intrusion of political considerations," and that through its existence "judgments were more likely to be given in accordance with the real force of the arguments submitted." In 1956 he went on record as saying that he would hardly have accepted the office as judge if the Statute had not taken over the Anglo-Saxon system of dissenting opinions.[31] A judge of the present Court has pointed out that this system "has come to be regarded as a safeguard of the individual responsibility of the Judges as well as of the integrity of the Court as an institution. . . . It precludes any charge of reliance on mere alignment of voting and lifts the pronouncements of the Court to the level of the inherent power of legal reason and reasoning."[32]

At the same time, the collective and anonymous drafting of the majority opinion has certain drawbacks. The opinion tends to be colourless and lack "character" and even cohesion, although there are exceptions, and our judgment is one of them. It is the product of compromise over words and phrases between a group of men who may be united only in their determination to reach a formally binding decision in the concrete case, but who remain in fact divided between themselves; and in such circumstances questions of semantics become of major importance. When this happens the opinion will appear excessively brief, for it will do no more than represent the common denominator of the divergent views of the judges, and exclude every redundant word. The problem which arises is the following: Should the Court strive for the largest possible majority for its decisions, at the cost of eliminating every word and thought that gives rise to controversy; or should it place the general cogency of the reasoning at the head of its concern, voting only on the operative clauses of the judgment, and leaving the reasons to the skill and energy of the individual judges? The Court has chosen the first course, and while it was probably a wise choice, it adds to the general significance of the individual opinions.

The individual opinions, whether they are separate or dissenting opinions, perform several functions. Thanks to the greater freedom of expression and emphasis enjoyed by the individual judges, many of them do no more than underpin the anonymous collective opinion of the majority, which, owing to the process by which it was put together, cannot always articulate fully and expressively the underlying principles which were applied. In other cases, the individual opinion may indicate other general underlying principles which its author believed should have been more appropriately applied in the concrete case. Such an opinion may have a value of its own in correcting any misleading impression which could be obtained from the majority opinion. The fact that certain ideas only appear in a separate opinion does not mean that the Court as a whole *rejected* them. It means nothing more than that the Court was not prepared to accept them for the purposes of its decision—something quite different. In another direction, one sometimes encounters individual opinions which flatly contradict both the underlying principles and their application by the majority and here, dependent on the author's general reputation and the cogency of his reasoning, the individual opinion may in the course of time come to be seen by enlightened and informed opinion as expressive of better law. Above all, the publication of these opinions focuses attention on the nature of the discussion in the Council Chamber. For a full understanding of the real implications of any judgment, the discerning reader will consult not merely the pleadings, which will show him how the parties presented the issues, but also the individual opinions appended to the majority judgment, which will show him the main lines of the discussion in the Court when it withdrew to deliberate on the case.

Here another factor has to be noticed. The figures of the final voting by the judges are an extremely deceptive guide to the strength of the two cases. In most instances of international litigation, the balance between the two parties' cases, from the point of view of abstract legal merit, is extremely fine. Countries do not become involved in international litigation, and certainly not plaintiff governments, if their case is not reasonably arguable! The fact that in the *Right of Passage* case the six clauses of the operative part of this judgment were reached by extremely large majorities, in no instance less than thirteen out of the seventeen judges who sat, is no test whatsoever of the strength of the Indian objections, all of which are much more plausible than a *cursory* reading of the judgment would suggest. How, then, is this phenomenon, of the large majorities in this and other cases, to be explained? The answer is in the overriding necessity of the Court to reach a decision which will be final and authoritative. This means that in the end a *choice* must be made—a choice which must be in accordance with the professional skill and the conscience of the individual judge. The care with which the issues are sifted by the Court during its deliberations, even before the writing of the judgment is taken in hand, is designed to enable the normal processes of free and equal discussion and persuasion to take their course. The right of the judges to express their own views on the case in the form of individual opinions thus is an important residuary power, and even a stimulus to the formation of large majorities on which the ultimate acceptability of a decision will depend. A government, and public opinion, will the more easily acquiesce in a decision reached by a large majority than in one reached by a narrow majority.

Not all these aspects are fully illustrated by the Judgment of 26 November 1957, in which, the division in the Court being clear-cut, there are no separate opinions, and only three dissenting opinions. But in the second judgment, on the merits, the situation was different.

The Court reaches its decision by applying international law. In the case of the preliminary objections in the present matter, the law applied was a limited and highly technical aspect of the law governing the compulsory jurisdiction of the Court. Broader issues of this character came out in the second phase of the case, and that will therefore be the most convenient place to discuss this aspect of the Court's working.

THE RESUMED PROCEEDINGS ON THE MERITS

The Judgment of 26 November 1957 had two automatic consequences. It terminated (with the force of *res judicata*) all further judicial discussion of the first four objections, which were thereby removed from the Court's agenda. On the other hand there was no *res judicata* on the fifth and sixth objections. It also resumed the proceedings on the merits, to which the two outstanding objections were now joined. New time-limits were therefore fixed—25 February 1958 for the Counter-Memorial, 25 May for the Reply and 25 July for the Rejoinder. In January, however, India asked for a month's extension to which Portugal consented provided it could have four months for the Reply, and the dates were correspondingly refixed, by an order of 10 February 1958.

The Counter-Memorial was accordingly filed on 25 March. This was a document of 153 pages, to which a further 250 or so pages of annexes were added. India now, for the first time, put forward its submission on the merits. This was short and to the point. The

Court was simply asked to declare that it had no jurisdiction to decide on the claim of Portugal, and, in the alternative, to declare the claim ill-founded. In that way the issues were joined without any direct complications, other than those resulting from the out-standing preliminary objections. On 25 July, Portugal filed its Reply—a pleading of 190 pages together with a further 250 pages of annexed material, but there was no new submission. The Indian Rejoinder was due for 25 September, but in August the Indian Agent asked for an extension of five months. This was opposed by Portugal, which was nevertheless prepared to agree to an extension of two months on the condition that the time allowed for the preparation of the oral arguments should not be less than that granted to India for the preparation of the Rejoinder. The Court, without accepting that condition, by an order of 28 August post-poned the date for the filing of the Rejoinder to 25 November. But that was not the end of this discussion, and in October an additional extension to 25 January 1959 was requested. This required a further consultation with the parties (especially as it then looked as though the Court would have a very heavy time-table for the year 1959 and might have difficulty in hearing the case), and by an order of 6 November, that extension was granted. On 17 January a further slight extension, to 5 February, was granted after Portugal had consented, and after this long process of gestation, the Rejoinder was finally filed, and the case became ready for hearing. This pleading is some 320 pages in length together with a further 660 pages of annexes—one of the longest Rejoinders filed in the present Court.

Let us now see how this case looked when it was ready for hearing. The Court had had presented to it something like 290 pages of pleading and 462 pages of annexes by Portugal, and 550 pages of pleading together with 1,340 pages of annexes by India; and if we add the oral pleadings in the preliminary objection phase, which were still of considerable relevance, we see that by this time the *dossier* contained nearly three thousand printed pages. A formidable case! And more was to come.

The written pleadings, especially the Reply and Rejoinder, had not succeeded in narrowing down the issues. In fact the position was very much to the contrary. What they did was to bring out two sharply differing concepts of the purpose of the case. Portugal was aiming at a decision which could protect it from the effects of the Indian policy of driving out the last vestiges of European coloni-zation in the Indian Peninsula. India, having failed to have the Portuguese case dismissed on the formal grounds advanced in the first, second and fourth objections, now concentrated on a more complicated double objective. The first was to try and isolate the incidents of 1954 from their general political background so that at the most a decision by the Court, if unfavourable to India, would be of limited implications. The second was not merely to challenge the Portuguese conception that it enjoyed sovereignty over the various districts and enclaved areas but also the corollary of that view, namely that Portugal had a *right* of passage over Indian territory: and in that connection there was a further development in that India made a determined attempt to break the right of passage up into a number of categories. The important thing for India was, if it were to lose the case, nevertheless to try and exclude from the right of passage the armed forces which had, for the first time, been specifically mentioned in the submissions of the Memorial (see p. 107 above). On the political level, India was still not in agreement with Portugal that *any* dispute between the two countries relating to the right of passage should be submitted to the Court. It was obliged to recognize the jurisdiction of the Court, but that did not mean that it had to look on the case in the same light as Portugal.

The change in date for the filing of the Rejoinder affected a number of other cases. On 3 February another case became ready for hearing: on 5 February the *Right of Passage* case became ready for hearing: and on 31 March yet a third case became ready for hearing. There was no difficulty over the case which became ready on 3 February: in accordance with the normal rule that had to be heard before the later cases (see p. 110 above). It was, however, obvious from the Indian Rejoinder that a considerable amount of preparatory work would be required both by the parties and by the Court before the hearings could profitably be opened. Arrangements were therefore made to take the third case before the summer vacation, and to postpone the *Right of Passage* case. In that way, incidentally, Portugal obtained satisfaction of the condition which it had made for consenting to the extension requested by India for the filing of the Rejoinder, without prejudicing the position of principle adopted by the Court.

The oral hearings accordingly commenced on 21 September and terminated on 6 November, occupying thirty-six meetings of the Court. Five persons shared the presentation of Portugal's case, and five that of India. The printed record covers some 840 pages. Final judgment was delivered on 12 May 1960.

A triennial election had intervened between the first judgment and the second, and the term of office of the former President had come to an end. There is a rule that the President shall continue to act as such if a case is begun before a periodic election, but it has long been the practice to regard the preliminary objections and the merits as two "cases"—even when, as in our matter, some of the objections are joined to the merits. For the same reason, although by the Statute the members of the Court shall continue to discharge their functions until their places have been filled, and though replaced shall finish any cases which they may have begun,[33] when a case is divided into two distinct phases, it is usual for the Court to sit on the second occasion in its new composition. As a result, the Court now sat under the Presidency of Judge Klaestad of Norway: two of the judges who had sat in 1957 had been replaced; there was one vacancy in the Court's ranks (which was filled only on 29 September, but that judge did not take part in the case); and one judge was absent after the first few sittings on account of sickness. The same two judges *ad hoc* continued to sit. The Court accordingly consisted this time of fifteen judges (the absence of two members from the bench may have had a decisive effect on the final outcome of this case).

MUST A STATE APPEAR?

It has been mentioned (p. 107 above) that theoretically India, instead of filing a Counter-Memorial, could have taken no action at all and let the case go by default. What would have happened then?

Provision is made for such an eventuality. It would have been pointless to have gone to the trouble of setting up an International Court and then to have opened the way to the frustration of its work by not closing this gap. Accordingly, the Statute lays down that whenever one of the parties does not appear before the Court, or fails to defend its case, the other party may call upon the Court to decide in favour of its claim. But before doing so, the Court must satisfy itself both that it has jurisdiction in accordance with the provisions of the Statute, and that the claim is well founded in fact and in law.[34] There has been only one instance of that, in the final phase of the *Corfu Channel* case, because States will not lightly risk the possibility that judgment will be given against them. It should however be noted that this procedure for giving judgment by default only applies if the Court has jurisdiction, and if the defaulting party has been duly notified of the hearing.

In the present case, it should not be assumed that the Court would have automatically held that it had jurisdiction in the event that India failed to appear. As it happened, there was on record a Note by the Swedish Government of 23 February 1956 in which that Government had stated that it regarded the third condition of the Portuguese acceptance of the compulsory jurisdiction as incompatible with the Statute, and on 5 July Portugal had replied thereto.[35] These documents had been circulated in the normal way by the Secretary-General of the United Nations, in his capacity of depositary of the acceptances of the compulsory jurisdiction. The Court would therefore in any event have had to have dealt with the issues presented by the first objection, and possibly by the second and fourth as well.[36] It is also not unlikely that some of the other objections would have been raised by the Court of its own initiative.

SETTLEMENT OUT OF COURT

Since Portugal was the applicant, Portugal could at any time have discontinued the proceedings by giving the Court notice to that effect. Before making the order recording the discontinuance, India would have first been asked if it had any objection. As applicant in the preliminary objection phase, India could likewise have discontinued the proceedings on the objections, in which event the proceedings on the merits would have been automatically resumed.[37] In addition to this, the two parties could have settled the case out of Court by agreement, and the Court would have placed this on record.[38] Instances of both these procedures are fairly common.

THE LAW APPLIED BY THE COURT

The Court being an international Court designed to serve the international community of States, the law which it applies is naturally international law. The Statute of the Court therefore contains some general directions on this aspect. According to this, the Court shall apply: (a) international conventions, whether general or particular, expressly recognized by the contesting States; (b) international custom, as evidence of a general practice recognized as law; (c) the general principles of law recognized by civilized nations; and (d) judicial decisions and the teachings of the most highly qualified publicists of the various nations, as subsidiary means for the determination of the rules of law.[39]

For theoretical reasons that enumeration has given rise to a not inconsiderable controversy. In practice, however, it is regarded as generally satisfactory, and indeed is frequently taken over into international arbitration agreements.[40] Heads (a), (b) and (c) refer to the rules of law itself. The real innovation that was introduced when the Statute was first drafted in 1920 related to head (c); its purpose was to remove any danger that the Court would be unable to give a decision on the mere ground that it could find no rule of law to govern the case.[41] This useful provision enables the Court to deal with entirely unprecedented situations, and through its pronouncements to keep the law abreast of the constantly changing developments.

Head *(d)*—which refers to two distinct aspects which are not on the same level, judicial decisions and the teachings of the highly qualified publicists—is a guide to explain how the law may be ascertained. However, it is far from exhaustive.[42] It is an interesting compromise between two approaches—of the Continental jurist on the one hand, who freely makes use of *doctrine*, theoretical literature, of publicists of repute and who attaches no formal authority to judicial decisions, and of the Common law which on the whole refuses to employ the writings of publicists in this way and indeed would even tend to look askance on their citation in a pleading or in a judgment, but which gives to judicial decisions the formal authority of a binding precedent. Nevertheless, the practical difference between these two schools of thought is not so great, for on the one hand the Continental jurist will tend to recognize the inherent as distinguished from the formal authority of judicial precedents, especially when the higher Courts are consistent in their decisions (the French call this *une jurisprudence constante*), whereas the American and English lawyer is second to none in his ability to "distinguish" one precedent from another.

International thinking tends to prefer the Continental approach in theory, and the Common law approach in practice. One reason for this is that in comparison with domestic litigation, international litigation is sparse, and for a judicial system which has given about one hundred decisions over a period of forty years to regard those decisions as constituting binding precedents would be little short of absurd. We therefore find that the International Court has refrained from saying that it was *obliged* to follow previous judicial decisions—of itself, of the Permanent Court, or of authoritative Arbitration Tribunals—although it has been very careful not to upset established jurisprudence unless it was convinced that there was good reason. For example, in the Judgment of 26 November 1957 on the preliminary objections of the *Right of Passage* case, two previous cases are quoted, and a further three are cited in the judgment of 12 April 1960 on the merits. Writings of publicists are almost never directly cited by the Court itself. The opinions of the individual judges are, naturally, freer in this regard, and the parties' pleadings even more so. This means that the non-citation of an earlier judgment or of important works of reputable publicists in the judgment itself does not imply that the Court was unaware of them, or wilfully ignored them.

The use of judicial decisions as precedents is subject to one important limitation—namely that a judicial decision itself has no "binding force" except between the parties and in respect of that particular case.[43] There is, however, no real contradiction. The "decision" which is only "binding" on the parties to a particular case is found in the operative clauses of the judgment. The Court's reasoning—its statement of what it regards as the correct legal position *and why*—enters into the general storehouse of public international law. That is why the decisions of the International Court have become one of the most important repertoires today for the rules of international law, and indeed one of the law's most powerful instruments for adaptation to the constantly changing conditions.[44]

The Court also has power, if the parties agree, to "decide a case *ex aequo et bono.*"[45] What this means is that if the parties expressly confer that power on the Court, it may lay down, in the form of a binding decision, a reasonable adjustment of the relations between the two parties, and not limit its decision to a statement of what those relations are on the basis of the law as it is. No instance has occurred of States conferring this power on the Court. The reason probably is that it is the normal function of diplomacy to bring such adjustments about, and it is not a judicial function to do so, and the normal processes of diplomacy have developed special machinery, such as conciliation and mediation machinery, to assist it.

In the merits of the *Right of Passage* case a number of significant general issues regarding the law applied by the Court arose.

One of the Indian arguments in connection with the fifth preliminary objection was, as seen, that a reasonably arguable cause of action based on the kind of legal rules which the Court has to apply had not been presented to the Court, and that in consequence there was no legal dispute which the Court could adjudicate. India further made it clear that it was not consenting to any adjustment of the situation *ex aequo et bono.* In the preliminary objection phase the Court had not considered this part of the argument, but it could not avoid doing so in the second phase. In the second part of the case India slightly changed the effect of this argument. It was no longer put forward exclusively as an argument against the jurisdiction of the Court, but rather as an argument for the dismissal of Portugal's claim on the merits. In consequence it became somewhat modified and contended that Portugal's claim was too vague and contradictory to enable the Court to pass judgment on it by application of any of the four categories of rules enumerated above. The

Court dismissed this part of India's contention and explained that while there was no doubt that the day-to-day exercise of the right of passage may give rise to delicate questions of application, that was not, in the view of the Court, sufficient ground for holding that the right itself was not susceptible of judicial determination with reference to the rules which the Court is authorized to apply. This is an important observation, for it shows that if the Court has jurisdiction it will not be deflected from its judicial task by exceptional difficulties, nor will it accept the argument that there are gaps in international law.

THE FINAL SUBMISSIONS ON THE MERITS

Portugal's final submissions were filed on 6 October at the end of the first pleading by Portugal—a pleading which itself had started on 21 September and had lasted over fourteen hearings. The submissions contained forty-seven "Whereases" and five operative clauses. Two of these asked for the dismissal of the remaining objections. As for the merits, the first submission asked for a declaration by the Court that the right of passage "as defined above" was a right possessed by Portugal which must be respected by India— that is to say a right "claimed only to the extent necessary for the exercise of Portuguese sovereignty over the enclaves". The second asked for a declaration that India had not complied with the obligations incumbent upon it by virtue of Portugal's right of passage. The third was more complicated and was divided into four parts. The Court was asked to hold that certain arguments by India relating to: *(a)* its right to adopt an attitude of neutrality in the conflict between the Portuguese Government and the insurgents in the enclaved territories; *(b)* the application of various provisions of the United Nations Charter relating to human rights and the right of self-determination of peoples; and *(c)* the existence of a provisional *de facto* local government in the enclaved territories, were all without foundation: and *(d)* on an argument that the exercise of the right of passage in "present circumstances" would cause grave dangers to India's public order, either to order India to end the suspension of the right of passage or to impose conditions for the temporary suspension of the right of passage until the danger to India passed. In reply to this India's final submissions, filed on 21 October after a further eleven days of pleading by India, contained forty-five "Whereases", leading to a single submission, that the Court was without jurisdiction, and alternatively that the claim was without foundation.

It should here be noted that between the application and this final submission, the Portuguese claim had undergone one fundamental modification. In the application Portugal asked for unconditional recognition by the Court for its right of passage (p. 101 above). But now, after all this strenuous pleading, the right claimed was conditional—"only to the extent necessary for the exercise of Portuguese sovereignty": and this was coupled with a reticent acknowledgment that in certain circumstances India did have the right to suspend the exercise of the right.

India's method of pleading had not been without effect. By bringing Portugal to these conclusions, India had gone a long way towards re-insuring itself against serious long-term adverse effects of a judgment in favour of Portugal. It is good diplomacy to be content with the possible. India's handling of the case *as a whole* had succeeded, come what might, in protecting India's national aspirations from any long-term harmful effects of the Portuguese surprise move of 1955.

THE JUDGMENT OF 12 APRIL 1960

After something like five months of deliberation, broken only for the Christmas vacation, the Court delivered its judgment on 12 April 1960. This judgment is 44 pages long, 24 of which are taken up by the formal parts. Short declarations were added by President Klaestad and Judges Basdevant, Badawi, Kojevnikov and Spiropoulos; Judge Wellington Koo appended a separate opinion and Judges Winiarski and Badawi (jointly), Armand-Ugon, Moreno Quintana, and Sir Percy Spender, and Judges *ad hoc* Chagla and Fernandes dissenting opinions. The whole text is 142 pages in length. By thirteen votes to two the Court dismissed the fifth preliminary objection and by eleven votes to four the sixth. On the merits, by eleven votes to four it found that Portugal had *in 1954* a right of passage, to the extent necessary for the exercise of Portuguese sovereignty over the enclaves and subject to the regulation and control of India, in respect of private persons, civil officials and goods in general. By the narrow margin of eight votes to seven it found that Portugal did not have *in 1954* such a right of passage in respect of armed forces, armed police and arms and ammunition. By nine votes to six it found that India had not acted contrary to its obligations resulting from the right of passage in respect of private persons, civil officials and goods in general. All the other Portuguese claims were dismissed without vote. Although both sides could cry victory—an important factor from the point of view of prestige—there is little doubt that India is the substantial victor in this case, and that if Portugal did obtain from the Court formal recognition of Portuguese sovereignty over the territories in question, the judgment effectively deprives Portugal of the means of enforcing that sovereignty.

How did the Court reach this judgment of Solomon? (That it was a judgment of Solomon the reader who is sceptical can see from the curious phenomenon of a dissenting opinion by each Judge *ad hoc*.)

The key lies in the delayed action effect of the sixth preliminary objection which, although (or perhaps because) it was dismissed, forced the Court to look very closely at the different elements of which the dispute was composed in order to decide precisely when it came into existence, and what were the facts and situations with which it was concerned. The answer to that would determine what was the dispute which the Court had to decide. The Court found that the *legal* dispute came into existence in 1954 against the background of the *political* dispute which came to a head in that year, and that the service of the Court was prayed in aid to redress the illegal situation which, in Portugal's view, flowed from India's failure *in 1954* to comply with its obligations in respect to the right of passage. That explains both the insertion of that date in the two fundamental operative clauses of the judgment, and the Court's refusal to consider all that part of Portugal's third submission on the merits which related not to the events of 1954, but to what had occurred later.

How did the Court reach its conclusion that a right of passage did exist on that date, and that it only applied to the "civilian" categories of transit?

As we have seen, specific reference to "armed forces" had appeared for the first time in the submission of the Memorial, and in subsequent pleadings the existence of the right, its historical origins going back to the earliest period of British India, was discussed not as an entity, but with reference to the different categories. The Court, after examination of the vast quantity of material placed before it (mostly of an historical character collected from various archives), reached the conclusion that the right only existed with regard to the civilian categories, and that Indian (or formerly British) permission had always been obtained for the transit of the "armed" categories. The fact that prior authorization was necessary made it impossible to say that for the "armed" categories the passage was exercised as of right.

Nevertheless, as the voting shows, it was this question which caused the major division in the Court. A swing of one vote would have produced an entirely different result. The case against the breakdown of the right of passage into the various categories, expounded in the individual opinions which deal with this aspect. is objectively speaking no less persuasive than the majority opinion. The balance is truly fine.

Two questions arise from this judgment. The first is: What has the Court done in relation to the *real* conflict between Portugal and India? The second is: Why, having regard to the actual decision, did the Court not seek an easier way out by accepting one of the preliminary objections, most of which have elements of plausibility about them not reflected in the size of the majorities by which they were dismissed?

By placing itself on the narrow basis of the events of 1954, the Court gave a limited decision referring to a particular incident, and avoided giving a legal decision on a much broader political conflict of interests. Had the parties been in agreement in conferring jurisdiction on the Court, it might have been able to deal with the other general Portuguese contentions which in fact related directly to the clash of aspirations, such as those concerning Indian "neutrality" in the conflict between the insurgents and the Portuguese authority, and the like. The persistence of the preliminary objections to the very end showed that there was no political agreement between the parties to confer such wide functions on the Court, and while, no doubt, India would have complied with its obligations under the Charter (see p. 43 above) in respect to *any* judgment rendered by the Court, that in itself is not sufficient authority for the Court to take upon itself any more than its collective judicial conscience recognizes to be consonant with the objective legal situation.[46] This is a significant instance of judicial caution, all the more striking in the light of the fact that in order to reach even its limited decision the Court still had to overcome no less than six preliminary objections.[47]

As for the second question, it is believed that the answer is to be found in long-term considerations of judicial policy. All these objections dealt exclusively with technical aspects of the compulsory jurisdiction. The first objection (and the second and fourth, closely associated with it) broke new ground relating, as they did, to the facility which a State, a member of the United Nations, possesses by a surprise move to subject itself to the compulsory jurisdiction: the Court in effect held that the element of surprise was not an abuse of rights, basing itself on a strict interpretation of the relevant texts.[48] The remaining objections are of a kind frequently raised, and the Court has well-developed patterns of approach towards them. This approach tends towards keeping them within reasonable limits, so as to avoid creating an easy way of frustrating an obligation to recognize the jurisdiction. It was probably an inarticulate desire to remain faithful to those patterns of jurisprudence which ultimately tipped the balance in favour of the rejection of those objections.

By the Judgment of 12 April 1960, the file in Case No. 32 was closed.

COSTS

The Court has general power to award costs, although the normal principle in international litigation is that each party bears its own costs.[49] This principle is an expression of the sovereign equality of the States at bar.

Neither party asked for costs in the present case, and no decision by the Court on that aspect was, therefore, required.

INTERPRETATION AND REVISION

The Judgment became binding on the parties with its delivery: and there is no appeal. It finally decided the issues between them with the force of *res judicata*.[50] But what could happen if difficulties arose over its implementation?

The Statute deals with that eventuality. If a dispute arises over the meaning or scope of a judgment, the Court has jurisdiction to construe it on the request of either party. Such a request may be submitted either by special agreement or by unilateral application, and the Court will decide on it by judgment.[51] This does not give the Court an unlimited power to re-open the case (for the judgment is final and without appeal), and the extent of what the Court can do by means of interpretation is in fact limited. The reason is to prevent a new dispute being submitted to the Court in the guise of a request to interpret an earlier judgment, for the jurisdiction to interpret derives directly from the Court's jurisdiction to decide the merits of the original case, and is not, to that extent, an independent jurisdiction. No encouragement must be given to its abuse, at all events so long as the international community does not accept the legal principle of compulsory jurisdiction. The present Court has had one case of interpretation (see p. 147 below).

The Court also has a general power to revise the judgment, under the same conditions as to jurisdiction, if some new fact of a decisive nature which was unknown to the Court and to the party producing it (provided that such ignorance was not due to negligence) is discovered within the period of ten years from the date of the judgment.[52]

THE EXTRA-JUDICIAL FUNCTION

No question arose in this case of inviting the Court to employ its extra-judicial function to assist the parties in reaching a settlement of their dispute. However, it may be mentioned, for the sake of completeness, that India has not been averse to the use of this procedure to assist it in achieving its national aspirations. In 1949 the French Government, formally as a matter of exclusive domestic sovereignty, decided to hold a referendum in the French Settlements in India to enable the populations to decide freely on their destiny and future status, and the Vice-President (the President being a French national) was asked to appoint a group of neutral observers to supervise it. The Vice-President carried out this assignment.[53]

In practice, the President will only accede to requests of this character if he is satisfied that the parties are in agreement that he makes the appointment.

NOTES

1. Rules of Court, Article 32 (2).
2. Statute, Article 39. Rules of Court, Articles 39, 58.
3. Statute, Article 42.   4. Statute, Article 40.
5. Rules of Court, Article 35 (5).
6. Statute, Article 62. Rules of Court, Articles 64-5.
7. Statute, Article 63. Rules of Court, Article 66.
8. Rules of Court, Articles 41-2.   9. Rules of Court, Article 44.
10. Rules of Court, Article 45.   11. Rules of Court, Article 61 (2).
12. The normal summer vacation is from 15 July to 15 September. Rules o Court, Article 25.
13. Rules of Court, Article 48.   14. Rules of Court, Article 46.
15. Statute, Articles 48-52. Rules of Court, Articles 49-50, 53-7.
16. A roneographed provisional record of the day's proceedings is distributed together with a translation by the Court, each evening. This is known as the C.R. (*compte rendu*). After correction by the speakers it is rapidly printed for the use of the members of the Court. This printed version is afterwards annexed to the formal minutes of the meetings and published. Statute, Article 47. Rules of Court, Article 60.
17. Rules of Court, Article 52.   18. Statute, Article 48.
19. Statute, Article 54.   20. Statute, Article 56.
21. Statute, Article 55.   22. Statute, Article 57.
23. Rules of Court, Article 30.   24. Rules of Court, Article 74.
25. The final text (which has not been republished by the present Court) can

be found in P.C.I.J., Series D., No. 1, Fourth ed. (1940), 42. It is reprinted in Sh. Rosenne, *The International Court of Justice* (Leyden, 1957), 419. For a description by a former Registrar of the Court, of how the deliberations are conducted, see E. Hambro, "The reasons behind the decisions of the International Court of Justice", *Current Legal Problems*, 7 (1954), 212. For a description of how the deliberations of the Permanent Court were conducted, see M. Hudson, *The Permanent Court of International Justice, 1920-1942* (New York, 1943), 579.

26. Statute, Article 58.   27. Rules of Court, Article 75.

28. *Ibid.* In the case of an advisory opinion notice of the date of the delivery of the opinion in open Court is given to the Secretary-General of the United Nations and the organization which requested it, and to the States which presented information in the course of the written or oral proceedings. One signed and sealed copy is retained in the archives of the Court, and one is sent to the requesting organization, and certified copies are sent by the Registrar to all members of the United Nations and to all other States, specialized agencies and other international organizations concerned. Rules of Court, Article 85. Orders are similarly signed and sealed but are not usually read in open Court, being communicated to the Agents by correspondence. In the case of an order indicating interim measures of protection, a signed and sealed copy is also sent to the Secretary-General of the United Nations for transmission to the Security Council.

Apart from these formal requirements, the Registry usually publishes a communiqué announcing a few days in advance when a judgment or advisory opinion is to be delivered.

29. Rules of Court, Article 22. The Registrar is responsible for the Court's publications, and the Registry includes a full Printing Department. For details of the publications of the Court, see p. 222 below. The Court's publications are obtainable through the United Nations local sales agents in each country.

30. The relevant date, 5 February 1930, is no more than the date on which India's first declaration accepting the jurisdiction of the Permanent Court of International Justice took effect. These objections are sometimes known as objections *ratione temporis*. For detailed discussion of this technical, but significant, aspect of the work of the Court, see Sh. Rosenne, *The Time Factor in the Jurisdiction of the International Court of Justice* (Leyden, 1960).

31. Quoted in Sir Hersch Lauterpacht, *The Development of International Law by the International Court* (London, 1958), 69.

32. *Ibid.*, 68-9.

33. See Statute, Article 13. Rules of Court, Article 13. In all the Court devoted 52 public meetings to the two phases of this case—the record in the present Court. The previous record was in the *Corfu Channel* case in which the Court held 46 public hearings devoted to three phases of the case.

34. Statute, Article 53.

35. Preliminary Objections, Annex B, Nos. 2 and 3.

36. As an instance of the interaction of two cases on one another, it may be mentioned that in the *Israel v. Bulgaria* case concerning the Aerial Incident of 27 July 1955, there took place a long discussion between the parties concerning the effect of the Court's decision of 1957 on an earlier Portuguese acceptance of the compulsory jurisdiction of 1920. The reason is that Bulgaria had also made a declaration at the same time, and had been admitted to the United Nations at the same time as Portugal, and Bulgaria was arguing that by the 1957 decision the Court had implicitly recognized that Portugal's 1920 declaration was no

longer in force, and that the same could apply to Bulgaria. In fact the 1920 declaration was not mentioned at all in the 1957 case.

37. Rules of Court, Article 69.   38. Rules of Court, Article 68.

39. Statute, Article 38 (1).

40. Cf. Article 10 of the Model Rules on Arbitral Procedure drawn up in 1958 by the International Law Commission, and referred to in Ch. I, n. 11 above.

41. The technical name for this kind of finding is *non liquet*—literally "it is not clear"—a term borrowed from Roman civil procedure. It is now generally accepted in international practice that an international tribunal is not allowed to bring in a finding of *non liquet*. Cf. Article 11 of the Model Rules referred to in the previous note.

42. In 1950 the International Law Commission, in response to a request from the General Assembly, attempted to formulate a list of the materials for ascertaining the content of modern customary international law. This list included: *(a)* texts of international instruments; *(b)* decisions of international courts; *(c)* decisions of national courts; *(d)* national legislation; *(e)* diplomatic correspondence; *(f)* opinions of national legal advisers (with some reserve); *(g)* practice of international organizations. Yearbook of the International Law Commission, 1950, II, 24, 367. Additions which may now be made include: *(h)* certain types of Resolutions of the United Nations and Specialized Agencies; *(i)* recommendations of the International Law Commission itself; and *(k)* (for some purposes, and with reserve) pleadings in the International Court and correspondence with the parties—this latter especially for the law and practice of international judicial procedure.

43. Statute, Article 59. This is expressly recalled in Article 38.

44. In this connection, see the literature cited in Ch. I, n. 26.

45. Statute, Article 38 (2). The words mean "right and equitable", and their implication is the application by the judge of a reasonable corrective to rules of law which have become out-dated. This concept should not be confused with the English concept of "equity", at least in its modern form.

46. It seems that only one Judge of the majority, the President, made express reserves to that part of the Court's reasoning which led it to limit its decision to the events of the year 1954.

47. It is believed that this is the first instance in the experience of the Permanent Court and the present Court in which each one of a multiple series of objections has been rejected and in which nevertheless the objecting State has emerged as the substantive victor.

48. At the same time it should be mentioned that other States have expressed disquiet over this development in the law—which seems unobjectionable in itself—and have taken steps to safeguard themselves against similar action. See the work cited in n. 30 above, at p. 21.

49. Statute, Article 64. Rules of Court, Article 77. There is in fact no instance in which costs have been awarded in the International Court.

50. Statute, Articles 59 and 60. Rules of Court, Article 76.

51. Statute, Article 60. Rules of Court, Articles 79, 80, 81.

52. Statute, Article 61. Rules of Court, Articles 78, 80, 81.

53. Yearbook of the International Court of Justice, 1948-9, 41.

CHAPTER VI

THE WORK OF THE COURT

BEFORE attempting to assess the part played by the Court since
1946 in the peaceful settlement of international disputes, let us first
survey briefly the cases that have come before it. The cases are
discussed in chronological order of their institution.

THE CORFU CHANNEL

On 22 October 1946 a squadron of British warships sailed through
a previously swept minefield in the Corfu Channel, which separates
Albania from Greece. In the course of this mission, two of the ships,
H.M.S. *Saumarez* and H.M.S. *Volage*, struck mines, subsequently
established to have been "recently laid", and were badly damaged.
Forty-four officers and men were killed and forty-two injured. The
British Government held Albania responsible, and after the failure
of diplomatic negotiations to lead to a settlement, referred the
matter to the Security Council in January, 1947. After a long and
complicated discussion, in which one draft resolution was vetoed
by the Soviet Union, the Council, on 3 April 1947, recommended
that the two governments should "immediately refer the dispute
to the International Court of Justice, in accordance with the provisions of the Statute of the Court." The resolution was adopted
by eight votes to none, with two abstentions (Poland and the
U.S.S.R.), the United Kingdom not participating in the vote in
accordance with Article 27 (3) of the Charter. During the proceedings Albania had accepted the formal invitation issued by the
Council under Article 32 of the Charter inviting it to participate
without vote in the discussion on condition that Albania accepted
all the obligations which a member of the United Nations would
have to assume in such a case. After the resolution was adopted,
the President of the Council observed that although Albania could
not be compelled to appear before the Court, by accepting the
obligations of a member it was obliged to comply with the provisions of the Charter and the Statute (cf. p. 76 above).

On 22 May, the United Kingdom filed in Court an application
instituting proceedings. In July the Albanian Government informed
the Court of its view that in proceeding unilaterally the United

Kingdom was not acting in conformity with the Statute, as required by the Security Council's resolution, and that accordingly Albania would be within its rights in holding that the case could not be brought without a special agreement. However, this notwithstanding, Albania, accepting the recommendation of the Security Council, was prepared to appear before the Court. Yet, when the time came to file the Counter-Memorial, Albania raised a preliminary objection which, in effect, repeated that attitude regarding the consequences of the initial irregularity of the manner in which the case had been instituted. In a judgment of 25 March 1948—the first delivered by the present Court—the objection was dismissed by fifteen votes to one, only the Albanian judge *ad hoc* dissenting, and the proceedings on the merits were resumed.

On the same day on which that judgment was delivered the parties concluded a special agreement by which they decided to put two questions to the Court. The first asked the Court to decide whether Albania was responsible under international law for the explosions which occurred on 22 October 1946 in Albanian waters and for the damage and loss of human life which resulted therefrom, and whether there was any duty to pay compensation. The second enquired whether the action of the United Kingdom in sending its warships through the Corfu Channel on 22 October, and whether its later action in re-sweeping the Channel on 12 and 13 November, violated Albanian sovereignty, and whether there was any duty to give satisfaction. The Court thereupon recognized that this special agreement constituted the basis for the future conduct of the case.

The pleadings showed—as had also been evident in the Security Council—that there were serious divergences between the parties on questions of fact, and it became necessary for the Court to hear witnesses and experts called by the parties. This was the first, and so far only, occasion in which witnesses have been heard in the International Court. Five witnesses and two witness-experts were called by the United Kingdom, and three witnesses and two experts by Albania, and as the differences of fact were not easily resolved, the Court decided to obtain an expert opinion on a number of contested points. Therefore, a committee of experts, consisting of senior officers of the Netherlands, Norwegian and Swedish Navies were appointed, and when their first report did not sufficiently clarify matters, they were requested to proceed to the scene, there to make further investigations. Although it was never fully established who had laid the mines which had damaged *Saumarez* and *Volage*, the Court in its judgment of 9 April 1949 found sufficient evidence to hold that in law Albania, as the territorial State, was responsible, and was under the duty of making compensation for the consequent loss and damage. The Court also found that the passage of the British warships through the Corfu Channel on 22 October was not a violation of Albanian sovereignty, but that the minesweeping activities of November "violated the sovereignty of the People's Republic of Albania, and that this declaration by the Court constitutes in itself appropriate satisfaction."

However, there had been no pleadings on the question of the amount of compensation to be paid—indeed Albania proceeded to argue that on a proper interpretation of the special agreement the Court did not have jurisdiction to assess the amount of compensation. In its judgment of 9 April the Court rejected that argument, and decided on a third phase of the case, limited to the question of compensation. Albania failed to present any pleadings in that phase of the case and, although duly notified, did not participate in the Court's hearing devoted to that question. This led the Court to apply the procedure for default of appearance (see p. 126 above) —the first instance of this. The question of jurisdiction had already been decided, but the figures advanced by the United Kingdom were found to raise questions of a technical nature for which expert opinion was required. The Court accordingly appointed another committee of experts consisting of two senior officers of the Netherlands Navy to examine the claim. The experts reached the conclusion that the amount claimed by the United Kingdom could be taken as a fair and accurate estimate of the damage sustained, and the Court, by a judgment of 15 December 1949, gave judgment in favour of the United Kingdom for the sum of £ 843,947.[1]

The compensation awarded to the United Kingdom has never been paid. Echoes of this were to be heard in the Court later (see p. 158 below).

The incidents in the Corfu Channel—among the earliest incidents of the Cold War—had caused a great deal of tension, and this had been exacerbated by the debates in the Security Council. The Security Council by itself was unable to remove the friction and therefore enlisted the aid of the Court by recommending the parties to refer the case to it. The special agreement opened the way to proceedings which could take account of Albania's complaints against the United Kingdom (in fact Albania could always have introduced its complaints in the proceedings, by way of a counter-claim), and the Court was enabled to deliver a judgment which gave partial satisfaction to both sides. To that extent, the combination of Court proceedings with those of the Security Council may be regarded as a successful innovation, and it may perhaps be regretted that the Security Council (or the General Assembly) has not found it possible to repeat it since.

This case raised expectations in some circles that with the emergence of the Soviet Union as a major power, the earlier attitude of reserve manifested towards the Permanent Court might be relaxed, at least to the extent that the Soviet Union would be prepared to conclude special agreements for referring specific disputes to the Court. However, later developments were to show that any such hopes were premature.

MEMBERSHIP IN THE UNITED NATIONS

Article 4 of the Charter lays down how new members can be admitted to the United Nations. Paragraph 1 specifies the conditions for membership—that the applicant State shall be peace-loving, have accepted the obligations contained in the Charter, and be able and willing to carry out those obligations. Paragraph 2 indicates the procedure—that admission to membership shall be effected by a decision of the General Assembly on the recommendation of the Security Council. Both these provisions have been interpreted by the Court.

From the beginning of 1946 the Security Council had been deadlocked on the question of the admission of new members, candidates proposed by the Communist States not receiving the necessary majority of votes (seven), and those proposed by the West encountering the veto. This gave rise to sharp discussions in the Security Council and later in the General Assembly which, on 17 November 1947, by forty votes to eight, with two abstentions, decided to ask the Court for an advisory opinion on the interpretation of the first paragraph. The question put to the Court was whether a member which is called upon to express itself by its vote, either in the Security Council or in the General Assembly, on the admission of a State to membership, was juridically entitled to make its consent to the admission dependent on conditions not expressly provided for in paragraph 1. In particular, could such a member, while recognizing the conditions to be fulfilled, subject its affirmative vote to the additional condition that other States will be admitted together with that State? This was designed to obtain a ruling on the "legality" of a possible "package deal", by which all outstanding applications for membership would be accepted.

The competence of the Court to give the advisory opinion was challenged on the grounds that the question was a political one and therefore fell outside the jurisdiction of the Court, that it was abstract, and that the Court is not entitled to interpret the Charter. The Court, in its advisory opinion of 28 May 1948, rejected these arguments, and then, by nine votes to six, proceeded to answer both questions put to it in the negative. But two individual opinions were given by judges forming part of the majority, and these seemed to indicate that despite the *juridical* answer, political considerations could not be regarded as irrelevant, and this led to considerable confusion over what the Court had actually decided, and why. Nevertheless, the General Assembly in a resolution of 8 December 1948, recommended that each member of the Security Council and of the General Assembly, in exercising its vote on the admission of new members, should act in accordance with the Court's opinion.[2]

In practice, the Court's opinion did not mean very much because all States could fully comply with it simply by explaining their negative vote on the basis of their view that the applicant State did not meet the conditions of paragraph 1. The political problem of the admission of new members did not originate in the explanations given for the negative vote, but in the underlying political situation for which those votes were merely an expression. The request for the advisory opinion did not, and indeed could not, bring out that aspect, and the practical wisdom displayed by the General Assembly in requesting the opinion and in trying to tie its hands on the question of the "package deal" is therefore highly questionable. On the other hand, the Court's decision rejecting the challenges to its jurisdiction rests on solid and convincing grounds.

The advisory opinion, then, could contribute little towards resolving the *political* problem of the admission of new members, and a move developed in the General Assembly urging that when the Security Council made no recommendation at all, the General Assembly could decide to admit new members. Although the language of paragraph 2 of Article 4 seems clear enough, the General Assembly decided to put the question to the Court by a resolution of 22 November 1949 which was adopted by forty-two votes to nine with six abstentions. In a brief and clear advisory opinion of 3 March 1950 the Court gave its opinion that admission to membership cannot be effected by a decision of the General Assembly when the Security Council has made no recommendation for admission, by reason of the candidate failing to secure the requisite majority or of a veto in the Security Council. The Court reached this decision by a majority of twelve votes to two. The Court summarily rejected challenges to its jurisdiction, similar to those which had been advanced in the first *Admission* case.[3]

There has been some criticism of the General Assembly in putting this question to the Court, on the ground that it did not raise a difficult point of law. That criticism is not justified. The putting of the question to the Court resulted from political considerations, and not from the difficulties of the legal question. The Court's opinion prevented extravagant claims being put forward in the General Assembly and performed a valuable function in keeping the dispute confined within given limits.

The deadlock over the admission of new members continued until the end of 1955 when the U.S.S.R. and the United States were able to agree between themselves on the means for bringing it to an end. A "package deal" was negotiated, and by a Resolution of 14 December 1955, sixteen new members were admitted. The advisory opinion of 1948 had been interpreted as excluding a package deal of this sort, and many people consider that the manner in which the problem was ultimately resolved was not in conformity with the legal interpretation of the Charter given by the Court. On the other hand, there was general relief that a solution had at last been found, and there is no serious disposition now to query its legality.

REPARATION FOR THE UNITED NATIONS

Following the assassination of Count Bernadotte, the United Nations Mediator in Palestine, in Israel, and the killing of other United Nations agents in Jordan and Egypt in the latter part of 1948, the question arose whether the United Nations could claim from the responsible governments reparation for the injuries it had suffered, and the General Assembly decided at the end of 1948 to refer a series of complicated legal questions to the Court for its opinion. The advisory opinion of 11 April 1949 is one of the Court's major opinions. In it the Court in effect held that the United Nations possesses international personality (thereby putting an end to a doctrinal controversy that had started in the days of the League of Nations), and that it has the capacity to bring an international claim against the responsible *de jure* or *de facto* government with a view to obtaining reparation due in respect of the damage caused to the United Nations and to the victim himself or those entitled through him, such claims being presentable both against members and against non-members of the United Nations. The opinion also indicated how to reconcile claims brought on behalf of the United Nations itself and those brought on behalf of other States injured by the acts, and mentioned the safeguards necessary to protect a defendant State against the possibility that it would have to pay double damages.[4]

On the basis of that opinion, the Secretary-General made proposals for the method by which the United Nations would claim the reparation due, and after approval by the General Assembly,

proceeded to present the claims against the responsible governments. None of the respondent governments contested the right of
the United Nations to present these claims, although only the
Government of Israel paid the damages claimed, the others contesting the basis on which they had been calculated.

FISHING IN THE NORTH SEA

On 28 September 1949 the United Kingdom filed an application
instituting proceedings against Norway, on the basis of the compulsory jurisdiction, the subject of the proceedings being the validity
or otherwise, under international law, of the Norwegian system of
delimitation of a Norwegian fisheries zone by a Decree of 1935.
Although disputes between British and Norwegian fishermen had
prevailed in one form or another for several centuries, it was only
since the beginning of the twentieth century, with the introduction
of modern methods of fishing and the increasing economic pressures
on the world's fish stocks, that Norway began to take more stringent
measures to protect its own fisheries interests in the sea areas adjacent
to its coast. After the decree of 1935 the dispute became more acute
and there was talk of referring it to the Permanent Court, but those
negotiations had not been completed when the Second World War
broke out. After the War, the danger of depletion of the fish stocks
through over-fishing had brought to a head a number of fishing
disputes, both in the North Sea and North Atlantic, and in other
parts of the world. Indeed, these disputes have become one of the
major concrete international issues now pending, although the
United Nations has only been obliquely concerned with them. The
Fisheries case was therefore partly a test-case on a matter of great
and general international interest.

Before the Norwegian Decree of 1935, it had been generally believed that the base-line from which the strip of territorial sea (over
which the coastal State has exclusive fishing rights) is measured is
the low-tide line on the coast, with a number of special rules for
dealing with bays, gulfs, estuaries and other indentations: and in
such cases, if artificial base-lines should be drawn, they should be
based on points on the mainland and as far as possible follow the
sinuosities of the coast, even if the coast is deeply indented by fjords
and lochs, as is the coast of Norway. The Decree of 1935, however,
proceeded on a different principle. It laid down a series of base-
points, 48 in all, many of them not being points on continental
Norway at all but on rocks out at sea and visible at low tide (drying
rocks, or low-tide elevations). The total length of these lines, which
did not follow the sinuosities of the coast but at most its general

direction, was some 600 miles. From these base-lines an exclusive fishing zone of four miles in width is claimed. This decree affected some 6,900 square kilometres of sea, in which are found important stocks of cod, saithe, haddock, halibut, plaice, herring, mackerel, seal and some types of whale.

The case was introduced in form unilaterally by the United Kingdom. But it appears that although the parties were unable to draw up a special agreement, there was diplomatic agreement to refer the dispute to the Court in this way, and the proceedings took their course without any complications. On 18 December 1951 the Court rendered its judgment in which, by ten votes to two, it upheld the Norwegian contentions.[5]

This is commonly regarded as one of the most important judgments rendered by the present Court. The issues far transcended the actual bipartite dispute of which the Court was seised, for since the end of the Second World War, as stated, questions of fishing rights have become a major international issue, and the implications of a judgment admitting that the new conception of base-lines on this extended scale was not contrary to international law, and even more so the reasons adopted by the Court, were general. In 1950 the General Assembly had decided to take up the whole question of the codification of the law of the sea, and the first phases of the work were entrusted to the International Law Commission. It soon became clear that the question of generalizing the rules applied by the Court in the *Fisheries* case for the delimitation of base-lines, and those applied earlier in the *Corfu Channel* case relating to the right of innocent passage through the territorial sea in general and through straits serving international navigation in particular, would encounter major political difficulties. In the end, the United Nations Conference on the Law of the Sea, which was in session for two months in Geneva in the spring of 1958, succeeded in achieving agreement on these vital aspects.[6] There can be little doubt that but for the Court's decision in 1951, the Conference would not have been able to complete its work with success. The Court, in deciding the concrete case, had expounded the principles which were applicable. Those principles were then taken up first by the International Law Commission (with political guidance from the General Assembly and from individual governments), and in that way generalized, and later finally approved, on the political level, by the 1958 Conference. Here is an important instance of the manner in which the Court, by its decision on a concrete dispute, makes a significant contribution to the development of international law, which itself is the basis for the prevention, or the settlement, of other international disputes.

To remove all doubt, it should be stated that the Court was not asked to decide, in 1951, what is the breadth of the territorial sea recognized by international law. That was not in issue in 1951. The sole question was the manner in which the inner, or landward, limit of the area of territorial sea may be fixed in cases where the coastline presents the special features of the coast of Norway.

FRENCH NATIONALS IN EGYPT

In October, 1949, France filed an application against Egypt, based on the Montreux Convention of 1937 for the abrogation of the Capitulations, asking for compensation for the damage suffered by a number of French nationals and protected persons, in their persons, property, rights and interests, as a result of measures taken by the Egyptian Government in May, 1948, in connection with the hostilities which broke out on the termination of the Mandate for Palestine. The proceedings were instituted after fifteen months of diplomatic negotiations had been in vain. In February, 1950, the oppressive measures were lifted. In those circumstances the proceedings were discontinued.[7]

A CASE OF DIPLOMATIC ASYLUM

On 3 October 1948 an unsuccessful military rebellion broke out in Peru at the instigation of a political party led by the well-known Peruvian politician Señor Victor Raúl Haya de la Torre. Judicial proceedings were thereupon opened against him, but he managed to evade arrest, and on 3 January 1949 sought, and was granted, political asylum in the Colombian Embassy in Lima, on the basis of certain Latin American customs and conventions regulating diplomatic asylum. The next day, the Colombian Ambassador made the usual demand for a safe-conduct so that he could leave the country. This was refused on the ground that he was not charged with political offences, and a dispute ensued between the two countries. On 31 August 1949 they concluded an agreement, called the Act of Lima, to refer the dispute to the Court, but being unable to determine the terms of the reference, agreed that either party might institute the proceedings unilaterally without that being regarded as an unfriendly act towards the other. On 15 October, Colombia, on the basis of the Act of Lima, filed an application instituting the proceedings, in the course of which the Court was to render three judgments in what became technically three separate cases.

In the application the Court was asked to decide, on the basis of the various legal rules binding the parties, whether Colombia was legally entitled, for the purpose of granting the asylum, to qualify the offence as a political offence and not as an ordinary offence (for which no asylum should be granted), and whether Peru as the territorial State was bound to give the necessary safe-conduct to enable Sr. Haya de la Torre to leave the country. In the course of the proceedings, Peru submitted a counter-claim, asking the Court to declare that the grant of asylum was in violation of the Havana Convention on Asylum of 1928. In the judgment of 20 November 1950, the Court found that Colombia was not entitled unilaterally, and in a manner binding on Peru, to qualify the nature of the offence, and accordingly it rejected the Colombian demand that Peru must give the necessary safe-conduct. On the other hand, while partly rejecting the Peruvian counter-claim, it nevertheless found that the grant of asylum was not made in conformity with the Havana Convention.[8]

This judgment left things as they were. This was not the fault of the Court, but was the consequence of the manner in which the case was presented. The agreement in principle to refer the dispute to the Court did not, apparently, go so far as to include any underlying agreement about the real issues on which the Court's decision could lay the basis for the political settlement. On 20 November, the day on which the judgment was delivered, Colombia filed an application for interpretation. The purpose of this was to obtain a decision from the Court on the manner of the termination of Sr. Haya de la Torre's continued enforced residence in the Colombian Embassy in Lima. In a judgment of 27 November 1950 the Court declared the request for interpretation to be inadmissible on the grounds that no dispute as to the meaning and scope of the judgment had been disclosed, and that new questions were raised, and not questions of the meaning of statements appearing in the judgment.[9]

The next day, Peru demanded the surrender of the refugee on the basis of the judgment of 20 November, and Colombia refused on the ground that neither of the judgments had dealt with the question of the surrender. This gave rise to a new dispute between the parties, and on 13 December 1950 Colombia filed a further application asking whether or not Colombia was bound to deliver Sr. Haya de la Torre to Peru. Jurisdiction was based on the Treaty of Friendship between the two countries of 24 May 1934. Colombia was willing to have a decision by the Court *ex aequo et bono* (see p. 129 above), but Peru did not agree to this course. On 13 March 1951 Cuba, as party to the Havana Convention of 1928 the construction of which was again in question, intervened, but the admissibility of the intervention was contested.

By a judgment of 13 June 1951, Cuba's intervention was first admitted, limited, however, to the new questions that had arisen, and not covering the interpretation of the Havana Convention which had been given in the first judgment. On the merits, the Court found that it was unable to give effect to submissions of both parties asking it to declare how the judgment of 20 November should be executed, on the ground that this was a submission couched in an interrogative form which implied a political choice which only the parties were in a position to appreciate. It was not part of the Court's judicial function to make such a choice. It went on to find that Colombia was not obliged to surrender the refugee to Peru, and that the asylum itself ought to have ceased after the judgment of 20 November.[10]

This had cleared up one point, but still left outstanding the major issue of how to bring the asylum to an end. This aspect reverted to the diplomatic channel. The reason for this again was the fact that the parties had been unable to agree what was the dispute to be referred to the Court. The Court, for its part, and consistent with its usual caution, did not feel itself empowered to do any more than declare the legal position between the parties. The Court nevertheless expressed the hope that after their mutual relations had been made clear the parties would be able to find a practical and satisfactory solution by seeking guidance from those considerations of courtesy and good-neighbourliness which, in matters of asylum, have always held a prominent place in the relations between the Latin-American republics. Over three more years were to elapse before Sr. Haya de la Torre was able to leave the Colombian Embassy, and the virtual state of siege under which it had been placed was lifted.

QUESTIONS OF HUMAN RIGHTS IN CERTAIN PEACE TREATIES

Starting in 1948 the General Assembly had been discussing the observance of the human rights clauses of the Peace Treaties with Bulgaria, Hungary and Rumania, which were being accused of grave violations of those provisions. The Peace Treaties each contained a clause for the settlement of disputes which provided, among other things, for the reference of a dispute to a three-man Commission of which the third member should be appointed by the Secretary-General of the United Nations in the event of disagreement. Attempts to refer the disputes to the Commissions having failed, owing to the refusal of Bulgaria, Hungary and Rumania to appoint their commissioners, the question arose in 1949 whether the Secretary-General could make the third appointment. In October, 1949, the General Assembly decided to ask for an advisory opinion on four legal questions: *(a)* Was the existence of disputes disclosed by the diplomatic correspondence? *(b)* If so, did the provisions of the Peace Treaties for the settlement of disputes come into operation? If the answer to those questions was in the affirmative, and if, after a delay of one month, the national commissioners had not been appointed, *(c)* was the Secretary-General authorized to proceed to the appointment of the "third" commissioner; and *(d)* if so, would such a Commission be competent? The General Assembly had adopted this resolution by forty-seven votes to five, with seven abstentions.

In its advisory opinion of 30 March 1950 the Court answered the first two questions in the affirmative, each time by a vote of eleven to three, and in a second opinion of 18 July, by eleven votes to two it answered the third question in the negative, and therefore did not consider the fourth question.[11]

As in the previous advisory opinions which originated in Cold War issues, here, too, the competence of the Court was challenged, on the ground, essentially, that if there were concrete disputes, the invocation of the advisory procedure was in fact an attempt to introduce surreptitiously a form of contentious case, and the Court was not authorized to deal with such a case in the absence of the consent of all the parties. The Court rejected these contentions in the present case. Its principal reason was that the advisory opinion as such was not binding, representing the participation of the Court in the work of the United Nations. The object of the request for the advisory opinion was to obtain enlightenment for the General Assembly, and in the present circumstances, the advisory opinion would not be substantially equivalent to deciding the questions in dispute between the parties.

The General Assembly had no alternative but to take note of the two advisory opinions, and in effect dropped the matter.[12]

As in a previous case, it may be considered that here too the questions put to the Court were on the whole not difficult from the legal point of view. The disputes were rooted in a more intractable political situation which all the organs of the United Nations were unable to solve. The real significance of this experience was that it showed once and for all that the Soviet Union and its Allies were not prepared to enable the advisory procedure to be employed to handle disputes relating to the Cold War, and the attempt to bring the Court into this aspect of contemporary international relations has not been repeated.

THE QUESTION OF SOUTH-WEST AFRICA

Questions relating to the Mandates system established by virtue of Article 22 of the Covenant of the League of Nations came before the Permanent Court in one instance only—the *Mavrommatis Palestine Concessions*—and although the Mandates system did not survive the liquidation of the League, being replaced by the International Trusteeship System set forth in Articles 75-91 of the Charter, the new Court has had before it no less than five cases to do with the legal status of the mandated territory of South-West Africa. Two of these cases are now pending.

On 17 December 1920 the League Council conferred this Mandate on South Africa and confirmed its terms. It was what was called a "C" class Mandate, under which the mandatory had full powers of administration and legislation over the territory as an integral portion of its own territory, subject to a number of obligations, and the League was to supervise the administration and see to it that the obligations were fulfilled. Difficulties over the interpretation and application of the Mandate had appeared already in the days of the League, but they only came to a head in the United Nations, when South Africa refused to convert the Mandate into a Trusteeship agreement, despite repeated urgings by the General Assembly.[13] In 1949 the General Assembly decided that for its further consideration of the question, the Court's opinion on a number of legal questions was desirable. On 11 July 1950 the Court gave an opinion on five questions. It found that the Mandate was still in force and that the obligations arising thereunder were still binding on South Africa; that under the Charter the territory could be placed under the Trusteeship system but that there was no legal obligation on South Africa to do so; and that South Africa, acting alone, does not have the competence to modify the international status of the territory, but that modifications in its international status could only be made with the consent of the United Nations.[14] The competence of the Court to give this opinion was not challenged.

The General Assembly then adopted the advisory opinion and commenced a long series of efforts to implement it.[15] In the course of these efforts further questions arose of the meaning of certain passages in the 1950 Opinion which had stated that the degree of supervision over the territory by the General Assembly should not exceed that which had previously been applied by the League and should conform as far as possible to the procedure of the League Council. On that basis the General Assembly had established the Committee on South-West Africa, broadly analogous to the Permanent Mandates Commission of the Council of the League. South Africa refused to co-operate with this Committee and to submit the annual reports which had been required by the League. This deprived the Committee of information necessary to enable it to discharge its functions. Other difficulties had arisen, because it was contended that the substitution in the United Nations of the two-thirds majority for the unanimity previously current in the League implied an increase in the degree of supervision, against which the Court in 1950 had uttered a warning. In 1954 the General Assembly therefore decided to ask the Court for an advisory opinion on that question—which the Court, in its Opinion of 7 June 1955, answered in the negative.[16]

After accepting this Opinion the General Assembly continued its efforts,[17] and the next year found it necessary to ask the Court whether it would be consistent with the 1950 Opinion for it to authorize the Committee on South-West Africa to grant oral hearings to petitioners (under the original Mandates system, petitioners could only submit their petitions in writing, and the question was whether oral petitions would constitute an excess in the degree of supervision).

The underlying purpose in granting oral hearings was to supplement the Committee's information on the situation on South-West Africa. In its Opinion of 1 June 1956 the Court answered the question put to it in the affirmative.[18]

These Opinions had certainly gone a long way towards clarifying the legal situation, but being advisory opinions these were not technically binding on South Africa, and the political conflict between the majority in the General Assembly and the Union started to grow sharper.[19] At its eleventh session (1956) the General Assembly decided to look for new ways to ensure that South Africa fulfil the obligations incumbent on it under the Mandate, and after detailed consideration of this aspect, in 1959, it drew the attention of member States to the possibility of their bringing a contentious case against the Union, based on the submission to the jurisdiction contained in the Mandate.[20] The question was then discussed at the Second African States Conference held at Addis Ababa in June, 1960, at which Ethiopia and Liberia announced their intention of initiating contentious proceedings, as recommended. The Conference established a steering committee of four African States, including Ethiopia and Liberia, to determine the procedure and tactics incident to the conduct of the case.

In November, 1960, the two contentious cases were accordingly instituted, and are now pending.[21] This action met with strong approval by the General Assembly, which also refused to see in the existence of the contentious proceedings at The Hague any reason to cause it to refrain from exercising its own responsibilities under the Charter for the supervision of the Territory of South-West Africa.[22]

This history well illustrates the extraordinary complications which beset a dispute having important legal elements between the majority of the General Assembly and a member State. It is understood that the underlying purpose in the contentious proceedings is to try and eradicate all ambiguity which flows from the formal non-binding character of the advisory opinions, and to obtain a binding decision from the Court, in the form of a judgment, on broadly similar issues. The future of this case will be awaited with great interest.

RIGHTS OF U.S. NATIONALS IN (FRENCH) MOROCCO

On 28 October 1950 France instituted proceedings against the United States, on the basis of the compulsory jurisdiction, asking for a definition of the rights of United States nationals in Morocco. The dispute originated in measures of currency control and control of imports introduced in 1948, but it also raised complicated questions concerning the extent to which United States citizens enjoyed rights of exterritoriality under the system of capitulations, and the method of evaluating imports for customs purposes under the so-called Act of Algeciras of 1906, and a number of related topics. The United States made a formal reservation about the applicability of the compulsory jurisdiction in this case, but nevertheless agreed to the questions being decided by the Court. The United States also raised a technical objection designed to ascertain whether the judgment would be binding not only on France but also on Morocco, and when this point was cleared up, the objection was withdrawn. In a long and complicated judgment of 27 July 1952, the Court gave its decision on the various issues presented to it.[23]

THE GENOCIDE CONVENTION

The Convention on the Prevention and Punishment of the Crime of Genocide which was signed on 9 December 1948 provided that it would come into force after twenty States had become parties to it. On the eve of the fifth session of the General Assembly in 1950 the Secretary-General was confronted with a novel problem: the number of States parties to the Convention was growing, but some of these had appended reservations to which other States had entered objections, and it seemed likely that he would run into difficulties in deciding whether in those circumstances the reserving States could be included in the twenty necessary to bring the Convention into force. On that basis he asked the General Assembly for directions. For practical purposes his difficulties were overcome on 14 October 1950 when five States ratified the Convention, bringing the total number up to twenty-four. Only two of these were affected by reservations, so there was no difficulty in determining the entry into force of the Convention. However the incident had disclosed great differences of opinion among the members about the applicable rules of law in circumstances such as these (which are fairly common), and it was decided to take the opinion of the Court on the basic question whether a reserving State could be regarded as being a party to the Convention if some of the other parties object to the reservation, but not others. Although the immediate problem of the Genocide Convention was therefore to some extent solved in fact, the questions were asked in relation to that Convention in order to enable the Court to consider the problems against a concrete background, and not entirely in the abstract. For the Court this became a normal question of treaty interpretation, of ascertaining the underlying intentions of the draftsmen, even though the issues involved were entirely novel. On 28 May 1951 the Court gave its opinion, which is mainly of technical interest to the professional international lawyer,[24] and the General Assembly subsequently gave instructions to the Secretary-General based on the opinion.[25]

Although technical, the underlying issues of this case are important for the smooth conduct of international affairs. However, the law has still not been sufficiently clarified and generalized, and the International Law Commission has been asked to deal with the matter in connection with its general codification of the international law of treaties.

A GREEK CITIZEN'S CLAIM FOR DAMAGES FOR BREACH OF CONTRACT

In 1919 a Greek shipowner, Nicholas Ambatielos, contracted with the British Government for the purchase of some steamships then abuilding, but the ships were not delivered as soon as anticipated and Mr. Ambatielos became indebted to the British Government for a considerable sum of money, part of which was secured by a mortgage on the ships. In the course of legal proceedings in London in 1920, certain interdepartmental minutes were not produced by the British Government—a fact which later gave rise to a claim by Ambatielos for "denial of justice". Ambatielos lost his case in the Court of Appeal in London, and made no attempt to take it to the House of Lords. Diplomatic correspondence then ensued, and at one time there was talk of referring the dispute to the Permanent Court, but the British Government took the position that there was no international dispute and did not consent to referring the matter to the Permanent Court. Proposals for arbitration were finally rejected by the British Government at the end of 1939. After the War the discussion was resumed, and on 9 April 1951 Greece instituted proceedings against the United Kingdom, basing the jurisdiction on a Treaty of Commerce and Navigation of 1926, which provided for the reference of certain disputes to the Permanent Court. The Court was asked to declare that by virtue of certain agreements between the parties, the United Kingdom was obliged to co-operate with Greece in establishing an Arbitration Commission to determine the merits of the dispute. It will thus be seen that the International Court itself was not asked to determine the merits of this complicated dispute: its task was limited to determining that a dispute existed between the parties for which the proper solution was to be found through a bilateral arbitration process.

The United Kingdom first challenged the jurisdiction of the International Court even for this limited purpose. In its judgment of 1 July 1952 the Court held that it was without jurisdiction to decide on the merits of the Ambatielos claim, but that it did have jurisdiction to decide whether the United Kingdom was under an obligation to submit the claim to arbitration.[26] The issues that arose in this phase of the case were mostly technical issues of international treaty law. In a second judgment of 19 May 1953 the Court found that the United Kingdom was under the obligation to submit the dispute to arbitration.[27] In the third phase of the proceedings before the arbitration commission (containing three "neutral" members), the final award was in favour of the United Kingdom.[28] It will be noted that the role of the International Court here was limited to deciding upon the "arbitrability" of the dispute, and its own jurisdiction to decide that issue. Since the parties had not agreed that it should decide the merits of the dispute, it was extremely careful in both its judgments not to encroach on the jurisdiction of the arbitral commission.

THE ANGLO-IRANIAN OIL CO.

Tension between Iran and the United Kingdom over the affairs of the Anglo-Iranian Oil Company has persisted throughout the present century. The original D'Arcy Concession was granted in 1901, and after the First World War the Iranian Government complained that the Company was not paying sufficient attention to Iran's national interests. In 1932 the dispute reached such a pitch that the United Kingdom Government contemplated referring it to the Permanent Court. In 1933 a new concession agreement was negotiated between Iran and the Company through the Council of the League, to which the United Kingdom had referred the dispute, and in 1949 a supplemental agreement, designed to increase Iran's benefits under the concession, was not ratified by the Iranian Parliament. Matters took a dramatic turn in March, 1951, when the Iranian Parliament enacted legislation, which received the Imperial assent on 1 May, for the nationalization of the oil industry throughout the country. The dispute became serious, and the British Government even started to make preparations for sending its armed forces into Iran in the event of danger to British nationals there.[29] Later, however, the British Government decided to refer the dispute to the Court, which it did by application instituting proceedings filed on 26 May. The application was based on the compulsory jurisdiction, which was said to be applicable by virtue of a somewhat complicated construction given in the document instituting the proceedings.

The filing of this application did not arrest the rapid deterioration in the situation, in the course of which there was a danger that the Company's installations would be damaged. Accordingly, on 22 June 1951 the British Government submitted to the Court an urgent request for an indication of interim measures of protection designed to protect the Company and its installations. The Iranian Government immediately denied that the Court had jurisdiction to deal with this request, and did not appear in the oral proceedings held on 30 June (nor was an Iranian judge *ad hoc* appointed at this stage). On 5 July the Court, being satisfied that it had jurisdiction for this purpose, made an order as requested.[30] This order was not implemented by Iran, and in September the United Kingdom referred to the Security Council the question of its enforcement, with the inconclusive results described earlier (p. 44 above).

In due course, the Iranian Government appointed its Agent and also designated a judge *ad hoc*, but instead of pleading to the merits, filed preliminary objections. In a judgment of 22 July 1952 the Court found that it had no jurisdiction on a number of grounds, mostly of a technical character. However, in the course of explaining its reasons, it had to deal with one facet of the dispute which was complicating the legal relations between the parties. As stated, the concession agreement of 1933 had been negotiated between the Iranian Government and the Company through the good offices of the Rapporteur appointed by the Council of the League of Nations, and it was argued that in consequence the concession agreement itself could be regarded as an international convention. The Court decided that question in the negative.[31]

Almost simultaneously with the filing of the British Government's application in this case, the Anglo-Iranian Oil Company applied to the President, asking him to appoint an umpire for the arbitration tribunal between the Company and the Iranian Government, in accordance with a provision in the 1933 concession conferring that power on the President of the *Permanent* Court. The President deferred his decision until after the termination of the British Government's case, and then, in the absence of the necessary consent on the part of the Iranian Government, found that he was not authorized to make the appointment.[32]

WHOSE ARE THE CHANNEL ISLETS: MINQUIERS AND ECREHOS?

On 5 December 1951 the United Kingdom filed the text of a special agreement concluded a year earlier with France by which a dispute over the sovereignty of these two islets lying between Jersey and the French coast was submitted to the Court (see p. 101 above). Underlying this dispute were not only fishing interests of the two countries—for the area contains valuable oyster beds—but also other economic interests including certain French plans to exploit the tides for the purpose of generating electricity. Furthermore, the interested party on the British side was not the United Kingdom itself, but the Island of Jersey, whose parliamentary organization actually approved the submission of the case to the Court, as far back as 1948, after diplomatic negotiations had broken down. The United Kingdom delegation included the Attorney-General of Jersey. On 17 November 1953 the Court gave judgment in favour of the claim of the United Kingdom.[33]

By a separate agreement of 30 January 1951, made independently of the special agreement to submit the case to the Court, the British and French Governments reached accord on the question of the fishing rights without prejudice to the question of sovereignty over the groups. This was an instance of the two parties appearing before the Court "arm-in-arm", in the words of the Attorney-General of the United Kingdom.

A GERMAN NATIONAL CLAIMS RESTORATION OF HIS SEQUESTERED PROPERTY

Herr Friedrich Nottebohm was born at Hamburg in September, 1881, of German nationality. In 1905 he established himself in Guatemala, where he continued to have his fixed abode until 1943 when, Guatemala having declared war on Germany in 1941, he was arrested, deported to the United States, and interned, and his substantial property sequestered under the equivalent of the trading with the enemy legislation. In March, 1939, he paid a visit to Germany, and in October, shortly after the outbreak of the War, he visited Liechtenstein where he applied for, and was granted, Liechtenstein nationality after undertaking to make certain annual payments by way of "naturalization tax". He then applied for a Guatemalan visa on his new passport with which he returned to Guatemala there to resume his business activities. After the War Liechtenstein attempted to recover the sequestered property, and on the failure of the diplomatic negotiations filed an application in Court on 17 December 1951, on the basis of the compulsory jurisdiction. Further negotiations having been unsuccessful, the pleadings commenced. In due course Guatemala filed a preliminary objection to the effect that since Guatemala's acceptance of the compulsory jurisdiction had expired after the institution of the proceedings, the Court no longer had jurisdiction, and by a judgment of 18 November 1953 the Court unanimously (there was no judge *ad hoc* for either party in this phase) dismissed the plea, which many lawyers believe to have been unarguable (a rare instance of this). In the next phase of the case, Guatemala contended that the claim was inadmissible on the ground that Liechtenstein was not entitled to rely against Guatemala on the nationality thus conferred for the purposes of exercising its right of diplomatic protection, so as to transform enemy (German) property into neutral property. The Court, in its judgment of 6 April 1955, upheld this contention.[34]

GOLD LOOTED FROM ROME IN 1943

In September, 1943, the Germans looted from a bank in Rome nearly 2,340 kilograms of monetary gold belonging to the National Bank of Albania and transferred it to Germany. The Paris Act on Reparation of 1946 provided that monetary gold found in Germany by the allied forces should be pooled for distribution as restitution proportionately among the countries which had lost gold through looting during the War. Both Italy and Albania were parties to the Paris Act, which established a Tripartite Commission, consisting of the United States, France and the United Kingdom, for the purpose of passing upon claims to a share out of the pool. Both Italy and Albania had claims, and since the Tripartite Commission was unable to solve them the Three Powers decided to submit the question to arbitration. On 20 February 1953 the arbitrator decided that the gold belonged to Albania.

At this point a complication appeared. The gold was in the hands of the Tripartite Commission, and the three Powers had agreed between themselves that if the arbitrator were to decide that the gold was Albanian, they would hand it over to the United Kingdom in partial satisfaction of the unpaid judgment debt in the *Corfu Channel* case, unless within a period of 90 days, either Albania or Italy instituted appropriate proceedings against them in the International Court, and for that purpose they agreed in advance to accept the Court's jurisdiction. Having lost before the arbitrator, the only way by which Italy could protect its claim to the gold was, therefore, by turning to the Hague Court, and on 19 May 1953 the proceedings were instituted against the three Governments. Albania, however, refused either to institute proceedings of its own, or to intervene in the Italian suit, and before filing the Memorial the Italian Government asked the Court to decide the preliminary question of whether, in such circumstances, it could exercise jurisdiction. In its judgment of 15 June 1954 the Court answered that question in the negative, on the ground that in the absence of Albania, a directly interested party, it could not decide a case directly involving the international responsibility of Albania. The future of the gold was therefore returned to the diplomatic channel.[35]

The importance of this case is not so much in the pronouncement of the Court, interesting though that is from the legal point of view, as in the action of the three Powers in developing novel procedures for securing satisfaction of a judgment debt previously awarded to one of them by the International Court. This was an instance of the adoption of measures of economic self-help, in which provision was made for the application of judicial controls at the request of interested parties, including possible competitive claimants.

FRANCE'S DIFFICULTIES IN THE LEBANON

On two occasions, in 1953 and again in 1959, France has referred to the Court disputes with the Lebanon arising out of Lebanese attempts to modify concessions agreements with French companies.

In both cases, the dispute was later settled out of Court, and the proceedings discontinued.[36] These are instances of Court procedures being invoked to bolster up diplomatic negotiations.

THE ADMINISTRATIVE TRIBUNALS

Two cases involving the decisions of the Administrative Tribunals —of the United Nations and of the International Labour Organization—have been referred to the Court for advisory opinion. The background for both is similar, namely, the rights of former staff members, in the first case of the United Nations and in the second of UNESCO, who had been discharged by the Secretary-General because of their refusal to answer questions put to them by an investigating committee of the United States Senate relating to membership in the Communist Party or subversive activities in the United States. All the staff members concerned were United States nationals. After their discharge they sought redress from the appropriate Administrative Tribunal, which in many instances found that the circumstances of the discharge gave rise to a claim for compensation.[37]

In accordance with the normal practice, the Secretary-General included in the 1953 budget appropriations to meet the sums awarded to the former United Nations staff members, but his action was challenged on the ground that the General Assembly was entitled to override the decisions of the Administrative Tribunal. The General Assembly thereupon decided to take the opinion of the Court on the legal issues, and in its advisory opinion of 13 July 1954, the Court reached the conclusion that the General Assembly had no right on any grounds to refuse to give effect to an award of compensation made by the Administrative Tribunal in favour of a staff member whose contract of service had been terminated without his assent.[38] Following that opinion, the General Assembly decided to introduce a system of review, by the Court, of the decisions of the Administrative Tribunal, as has been described earlier (p. 94 above). No instance of formal review being requested of the Court has occurred, although the Committee which was then established to see if any case warranted recourse to the Court has met several times.

In the second case, the recourse to the Court was initiated in 1955 by the Executive Board of UNESCO which wanted to avail itself of the procedure for review existing under the current rules for the I.L.O. Administrative Tribunal and challenge decisions by the Tribunal confirming its own jurisdiction. In its advisory opinion of 23 October 1956, the Court, after first deciding that the exercise of the advisory function in this type of case was compatible with its judicial role, found that the Administrative Tribunal was competent, and that the validity of its decisions in the cases in question was no longer open to question.[39]

In this case, the interesting feature is the special procedure which was devised to enable the interested persons, who had already obtained judgments in their favour in the Administrative Tribunal, to present their views to the Court. The Executive Board had decided, when it adopted the request for the advisory opinion, to enable these persons to submit their statements to UNESCO which would annex them to its own statement without comment, and this was done. The Court later decided not to hold oral proceedings, but instead to make provision for a second round of written pleadings, in which both UNESCO and the interested persons were able to comment briefly on the statements made in the first round of statements. The problem which the Court then faced was whether it could give the advisory opinion and remain faithful to the requirements of its judicial character as a Court in which only States can litigate their differences. Without prejudice to its future action, the Court found that in the circumstances it could, and that if there was any inequality between the "parties"—UNESCO on the one hand and the staff members on the other—it was purely nominal and did not affect the exercise by the Court of its judicial functions.

The important consequence of these two opinions has been to safeguard the judicial character of the two Administrative Tribunals, and this, in turn, is an important contribution towards the creation of an independent international civil service on which the effective functioning of the system of international organization depends.

THE IRON CURTAIN OVERFLOWN (I)—MILITARY AIRCRAFT

It has been seen (p. 80 above) that the procedure of the Court makes it possible for proceedings to be instituted even though there is at the time no basis for the jurisdiction of the Court, the application instituting proceedings containing an invitation to the defendant to confer jurisdiction on the Court to decide that concrete dispute. The first instances of this occurred on 3 March 1954, when the United States filed applications against the U.S.S.R., and Hungary relating to the treatment of aircraft and crew of the United States in Hungary. These applications referred to an in-

Balloting in the General Assembly 1960

The Court deliberating in the Salle "Bol"

The Indian Delegation

cident which had occurred in 1951 when a United States military aircraft had been shot down over Hungary and its crew subjected to treatment which the United States regarded as contrary to international law. Attempts to reach a solution of these differences through the diplomatic channels had been unsuccessful. The defendant governments declined the invitation to adjudicate the dispute, and the Court was left with no alternative but to order the two cases to be removed from the list.[40]

Further incidents of this kind continued, and in September, 1954, the United States asked the Security Council to deal with a situation which it thought could constitute a danger to the maintenance of international peace and security. The debate, in the Council's 679th and 680th meetings on 10 September, was inconclusive, and no resolution was proposed. Since then, the United States has instituted three similar cases against the Soviet Union and one against Czechoslovakia, between 1956 and 1959. In no case has the defendant government consented to confer jurisdiction on the Court, which could therefore take no action except to order the cases to be removed from the list.[41]

THE ANTARCTICA

Similar was the action of the United Kingdom in instituting proceedings against Argentina and Chile on 4 May 1955. In these applications the Court was asked to declare that the sovereignty over the disputed Falkland Islands Territories and other areas of the Antarctic belonged to the United Kingdom and that the claims of Argentina and Chile to those territories were, as against the United Kingdom, invalid. After the proceedings were instituted, the United Kingdom continued to make strenuous efforts to obtain the consent of the defendant governments to litigate the dispute, but finally conceded that the Court did not have jurisdiction, and the cases were accordingly removed from the list.[42]

As in the *Aerial Incident* cases, the effect of this action is to place the claim, and the main grounds on which it is based, on public record. The action of the United Kingdom may be regarded as a diplomatic phase in a dispute which has been in existence for some time.

SOME NORWEGIAN LOANS

The origins of this dispute lie in a flotation of loans by Norway at the turn of the century on various foreign markets, including that of Paris. The bonds contained a "gold clause". During the financial instability of the First World War, and again in the financial crisis of 1931, the convertibility of the notes was suspended, and has remained so. Diplomatic correspondence claiming fulfilment of the gold clause proceeded intermittently since 1925, in the course of which Norway rejected all proposals to submit the dispute to arbitration or adjudication on the ground that the matter came within its exclusive jurisdiction. On 6 July 1955 France instituted proceedings on the basis of the compulsory jurisdiction, and in due course Norway raised four objections to the jurisdiction and to the admissibility of the suit. However, by agreement between the parties, Norway agreed to postpone the decision on these objections until the merits.

The French declaration accepting the jurisdiction had contained a clause (since revoked) by which France excluded from the jurisdiction disputes relating to matters which are essentially within the national jurisdiction as understood by the French Government (see p. 82 above). One of the Norwegian objections was that the loan contracts were governed by domestic law and not by international law, but in the course of pleading that objection the Norwegian Government had sought to rely, in a subsidiary manner, on the subjective element of the French declaration (which Norway was entitled to invoke on the basis of reciprocity), and thus exclude the jurisdiction. In its judgment of 6 July 1957, the Court upheld that contention and found that it was without jurisdiction.[43]

RIGHT OF PASSAGE

This case, which was instituted by application filed by Portugal on 22 December 1955, is discussed in chapter V.

WHO SHALL APPOINT A GUARDIAN OVER AN INFANT?

This dispute, which did not reflect any political tension between the two countries, had its origins in a family squabble between two branches of a mixed Dutch-Swedish family about the right to appoint a guardian over an infant born in May 1945. The child, who was the issue of a marriage between a Dutchman and a Swedish woman and was of Dutch nationality, had lived all its life in Sweden. After the death of the mother in 1953 the father became guardian by Dutch law, but later a female guardian was appointed by a Dutch civil Court dealing with children. However, about the

same time a Swedish Court instituted measures of protective up-
bringing based on a Swedish Law of 1924 for the protection of
children. The Swedish authorities refused to allow the child to be
transferred to the Netherlands. The dispute was then taken up
through the diplomatic channels, and on 9 July 1957 the Netherlands instituted proceedings against Sweden on the basis of the
compulsory jurisdiction. The legal questions at issue related to the
Hague Convention of 1902 on the Guardianship of Infants. In its
judgment of 28 November 1948 the Court rejected the claim of the
Netherlands, and decided to leave the existing arrangements untouched.[44]

The view is occasionally expressed that a case of this nature is
somewhat trivial for the International Court. Such opinions must
be examined with care. There is no doubt that the dispute raised
difficult issues of interpretation of the Guardianship Convention of
1902, and there is no reason why the Court should not be asked to
decide them. Although the dispute had no political implications,
it should also be remembered that it involved conflicting decisions
of the competent judicial authorities of two friendly States, and it
seems clear that international legal proceedings are especially appropriate for overcoming that kind of difficulty.

THE INTERHANDEL COMPANY'S ASSETS

In 1942 the United States Government, acting under the Trading
with the Enemy Act, vested in itself nearly all the shares of the
General Aniline and Film Company, incorporated in the United
States, on the ground that in reality they belonged to or were controlled by the I.G. Farbenindustrie of Frankfurt. Until 1940 I.G.
Farben certainly controlled General Aniline and Film through a
company incorporated in Switzerland, later known as Interhandel,
but the Swiss Government alleged that in 1940 Interhandel severed
its links with the German Company, so that the General Aniline
assets became Swiss, and neutral, and were not enemy property
when they were seised. Towards the end of the War property of
Germans in Switzerland was blocked as a result of an agreement
between Switzerland and the Western Allies, but the Swiss Compensation Office accepted the view that Interhandel was Swiss, and
its assets there were not blocked. An agreement of 1946 provided
for the unblocking of Swiss assets in the United States, and further
discussions ensued regarding the character of Interhandel. No
agreement was reached, and in 1948 proceedings were instituted
in the United States Courts by Interhandel. One of the obstacles

to those proceedings was the refusal of Interhandel to produce certain documents on the ground that their production would be a violation of Swiss law. In the course of the diplomatic correspondence between the two governments, the United States informed Switzerland (prematurely, as it later transpired) that in fact Interhandel had failed in its suit. Accordingly, on 2 October 1957 Switzerland instituted proceedings in reliance on the compulsory jurisdiction, asking for the restoration of Interhandel's assets. The next day Switzerland requested interim measures of protection asking the United States Government to take no steps to part with the property and in particular not to sell the shares which were being claimed as Swiss property. The United States immediately made a determination that the matters referred to came within the domestic jurisdiction of the United States, in accordance with the condition appearing in its acceptance of the compulsory jurisdiction (see p. 82 above).

Oral proceedings on the question of the measures of protection were held on 12 and 14 October 1957, and on 16 November the Court was informed that the Supreme Court had, on the 14th, but many hours after the International Court had terminated its meeting, issued an order readmitting Interhandel into its suit, and the United States informed the Court that it would not be proceeding to the sale of the shares. In those circumstances, and holding that there was no urgency, the Court, by an order of 24 October 1957, found that there was no need to indicate interim measures of protection.[45]

In due course the United States filed four preliminary objections, three arguing that the Court lacked jurisdiction, and one contending that the suit was inadmissible on the ground that Interhandel had not exhausted the local remedies provided by the law of the United States before Switzerland instituted the proceedings at The Hague. The three objections to the jurisdiction were each dismissed, but the Court, influenced by the fact that the legal proceedings in the United States were continuing, accepted the objection to the admissibility, and the suit was dismissed.[46] The domestic litigation is still proceeding in the United States, and future proceedings in The Hague will depend on the outcome of the domestic litigation.

THE IRON CURTAIN OVERFLOWN (II) — CIVIL AIRCRAFT

On 27 July 1955 an Israel civil aircraft on a scheduled commercial flight was shot down by the Bulgarian aerial defence service, having inadvertently penetrated into the Bulgarian airspace. All its fifty-eight occupants were killed. The victims were nationals of Israel, Austria, Belgium, Canada, France, Germany, South Africa, Sweden, the United Kingdom, and the United States. A few days later the Bulgarian Government announced that its armed forces had shot the aircraft down, those armed forces having acted in haste and without taking all the necessary measures. The Bulgarian Government undertook to identify and punish the culpable persons, and to pay the compensation due. Negotiations and diplomatic correspondence followed in attempts by the various claimant governments to reach a friendly solution, but to no avail. On 16 October 1957, Israel instituted proceedings against Bulgaria with regard to the destruction of this aircraft. On 28 October and on 21 November, the United States and the United Kingdom also instituted proceedings in respect to the damage suffered by their nationals arising out of the destruction of the aircraft. Israel had invoked the compulsory jurisdiction, relying on a Bulgarian declaration of 1921 and the provisions contained in the present Statute for maintaining continuity in the domain of international jurisdiction (see p. 84 above). These were three separate proceedings: although they all arose out of the same incident, the three governments each represented different interests. Israel, in addition to claiming on behalf of its injured nationals, which included both the airline and the Israeli passengers and crew, was also interested in protecting its flag; whereas the other governments were interested in protecting the rights of their injured nationals. As a consequence, the three cases each took a separate course, and never remained in the same procedural stage.

When the time came for Bulgaria to reply to the Israel Memorial, that government filed five preliminary objections, two relating to the jurisdiction and three contesting the admissibility of the suit. One of the objections was that since Bulgaria had become a member of the United Nations and a party to the Statute of the Court ten years after the Charter had come into force (Bulgaria was admitted to the United Nations on 14 December 1955), the clause in the Statute providing for the maintenance in force of declarations accepting the jurisdiction of the Permanent Court did not apply to it. In its judgment of 26 May 1959, the Court upheld that objection to its jurisdiction.[47]

Following that judgment, the United Kingdom, without prejudice to its international claim, decided to discontinue its suit against Bulgaria.[48] The United States, however, on the basis of the rule that the judgment in the Israel case was only binding as between Israel and Bulgaria (see p. 129 above), continued with its case, and in due course Bulgaria filed four preliminary objections, one based on the very ground which the Court had upheld in the Israel case. Another of these objections pleaded, on the basis of reciprocity and following the Court's decision in the *Norwegian Loans* case, that Bulgaria was entitled as against the United States to determine that the matter came within the domestic jurisdiction of Bulgaria, and that the Court had no jurisdiction. The United States was originally prepared to contest this plea, but shortly before the case became ready for hearing had second thoughts, and entered notice of discontinuance.[49]

BAERLE-DUC AND BAARLE-NASSAU—BELGIAN OR DUTCH?

On 26 November 1957 a special agreement between the Netherlands and Belgium was filed, asking the Court to decide whether sovereignty over certain parcels of land on the frontier, about 14 hectares (33 acres) in area, belonged to the Dutch Commune of Baarle-Nassau or the Belgian Commune of Baerle-Duc. In a judgment of 20 June 1959, the Court found in favour of Belgium.[50]
     Neither side appointed a judge *ad hoc* in this case.

THE FRONTIER BETWEEN HONDURAS AND NICARAGUA

The roots of this dispute go back to the distant past—to the period of Spanish rule in South America. In 1906 the King of Spain was asked to arbitrate the differences between the two countries, and in his award he fixed the frontier, for the greater part to the advantage of Honduras.[51] The frontier thus fixed was not delimited, however, and from about 1912 onwards Nicaragua began to challenge the regularity of the arbitration proceedings before the King of Spain and the validity of the arbitral award he had rendered. Various attempts to reach a settlement of this dispute failed, and in 1957 hostilities broke out between the two countries over the disputed territory. This incident was brought before the competent organs of the Organization of American States through the good offices of which the parties, in July 1957, agreed to submit their dispute to the International Court. It was further agreed that Honduras would submit its claim that the arbitral award should be carried out, and that Nicaragua would answer the claim in the normal course. On 1 July 1958 Honduras accordingly instituted the proceedings by application based on the Washington Agreement of 1957. The pleadings in this case were heavy, but proceeded without complication, and judgment was given on 18 November

1960. The Court was virtually unanimous in finding that the King of Spain's award was valid and binding and that Nicaragua was under an obligation to give effect to it.[52]

The interesting feature of this case is the manner in which the procedures of an international political organization—the Organization of American States—were used first to bring acts of hostility to an end, and then to persuade the parties to submit their differences to the Court which, in the guise of determining the validity of an earlier arbitral award, was in fact empowered to render a definitive settlement of an important territorial dispute.

Both sides appointed a judge *ad hoc*, but neither of them was a national of the country appointing him. One of the judges *ad hoc* was not even the national of one of the States of Latin America.

THE AFFAIRS OF THE BARCELONA TRACTION, LIGHT AND POWER COMPANY

The above company was established in Toronto in 1911, but for the last twenty-five years most of its shares have been in Belgian hands. The Belgian Government alleged that it had been subjected to a variety of vexatious measures at the hands of the Spanish authorities, and was subsequently, in 1948, adjudicated bankrupt in Spain, and that in the measures of liquidation it was despoiled of its assets which were transferred to a Spanish group. On 23 September 1958 Belgium instituted proceedings against Spain, founding jurisdiction on the Treaty of Conciliation, Judicial Settlement and Arbitration between the two countries of 19 July 1927. In that application, Belgium asked for the restoration of the desspoiled assets or alternatively for compensation. In due course Spain raised a number of preliminary objections, but before Belgium replied to them the dispute was settled and Belgium filed notice of discontinuance.[53] Further negotiations were abortive, and in the summer of 1962 new proceedings were initiated, and are now pending.

THE MARITIME SAFETY COMMITTEE

The Constitution of the Intergovernmental Maritime Consultative Organization establishes as one of the main organs of the Organization the Maritime Safety Committee on which are to be represented, among others, the eight largest ship-owning nations. At the first meeting of the IMCO Assembly in 1959 the question of the meaning of that phrase arose—whether it meant the nations possessing the largest amount of registered tonnage or those beneficially owning the largest amount of tonnage. Beneath this formal dispute lay the vexed question of "flags of convenience", i.e. the registration of ships in a foreign country, usually for purposes of tax relief or for other reasons. If the first interpretation were adopted, Liberia and Panama, under whose flags over ten million and over four millions of tons of merchant shipping respectively are registered, would be entitled to be members of the Maritime Safety Committee. In the elections held in January, 1959, neither of those countries had been elected to the Committee, but at the same time the Assembly, recognizing that differences of opinion had arisen regarding the correct interpretation of the Constitution, decided to request an advisory opinion. In its opinion of 8 June 1960 the Court held that the Committee had not been properly constituted, and that as the proper criterion was registered tonnage, Liberia and Panama were entitled to be elected.[54]

The significance of this case is that it is the first instance in which the International Court has held to be unconstitutional action taken by an international organization. On the other hand, the advisory opinion makes no attempt to solve the legal problems arising from the existence of the flags of convenience: the Court's opinion was for the most part based on a textual analysis of the relevant clause of the IMCO Constitution.

THE TEMPLE OF PREAH VIHEAR

On 6 October 1959 Cambodia, invoking the compulsory jurisdiction, instituted proceedings against Thailand alleging violation on the part of Thailand of Cambodia's territorial sovereignty over the region of the Temple of Preah Vihear and its precincts. The Court first dismissed challenges to its jurisdiction by judgment of 26 May 1961 and then went on to dispose of the merits. In a judgment of 15 June 1962, the Court found that the Temple was situated in territory under the sovereignty of Cambodia, and made various consequential findings. This decision caused great disappointment to Thailand. However, on 3 July 1962 the Government of Thailand announced that despite its profound sorrow at the result of the case it considered that "as a member of the United Nations, Thailand is bound to honour its obligations under the United Nations Charter. It will do so under protest and with reservation of her intrinsic rights."[55]

THE NORTHERN CAMEROONS

As this case, too, is pending, it will be sufficient to say that on 30 May 1961 Cameroun filed an application instituting proceedings against the United Kingdom alleging that the United Kingdom had failed to respect certain obligations directly or indirectly flowing from the Trusteeship Agreement of 1946 for the Territory of the Cameroons under British Administration.

THE U.N. BUDGET

After the crisis in the Middle East at the end of 1956, the General Assembly established the United Nations Emergency Force (UNEF). The financing of UNEF presented what the Court called "perplexing problems". In the middle of 1960, the United Nations commenced its activities in the Congo, for which purpose it established another Force known as ONUC. The expenses of these two Forces became very heavy and the question of how to meet them gave rise to very serious difficulties, both for political and for legal reasons. In the summer of 1961, a Working Group appointed by the General Assembly reached the conclusion that, having regard to the differences of opinion which had been expressed about the legal nature of the financial obligations arising out of the peace-keeping operations, the General Assembly should request an advisory opinion from the Court, the precise formulation of the question being for the General Assembly to decide. In a Resolution of 21 December 1961, adopted by 52 votes to 11 with 32 abstentions, the General Assembly asked the Court whether certain expenditures authorised in a number of given Resolutions relating to ONUC and relating to UNEF constituted "expenses of the Organization" within the meaning of Article 17 (2) of the Charter. The power of the Court to give the Opinion in the terms requested was challenged both in the General Assembly and before the Court, although it will be noted that these challenges did not, as had been the case in the years 1948-50, question the power of the Court to interpret the Charter itself. In its Advisory Opinion of 20 July 1962 the Court dismissed all the challenges to its competence and, by nine votes to five, answered the question put to it in the affirmative. The Court found that it was required to answer a concrete question and, contrary to the practice adopted in all previous Advisory Opinions on the interpretation of the Charter, proceeded to deal with almost all the major legal contentions which had been advanced in the previous discussions. This case provided the first occasion since the establishment of the Permanent Court of International Justice for participation by a representative of the Soviet Union in the oral proceedings. The matter will now come before the 17th Session of the General Assembly.[56]

EVALUATION

During the first fifteen years of the existence of the present Court, from 1946 to the end of 1961, 48 cases were referred to the Court. Twelve of these were requests for advisory opinions, and the remaining 36 were contentious cases (eight of them cases in which the Court would only have jurisdiction if the defendant accepted the invitation to litigate, contained in the application instituting proceedings). These figures, especially when compared with those of the Permanent Court (see Appendix 4), have led many observers to the view that the contribution which the present Court has been enabled to make to the maintenance of international peace has been less than was the case for the Permanent Court. However, in the long run, the bare figures may be misleading as the point of departure for an evaluation of the role of the Court in the contemporary international scene.

The figures themselves are not without interest. On the one hand they show virtual consistency in the number of *contentious* cases sought to be referred by States to the decision of each Court. On the other hand, the real and substantial decline is in the number of matters referred collectively to the present Court for *advisory* opinion. It might fairly be concluded from this that, contrary to a widespread impression, there is no real falling-off in the readiness of States to refer appropriate bilateral disputes to the decision of the Court. Against this, it is quite clear that in the modern political organs, above all the General Assembly and the Security Council, the political difficulties in securing a majority to support properly drafted legal questions for advisory opinion as an incident in the settlement of political disputes or situations referred to them, are virtually insuperable in the absence of agreement of the parties to the dispute in question. Bearing in mind that the effectiveness of the judicial method of settling international disputes depends exclusively on the agreement of the parties to invoke judicial procedures, it is not a cause for dismay that, in the absence of such agreement, the General Assembly and the Security Council have shown themselves averse to employing even the indirect system of access to the Court provided by the advisory competence. In the League's practice there was found a tendency, which was not beyond criticism, for the political and judicial processes to coalesce through the advisory procedure. But United Nations practices (especially the manner in which debates are conducted and decisions reached) demonstrate the opposite tendency—to differentiate between the two types of pacific solution for international disputes. Today States which refer disputes or situations to the political organs do so because they want a political and not a judicial settlement, and the way these organs work affords them plenty of opportunities to concentrate their diplomatic endeavours in an exclusively political direction. That differentiation, the lines for which are more firmly drawn in the Charter than they were in the Covenant, has been further accentuated by the repeated emphasis placed by these organs on the primacy and exclusiveness of their political character. This is not a matter for value-judgment here: it is simply stated as a fact.

The reasons for this state of affairs are undoubtedly many and complex, but the impression is inescapable that their origin lies in the relentless quest after security which is the major preoccupation of all responsible statesmen and of all peoples, and the lack of general spiritual calmness engendered by it. The lawyer may regret that more use is not made of legal and judicial techniques in contemporary international affairs (although the unwary may fall into the trap of too readily assuming that too little use is made of those techniques). But he should not permit himself to be blinded into the mistaken belief that legal and judicial techniques by themselves are inherently superior or more effective in keeping international situations of tension under control than others which modern political and diplomatic experience has evolved. An assertion of that kind, unsupported by the evidence of history, runs the risk of assuming that which has to be proved. In the lawyer's language, it would be a *petitio principii*, begging the question.

To turn from the figures to the substance, there are some striking differences between the kind of dispute which the present Court has had to settle and the kind of dispute which came the way of its predecessor. As we have seen earlier, the Permanent Court had a great deal to do with marginal disputes that were closely connected with the major sources of international tension prevalent in the inter-War period. It had little to do with the central issues of other important conflicts. It is significant that the present Court, after a hesitant start which was not particularly successful, has not been asked by interested States to deal with disputes relating even marginally to the major international tension which has emerged since the end of the Second World War. The Court is not now being invoked to deal with Cold War problems, and when attempts have been made to invoke it, these have for the most part been completely inconclusive. This fact, on the one hand, has naturally reduced the amount of business brought before the Court. On the other hand, this is not necessarily disadvantageous, for it has freed the Court from what might be misdirected efforts to find legal solutions for problems which are not in reality legal problems at all.

On the other hand (and leaving aside what might be termed routine legal disputes between States, of which the Court has possibly had more than its predecessor), the present Court has been asked to decide the central issues of several major international disputes which were not directly connected with the Cold War. Some of these, being in reality conflicts of interest and of national aspirations, even contained a sufficient number of elements to give rise to concern that they might constitute a threat to international peace, if not on a universal scale then at least on a regional scale. In situations of great tension and conflict, diplomacy has two ways of proceeding. It can by deliberate choice leave the dispute unsettled, while trying not to let it get out of hand. Alternatively, it can try to reach a definitive settlement. The timing and the method of the change from one approach to the other is usually a matter of the greatest delicacy, and depends upon considerations of domestic politics no less than on international factors. The International Court has shown that when States are agreed that the time has come for a final settlement of a given dispute, it is perfectly capable of assisting them, if they so desire, to reach their objective. This is the lesson of major conflicts settled by the Court, such as the *Fisheries* and *Honduras-Nicaragua Frontier* cases. On the other hand, if there is no underlying political agreement, as in the *Anglo-Iranian* and *Right of Passage* cases, the Court has shown that its procedures can be invoked not so much to reach a definitive settlement as to deflect into peaceful channels a phase of a complex diplomatic situation, and prevent that from getting out of hand and endangering world peace. Two contentious cases, *Anglo-Iranian* and the *Honduras-Nicaragua Frontier* cases, came before the Court either in close connection with fear that force would be used (the first of them) or after hostilities had actually broken out (the second of them). The *Right of Passage* sometimes conveys the impression that Portugal had recourse to the Court as a deliberate alternative to the Security Council, presumably out of a belief that its diplomacy would be the more likely to achieve its aims in a (for it) deteriorating situation at The Hague than at New York.

The Permanent Court never had contentious cases of this character referred to it.

Another striking thing about the work of the present Court is its variety.

The substantive work of the Court is far from being confined to mere questions of treaty interpretation, which many people consider to have been the most prominent feature of the work of the Permanent Court. A great number of completely novel problems have come before it, covering vast areas of international legal and social relations previously untouched by the international judge.

Geographically, too, the substance of the Court's work is covering a wider area than its predecessor. All the cases before the Permanent Court (except one) were litigated exclusively between European States although some of them related to interests outside Europe. It is true that the majority of cases before the present Court relate to European affairs, but there have been a significant number of cases in which one of the parties has not been a European power. A complete innovation is the fact that two cases have concerned exclusively Latin-American powers, and one case concerns exclusively South-East Asian powers. Since 1960 a further development is noticeable in that African powers have started seeing in the Court an instrument which their diplomacy can employ in their disputes with European powers. This applies not only to the cases concerning South-West Africa and the Northern Cameroons, but also to the case on the constitution of the Maritime Safety Committee of IMCO, in which the main protagonists were Liberia and the United Kingdom. The Court is now truly universal.

On the negative side of the Court's work to date, noticeable is the fact that, albeit on technical grounds of lack of jurisdiction or inadmissibility, the Court has not found it possible to decide on the substance of any dispute relating to events occurring during the Second World War, whether or not that dispute ended up also by being a Cold War dispute (the *Monetary Gold from Rome*, *Nottebohm* and *Interhandel* cases). But this negative conclusion too requires further examination, for it is possibly not accidental. As a matter of fact, Article 107 of the Charter of the United Nations (of which the Statute of the Court is an integral part) can be interpreted as excluding from the normal competence of the United Nations and its different organs actions taken during the Second World War against enemy States. Although the Court has never directly referred to this Article, its action in declining to decide the merits of this type of case cannot necessarily be regarded as being contrary to the spirit of the Charter.

It is usual today to say that the expectations generated by the decision of the San Francisco Conference to make the Court a principal organ of the United Nations, and which led to the assumption that the new Court would be able to play a major role in the pacific settlement of international disputes, have not been fully realized. The reason for this state of affairs are many and complex, and are only partly due to the general attitude of reserve towards the Court manifested by some of the major contemporary world Powers. There is prevalent in the world today a widespread questioning of the contemporary international law. This feeling is based on the view that for the greater part international law is the product of European imperialism and colonialism and does not take sufficient account of the completely changed pattern of international relations which now exists. This feeling has been very marked in the prolonged discussions in the United Nations over questions of the codification of different aspects of international law. Its existence is not conducive to recourse to the Court. Whereas before the Second World War it was on the whole the small Powers who were inclined to look to international law and its organs as a means to protect themselves against the rapacity of the Great Powers, paradoxically enough the situation today is changing rapidly, and it is the Great Powers who are inclined to take refuge behind a formal position based on traditional international law when faced with claims by small and new States who object to the traditional position. This is particularly evident in the sphere of international economic relations.

What is perhaps not sufficiently known is that in this type of case the International Court has shown itself sympathetic towards the psychological attitudes of the new and of the small States. Careful scrutiny of the record of the Court may lead to the conclusion that it has displayed quite a remarkable sense of appreciation of the changing currents of internationalist thought. In this respect it has performed a major service to the international community as a whole, because the need to bring international law into line with present-day requirements and conditions is real and urgent. Here we recall our basic assumption that in most instances of international litigation the legal cases of the two parties are evenly balanced and that the decision is reached by a process of choice which enables the majority of the Court to reach a result which it considers just and tenable in the circumstances. Many observers feel that several of the great cases decided since 1946 which raised this type of issue would have been decided differently had they been brought before the Permanent Court. The International Court does not support the charge of rigid conservatism said to be characteristic of lawyers. If anything, it is the International Court, more than any other organ of the United Nations, which has infused new dynamism into the international law of today. As we have seen, but for the decisions of the Court it is extremely doubtful if the Conferences on the Law of the Sea would have succeeded in reaching agreement on a vast number of problems satisfactory to the extremely diversified international community of today. Other branches of law on which the Court has already pronounced itself are awaiting treatment by the codification organs of the United Nations.

Above all, in considering the work of the Court and the role which it has been called upon to play, it has to be remembered that, unlike the situation after the First World War, when, after a few years, the illusion of general pacification and relaxation of tension became commonplace, the period since the Second World War has been marked by unceasing international tension and unrelieved anxiety on the part of all statesmen and on the part of the public at large over what the future might bring. The international situation has lacked any element of relaxation and tranquility. The development of this situation has been marked by continuous weakening of the authority of all the international institutions established to deal with the intercourse of States in time of peace. This general atmosphere is not propitious for any extended use of international judicial techniques. In the light of the general international situation, the wonder perhaps is not so much what the Court has been able to do, as that in fact States continue to show willingness to refer a number of major disputes to its decision, and great interest in all that pertains to the Court. This is the encouraging feature of the experience of the International Court, for it shows that even if its jurisdiction is not compulsory, its permanency as an international organ enables it to play its own constructive role in the pacific settlement of international disputes despite the constantly disintegrating international situation.

NOTES

1. For the proceedings in the Security Council, see the *Official Records* of its 95th, 107th, 109th, 111th, 114th, 120th - 122nd and 125th meetings, between 20 January and 3 April 1947. For the three judgments of the Court, see Rep. 1948, 15; 1949, 4, and 244; and for the orders regarding the appointment of the committees of experts, Rep. 1948, 124, and 1949, 237.

2. For the decisions of the General Assembly, see Resolutions 113 B (II) of 17 November 1947 and 197 (III) of 8 December 1948. For the opinion of the Court, see Rep. 1948, 57. In these proceedings, written statements were submitted by China, El Salvador, Guatemala, Honduras, India, Canada, the United States of America, Greece, Yugoslavia, Belgium, Iraq, the Ukrainian S.S.R., U.S.S.R., and Australia. Oral statements were made on behalf of the Secretary-General of the United Nations, and France, Yugoslavia, Belgium, Czechoslovakia and Poland.

3. See General Assembly Resolution 296 J (IV) of 22 November 1949. For the opinion of the Court, see Rep. 1950, 4. In these proceedings, written statements were submitted by the Secretary-General and by the Byelorussian S.S.R., Czechoslovakia, Egypt, the Ukrainian S.S.R., U.S.S.R., the United States, Argentina and Venezuela. An oral statement was made by France.

4. Resolution 258 (III) of 3 December 1948, adopted unanimously by fifty-three votes with no abstention. For the opinion of the Court, see Rep. 1949, 174. In these proceedings, written statements were submitted by India, China, the United States, the United Kingdom, France. Oral statements were made on

behalf of the Secretary-General, and Belgium, France and the United Kingdom. For the action subsequently taken by the General Assembly, see Resolution 365 (IV) of 1 December 1949.

5. Rep. 1951, 116.

6. See the Geneva Convention of 1958 on the Territorial Sea and Contiguous Zone. Both these issues were discussed in the Conference's First Committee. See *Official Records*, vol. III, *passim*. It may be noted that this Conference also dealt with another aspect of the law of the sea, emerging from the decision of the Permanent Court of International Justice in the *Lotus* case. There it had been held that a State could exercise criminal jurisdiction over a foreign ship on the high seas, if as a result of a collision on the high seas its nationals were injured. That decision was badly received in maritime circles, but the general rule of international law which the Court found to be applicable could only be changed by an international convention. The 1958 Convention on the High Seas (Article 11) now limits the jurisdiction, in such circumstances, to the flag State or the State of which the ship's officer concerned was a national.

7. Rep. 1950, 59.   8. Rep. 1950, 266.

9. Rep. 1950, 395.   10. Rep. 1951, 71.

11. See General Assembly Resolution 294 (IV) of 22 October 1949. For the opinions of the Court, see Rep. 1950, 65, 221. In the first stage of these proceedings, written statements were submitted by the United States, the United Kingdom, Bulgaria, the Ukrainian S.S.R., U.S.S.R., the Byelorussian S.S.R., Rumania, Czechoslovakia, Hungary and Australia. Oral statements were made on behalf of the Secretary-General, the United States and the United Kingdom. In the second phase, a further written statement was submitted by the United States, and oral statements were made on behalf of the Secretary-General, the United States and the United Kingdom.

12. Resolution 385 (V) of 3 November 1950.

13. See Resolutions 65 (I) of 14 December 1946, 141 (II) of 1 November 1947, 227 (III) of 26 November 1948, and 337 (IV) of 6 December 1949.

14. See General Assembly Resolution 338 (IV) of 6 December 1949. The Resolution was adopted by forty votes to seven, with four abstentions. For the Court's opinion, see Rep. 1950, 128. Written statements were submitted by Egypt, South Africa, the United States, Poland, and India. Oral statements were made on behalf of the Secretary-General, the Philippines and South Africa.

15. Resolutions 449 (V) of 13 December 1950, 570 (VI) of 19 January 1952, 651 (VII) of 20 December 1952, 749 (VIII) of 28 November 1953, 851 (IX) and 852 (IX) of 23 November 1954.

16. See Resolutions 844 (IX) of 11 October 1954 and 904 (IX) of 23 November 1954. That Resolution was adopted by twenty-five votes to eleven, with twenty-one abstentions. For the Court's opinion, see Rep. 1955, 67. Written statements were submitted by the United States, Poland, India, Israel, China, Yugoslavia and the Secretary-General. No State requested to make an oral statement.

17. Resolutions 934 (X), 940 (X) and 941 (X), of 3 December 1955.

18. See Resolution 942 (X) of 3 December 1955, adopted by thirty-two votes to five, with nineteen abstentions. For the Court's opinion, see Rep. 1956, 23. In addition to the Secretary-General's statement, written statements were submitted by the United States, China and India, and an oral statement was made on behalf of the United Kingdom.

19. See Resolutions 1047 (XI) of 23 January 1957, 1054 (XI), 1055 (XI), 1059 (XI), and 1061 (XI) of 26 February 1957, 1141 (XII) and 1143 (XII) of

25 October 1957, 1246 (XIII) of 30 October 1958, 1359 (XIV) and 1360 (XIV) of 17 November 1959, 1568 (XV) of 18 December 1960.

20. Resolution 1361 (XIV) of 17 November 1959.

21. Although initiated as two separate cases, the Court, after the Memorials has been filed, decided that as they were substantially identical they should be consolidated into a single case. Rep. 1961, 13. Late in 1961 South Africa filed a number of preliminary objections, on which the Court's decision is now expected.

22. See Resolutions 1565 (XV) and 1568 (XV) of 18 December 1960, and 1596 (XV) of 7 April 1961.

23. Rep. 1951, 109, 1952, 176. Questions relating to the Act of Algeciras were also raised before the Permanent Court in the *Phosphates in Morocco* case (1938).

24. See Resolution 478 (V) of 16 November 1950, adopted by a majority of forty-seven votes to five with five abstentions. For the Court's opinion, see Rep. 1951, 15. Written statements were submitted by the United Nations, the Organization of American States and the International Labour Organization, and by the United States, U.S.S.R., Jordan, United Kingdom, Israel, Poland, Czechoslovakia, the Netherlands, the Ukrainian S.S.R., Bulgaria, the Byelorussian S.S.R., and the Philippines. Oral statements were made on behalf of the Secretary-General, Israel, United Kingdom and France. In its opinion the Court dismissed challenges to its jurisdiction, which were similar to those put forward in the *Peace Treaties* case.

25. See Resolution 598 (VI) of 12 January 1952 as amended by Resolution 1452 B (XIV) of 7 December 1959.

26. Rep. 1952, 28.   27. Rep. 1953, 10.

28. Award of 6 March 1956, *International Law Reports*, 1956, 306.

29. C.R. Attlee, *As it Happened* (New York, 1954), 246. See also I.S. Macadam and H. Latimer, *The Annual Register, 1951* (London, 1952), 50.

30. Rep. 1951, 89.   31. Rep. 1952, 93.

32. International Court of Justice, Yearbook, 1952-3, 45. In the new agreement of September 1954, by which the dispute was finally settled, a similar power was conferred on the President of the present Court. For text, see J. C. Hurewitz, *Diplomacy in the Near and Middle East*, II (New York, 1956), 348.

33. Rep. 1953, 47.   34. Rep. 1953, 111, 1955, 4.

35. Rep. 1954, 19. For the arbitral award, see *International Law Reports*, 1953, 441.

36. Rep. 1954, 107, 1960, 186.

37. For the cases in the U.N. Administrative Tribunal, see *International Law Reports*, 1953, 493 ff. For the cases in the I.L.O. Administrative Tribunal, see *ibid.*, 1955, 768, etc.

38. Resolution 785 A (VIII) of 6 December 1953, adopted by forty-one to six, with thirteen abstentions. For the Court's opinion, see Rep. 1954, 47. Written statements were presented by the United Nations, the I.L.O., France, Sweden, the Netherlands, Greece, the United Kingdom, the United States, the Philippines, Mexico, Chile, Iraq, China, Guatemala, Turkey, Ecuador, Canada, U.S.S.R., Czechoslovakia and Egypt. Oral statements were made on behalf of the United Nations, France, the United States, Greece, the United Kingdom and the Netherlands.

39. Resolution of the Executive Board of UNESCO of 25 November 1955, adopted by twelve votes to five, with four abstentions. For the Court's opinion, see Rep. 1956, 77. Written statements were submitted by UNESCO, the United

States, France, the United Kingdom, and China. No oral proceedings were held.

40. Rep. 1954, 99, 103.   41. See Rep. 1956, 6, 9, 1958, 158 and 1959, 276.

42. Rep. 1956, 12, 15.   43. Rep. 1957, 9.

44. Rep. 1958, 55.   45. Rep. 1957, 105.   46. Rep. 1959, 6.

47. Rep. 1959, 127. In the course of the proceedings, Bulgaria withdrew the other objection to the jurisdiction, and agreed to defer consideration of two of the three objections to the admissibility until the proceedings on the merits.

48. Rep. 1959, 264.   49. Rep. 1960, 146.   50. Rep. 1959, 206.

51. Award of 23 December 1906. For text, see British and Foreign State Papers, 100 (1906-7), 1096.

52. Rep. 1960, 192.   53. Rep. 1961, 9.

54. See Resolution A.12 (I) adopted by the Assembly of IMCO on 19 January 1959. For the Court's opinion, see Rep. 1960, 150. Written statements were presented by Belgium, France, Liberia, the United States, China, Panama, Switzerland, Italy, Denmark, the United Kingdom, Norway, the Netherlands, and India. Oral statements were made on behalf of Liberia, the United States, Panama, Italy, the Netherlands, Norway, and the United Kingdom. The Resolution of the IMCO Assembly was adopted unanimously, with one abstention. In April, 1961, the IMCO Assembly dissolved the Maritime Safety Committee and reconstituted it to conform to the terms of the advisory opinion.

55. For the Court's judgment see Rep. 1961, 17 and 1962, 6. For the statements of the Thailand government see *Foreign Affairs Bulletin* issued by the Thailand Ministry for Foreign Affairs, vol. 1 No. 6, June-July 1962, 129.

56. General Assembly Resolution 1731 (XVI) of 20 December 1961, adopted by 52 votes to 11 with 32 abstentions. For the advisory opinion, see Rep. 1962, 151. Written statements were submitted by Australia, Bulgaria, Byelorussia, Canada, Czechoslovakia, Denmark, France, Ireland, Italy, Japan, Mexico, Netherlands, Philippines, Poland, Portugal, Romania, South Africa, Spain, Ukraine, USSR., United Kingdom, United States and Upper Volta, and the Secretary-General submitted a comprehensive introductory note to the documentation. In the oral proceedings statements were made by Australia, Canada, Ireland, Italy, Netherlands, Norway, USSR., United Kingdom and United States.

CHARTER OF THE UNITED NATIONS

WE THE PEOPLES OF THE UNITED NATIONS

DETERMINED

> to save succeeding generations from the scourge of war, which twice in our lifetime has brought untold sorrow to mankind, and
> to reaffirm faith in fundamental human rights, in the dignity and worth of the human person, in the equal rights of men and women and of nations large and small, and
> to establish conditions under which justice and respect for the obligations arising from treaties and other sources of international law can be maintained, and
> to promote social progress and better standards of life in larger freedom,

AND FOR THESE ENDS

> to practice tolerance and live together in peace with one another as good neighbors, and
> to unite our strength to maintain international peace and security, and
> to ensure, by the acceptance of principles and the institution of methods, that armed force shall not be used, save in the common interest, and
> to employ international machinery for the promotion of the economic and social advancement of all peoples,

HAVE RESOLVED TO COMBINE OUR EFFORTS

TO ACCOMPLISH THESE AIMS.

Accordingly, our respective Governments, through representatives assembled in the city of San Francisco, who have exhibited their full powers found to be in good and due form, have agreed to the present Charter of the United Nations and do hereby establish an international organization to be known as the United Nations.

CHAPTER I

Purposes and Principles

Article 1

The Purposes of the United Nations are:

1. To maintain international peace and security, and to that end: to take effective collective measures for the prevention and removal of threats to the peace, and for the suppression of acts of aggression or other breaches of the peace, and to bring about by peaceful means, and in conformity with the principles of justice and international law, adjustment or settlement of international disputes or situations which might lead to a breach of the peace;

2. To develop friendly relations among nations based on respect for the principle of equal rights and self-determination of peoples, and to take other appropriate measures to strengthen universal peace;

3. To achieve international cooperation in solving international problems of an economic, social, cultural, or humanitarian character, and in promoting and encouraging respect for human rights and for fundamental freedoms for all without distinction as to race, sex, language, or religion; and

4. To be a center for harmonizing the actions of nations in the attainment of these common ends.

Article 2

The Organization and its Members, in pursuit of the Purposes stated in Article 1, shall act in accordance with the following Principles.

1. The Organization is based on the principle of the sovereign equality of all its Members.

2. All Members, in order to ensure to all of them the rights and benefits resulting from membership, shall fulfil in good faith the obligations assumed by them in accordance with the present Charter.

3. All Members shall settle their international disputes by peaceful means in such a manner that international peace and security, and justice, are not endangered.

4. All Members shall refrain in their international relations from the threat or use of force against the territorial integrity or political independence of any state, or in any other manner inconsistent with the Purposes of the United Nations.

5. All Members shall give the United Nations every assistance in any action it takes in accordance with the present Charter, and shall refrain from giving assistance to any state against which the United Nations is taking preventive or enforcement action.

6. The Organization shall ensure that states which are not Members of the United Nations act in accordance with these Principles so far as may be necessary for the maintenance of international peace and security.

7. Nothing contained in the present Charter shall authorize the United Nations to intervene in matters which are essentially within the domestic jurisdiction of any state or shall require the Members to submit such matters to settlement under the present Charter; but this principle shall not prejudice the application of enforcement measures under Chapter VII.

CHAPTER II

Membership

Article 3

The original Members of the United Nations shall be the states which, having participated in the United Nations Conference on International Organization at San Francisco, or having previously signed the Declaration by United Nations of January 1, 1942, sign the present Charter and ratify it in accordance with Article 110.

Article 4

1. Membership in the United Nations is open to all other peace-loving states which accept the obligations contained in the present Charter and, in the judgment of the Organization, are able and willing to carry out these obligations.

2. The admission of any such state to membership in the United Nations will be effected by a decision of the General Assembly upon the recommendation of the Security Council.

Article 5

A Member of the United Nations against which preventive or enforcement action has been taken by the Security Council may be suspended from the exercise of the rights and privileges of membership by the General Assembly upon the recommendation of the Security Council. The exercise of these rights and privileges may be restored by the Security Council.

Article 6

A Member of the United Nations which has persistently violated the Principles contained in the present Charter may be expelled from the Organization by the General Assembly upon the recommendation of the Security Council.

CHAPTER III

Organs

Article 7

1. There are established as the principal organs of the United Nations: a General Assembly, a Security Council, an Economic and Social Council, a Trusteeship Council, an International Court of Justice, and a Secretariat.

2. Such subsidiary organs as may be found necessary may be established in accordance with the present Charter.

Article 8

The United Nations shall place no restrictions on the eligibility of men and women to participate in any capacity and under conditions of equality in its principal and subsidiary organs.

CHAPTER IV

The General Assembly

Composition

Article 9

1. The General Assembly shall consist of all the Members of the United Nations.

2. Each Member shall have not more than five representatives in the General Assembly.

Functions and Powers

Article 10

The General Assembly may discuss any questions or any matters within the scope of the present Charter or relating to the powers and functions of any organs provided for in the present Charter, and, except as provided in Article 12, may make recommendations to the Members of the United Nations or to the Security Council or to both on any such questions or matters.

Article 11

1. The General Assembly may consider the general principles of cooperation in the maintenance of international peace and security, including the principles governing disarmament and the regulation of armaments, and may make recommendations with regard to such principles to the Members or to the Security Council or to both.

2. The General Assembly may discuss any questions relating to the maintenance of international peace and security brought before it by any Member of the United Nations, or by the Security Council, or by a state which is not a Member of the United Nations in accordance with Article 35, paragraph 2,

and, except as provided in Article 12, may make recommendations with regard to any such questions to the state or states concerned or to the Security Council or to both. Any such question on which action is necessary shall be referred to the Security Council by the General Assembly either before or after discussion.

3. The General Assembly may call the attention of the Security Council to situations which are likely to endanger international peace and security.

4. The powers of the General Assembly set forth in this Article shall not limit the general scope of Article 10.

Article 12

1. While the Security Council is exercising in respect of any dispute or situation the functions assigned to it in the present Charter, the General Assembly shall not make any recommendation with regard to that dispute or situation unless the Security Council so requests.

2. The Secretary-General, with the consent of the Security Council, shall notify the General Assembly at each session of any matters relative to the maintenance of international peace and security which are being dealt with by the Security Council and shall similarly notify the General Assembly, or the Members of the United Nations if the General Assembly is not in session, immediately the Security Council ceases to deal with such matters.

Article 13

1. The General Assembly shall initiate studies and make recommendations for the purpose of:
   a. promoting international cooperation in the political field and encouraging the progressive development of international law and its codification;
   b. promoting international cooperation in the economic, social, cultural, educational, and health fields, and assisting in the realization of human rights and fundamental freedoms for all without distinction as to race, sex, language, or religion.

2. The further responsibilities, functions, and powers of the General Assembly with respect to matters mentioned in paragraph 1 (*b*) above are set forth in Chapters IX and X.

Article 14

Subject to the provisions of Article 12, the General Assembly may recommend measures for the peaceful adjustment of any situation, regardless of origin, which it deems likely to impair the general welfare or friendly relations among nations, including situations resulting from a violation of the provisions of the present Charter setting forth the Purposes and Principles of the United Nations.

Article 15

1. The General Assembly shall receive and consider annual and special reports from the Security Council; these reports shall include an account of the measures that the Security Council has decided upon or taken to maintain international peace and security.

2. The General Assembly shall receive and consider reports from the other organs of the United Nations.

Article 16

The General Assembly shall perform such functions with respect to the international trusteeship system as are assigned to it under Chapters XII and XIII, including the approval of the trusteeship agreements for areas not designated as strategic.

Article 17

1. The General Assembly shall consider and approve the budget of the Organization.

2. The expenses of the Organization shall be borne by the Members as apportioned by the General Assembly.

3. The General Assembly shall consider and approve any financial and budgetary arrangements with specialized agencies referred to in Article 57 and shall examine the administrative budgets of such specialized agencies with a view to making recommendations to the agencies concerned.

Voting

Article 18

1. Each member of the General Assembly shall have one vote.

2. Decisions of the General Assembly on important questions shall be made by a two-thirds majority of the members present and voting. These questions shall include: recommendations with respect to the maintenance of international peace and security, the election of the non-permanent members of the Security Council, the election of the members of the Economic and Social Council, the election of members of the Trusteeship Council in accordance with paragraph 1 (*c*) of Article 86, the admission of new Members to the United Nations, the suspension of the rights and privileges of membership, the expulsion of Members, questions relating to the operation of the trusteeship system, and budgetary questions.

3. Decisions on other questions, including the determination of additional categories of questions to be decided by a two-thirds majority, shall be made by a majority of the members present and voting.

Article 19

A Member of the United Nations which is in arrears in the payment of its financial contributions to the Organization shall have no vote in the General Assembly if the amount of its arrears equals or exceeds the amount of the contributions due from it for the preceding two full years. The General Assembly may, nevertheless, permit such a Member to vote if it satisfied that the failure to pay is due to conditions beyond the control of the Member.

Procedure

Article 20

The General Assembly shall meet in regular annual sessions and in such special sessions as occasion may require. Special sessions shall be convoked by the Secretary-General at the request of the Security Council or of a majority of the Members of the United Nations.

Article 21

The General Assembly shall adopt its own rules of procedure. It shall elect its President for each session.

Article 22

The General Assembly may establish such subsidiary organs as it deems necessary for the performance of its functions.

CHAPTER V

The Security Council

Composition

Article 23

1. The Security Council shall consist of eleven Members of the United Nations. The Republic of China, France, the Union of Soviet Socialist Republics, the United Kingdom of Great Britain and Northern Ireland, and the United States of America shall be permanent members of the Security Council. The General Assembly shall elect six other Members of the United Nations to be non-permanent members of the Security Council, due regard being specially paid, in the first instance to the contribution of Members of the United Nations to the maintenance of international peace and security and to the other purposes of the Organization, and also to equitable geographical distribution.

2. The non-permanent members of the Security Council shall be elected for a term of two years. In the first election of the non-permanent members, however, three shall be chosen for a term of one year. A retiring member shall not be eligible for immediate re-election.

3. Each member of the Security Council shall have one representative.

Functions and Powers

Article 24

1. In order to ensure prompt and effective action by the United Nations, its Members confer on the Security Council primary responsibility for the maintenance of international peace and security, and agree that in carrying out its duties under this responsibility the Security Council acts on their behalf.

2. In discharging these duties the Security Council shall act in accordance with the Purposes and Principles of the United Nations. The specific powers granted to the Security Council for the discharge of these duties are laid down in Chapters VI, VII, VIII and XII.

3. The Security Council shall submit annual and, when necessary, special reports to the General Assembly for its consideration.

Article 25

The Members of the United Nations agree to accept and carry out the decisions of the Security Council in accordance with the present Charter.

Article 26

In order to promote the establishment and maintenance of international peace and security with the least diversion for armaments of the world's human and economic resources, the Security Council shall be responsible for formulating, with the assistance of the Military Staff Committee referred to in Article 47, plans to be submitted to the Members of the United Nations for the establishment of a system for the regulation of armaments.

Voting

Article 27

1. Each member of the Security Council shall have one vote.

2. Decisions of the Security Council on procedural matters shall be made by an affirmative vote of seven members.

3. Decisions of the Security Council on all other matters shall be made by an affirmative vote of seven members, including the concurring votes of the per-

manent members; provided that, in decisions under Chapter VI, and under paragraph 3 of Article 52, a party to a dispute shall abstain from voting.

Procedure

Article 28

1. The Security Council shall be so organized as to be able to function continuously. Each member of the Security Council shall for this purpose be represented at all times at the seat of the Organization.

2. The Security Council shall hold periodic meetings at which each of its members may, if it so desires, be represented by a member of the government or by some other specially designated representative.

3. The Security Council may hold meetings at such places other than the seat of the Organization as in its judgment will best facilitate its work.

Article 29

The Security Council may establish such subsidiary organs as it deems necessary for the performance of its functions.

Article 30

The Security Council shall adopt its own rules of procedure, including the method of selecting its President.

Article 31

Any Member of the United Nations which is not a member of the Security Council may participate, without vote, in the discussion of any question brought before the Security Council whenever the latter considers that the interests of that Member are specially affected.

Article 32

Any Member of the United Nations which is not a member of the Security Council or any state which is not a Member of the United Nations, if it is a party to a dispute under consideration by the Security Council, shall be invited to participate, without vote, in the discussion relating to the dispute. The Security Council shall lay down such conditions as it deems just for the participation of a state which is not a Member of the United Nations.

CHAPTER VI

Pacific Settlement of Disputes

Article 33

1. The parties to any dispute, the continuance of which is likely to endanger the maintenance of international peace and security, shall, first of all, seek a solution by negotiation, enquiry, mediation, conciliation, arbitration, judicial settlement, resort to regional agencies or arrangements, or other peaceful means of their own choice.

2. The Security Council shall, when it deems necessary, call upon the parties to settle their dispute by such means.

Article 34

The Security Council may investigate any dispute, or any situation which might lead to international friction or give rise to a dispute, in order to determine whether the continuance of the dispute or situation is likely to endanger the maintenance of international peace and security.

Article 35

1. Any Member of the United Nations may bring any dispute, or any situation of the nature referred to in Article 34, to the attention of the Security Council or of the General Assembly.

2. A state which is not a Member of the United Nations may bring to the attention of the Security Council or of the General Assembly any dispute to which it is a party if it accepts in advance, for the purposes of the dispute, the obligations of pacific settlement provided in the present Charter.

3. The proceedings of the General Assembly in respect of matters brought to its attention under this Article will be subject to the provisions of Articles 11 and 12.

Article 36

1. The Security Council may, at any stage of a dispute of the nature referred to in Article 33 or of a situation of like nature, recommend appropriate procedures or methods of adjustment.

2. The Security Council should take into consideration any procedures for the settlement of the dispute which have already been adopted by the parties.

3. In making recommendations under this Article, the Security Council should also take into consideration that legal disputes should as a general rule be referred by the parties to the International Court of Justice, in accordance with the provisions of the Statute of the Court.

Article 37

1. Should the parties to a dispute of the nature referred to in Article 33 fail to settle it by the means indicated in that Article, they shall refer it to the Security Council.

2. If the Security Council deems that the continuance of the dispute is in fact likely to endanger the maintenance of international peace and security, it shall decide whether to take action under Article 36 or to recommend such terms of settlement as it may consider appropriate.

Article 38

Without prejudice to the provisions of Articles 33 to 37, the Security Council may, if all the parties to any dispute so request, make recommendations to the parties with a view to a pacific settlement of the dispute.

CHAPTER VII

Action with Respect to Threats to the Peace, Breaches of the Peace, and Acts of Aggression

Article 39

The Security Council shall determine the existence of any threat to the peace, breach of the peace, or act of aggression, and shall make recommendations, or decide what measures shall be taken in accordance with Articles 41 and 42, to maintain or restore international peace and security.

Article 40

In order to prevent an aggravation of the situation, the Security Council may, before making the recommendations or deciding upon the measures provided for in Article 39, call upon the parties concerned to comply with such provisional measures as it deems necessary or desirable. Such provisional measures shall be without prejudice to the rights, claims, or position of the parties concerned. The Security Council shall duly take account of failure to comply with such provisional measures.

Article 41

The Security Council may decide what measures not involving the use of armed force are to be employed to give effect to its decisions, and it may call upon the Members of the United Nations to apply such measures. These may include complete or partial interruption of economic relations and of rail, sea, air, postal, telegraphic, radio, and other means of communication, and the severance of diplomatic relations.

Article 42

Should the Security Council consider that measures provided for in Article 41 would be inadequate or have proved to be inadequate, it may take such action by air, sea, or land forces as may be necessary to maintain or restore international peace and security. Such action may include demonstrations, blockade, and other operations by air, sea, or land forces of Members of the United Nations.

Article 43

1. All Members of the United Nations, in order to contribute to the maintenance of international peace and security, undertake to make available to the Security Council, on its call and in accordance with a special agreement or agreements, armed forces, assistance, and facilities, including rights of passage, necessary for the purpose of maintaining international peace and security.

2. Such agreement or agreements shall govern the numbers and types of forces, their degree of readiness and general location, and the nature of the facilities and assistance to be provided.

3. The agreement or agreements shall be negotiated as soon as possible on the initiative of the Security Council. They shall be concluded between the Security Council and Members or between the Security Council and groups of Members, and shall be subject to ratification by the signatory states in accordance with their respective constitutional processes.

Article 44

When the Security Council has decided to use force it shall, before calling upon a Member not represented on it to provide armed forces in fulfilment of the obligations assumed under Article 43, invite that Member, if the Member so desires, to participate in the decisions of the Security Council concerning the employment of contingents of that Member's armed forces.

Article 45

In order to enable the United Nations to take urgent military measures, Members shall hold immediately available national air-force contingents for combined international enforcement action. The strength and degree of readiness of these contingents and plans for their combined action shall be determined, within the limits laid down in the special agreement or agreements referred to in Article 43, by the Security Council with the assistance of the Military Staff Committee.

Article 46

Plans for the application of armed force shall be made by the Security Council with the assistance of the Military Staff Committee.

Article 47

1. There shall be established a Military Staff Committee to advise and assist the Security Council on all questions relating to the Security Council's military requirements for the maintenance of international peace and security, the employment and command of forces placed at its disposal, the regulation of armaments, and possible disarmament.

2. The Military Staff Committee shall consist of the Chiefs of Staff of the permanent members of the Security Council or their representatives. Any Member of the United Nations not permanently represented on the Committee shall be invited by the Committee to be associated with it when the efficient discharge of the Committee's responsibilities requires the participation of that Member in its work.

3. The Military Staff Committee shall be responsible under the Security Council for the strategic direction of any armed forces placed at the disposal of the Security Council. Questions relating to the command of such forces shall be worked out subsequently.

4. The Military Staff Committee, with the authorization of the Security Council and after consultation with appropriate regional agencies, may establish regional subcommittees.

Article 48

1. The action required to carry out the decisions of the Security Council for the maintenance of international peace and security shall be taken by all the Members of the United Nations or by some of them, as the Security Council may determine.

2. Such decisions shall be carried out by the Members of the United Nations directly and through their action in the appropriate international agencies of which they are members.

Article 49

The Members of the United Nations shall join in affording mutual assistance in carrying out the measures decided upon by the Security Council.

Article 50

If preventive or enforcement measures against any state are taken by the Security Council, any other state, whether a Member of the United Nations or not, which finds itself confronted with special economic problems arising from the carrying out of those measures, shall have the right to consult the Security Council with regard to a solution of those problems.

Article 51

Nothing in the present Charter shall impair the inherent right of individual or collective self-defense if an armed attack occurs against a Member of the United Nations, until the Security Council has taken the measures necessary to maintain international peace and security. Measures taken by Members in the exercise of this right of self-defense shall be immediately reported to the Security Council and shall not in any way affect the authority and responsibility of the Security Cuoncil under the present Charter to take at any time such action as it deems necessary in order to maintain or restore international peace and security.

CHAPTER VIII

Regional Arrangements

Article 52

1. Nothing in the present Charter precludes the existence of regional arrangements or agencies for dealing with such matters relating to the maintenance of international peace and security as are appropriate for regional action, provided that such arrangements or agencies and their activities are consistent with the Purposes and Principles of the United Nations.

2. The Members of the United Nations entering into such arrangements or constituting such agencies shall make every effort to achieve pacific settlement of local disputes through such regional arrangements or by such regional agencies before referring them to the Security Council.

3. The Security Council shall encourage the development of pacific settlement of local disputes through such regional arrangements or by such regional agencies either on the initiative of the states concerned or by reference from the Security Council.

4. This Article in no way impairs the application of Articles 34 and 35.

Article 53

1. The Security Council shall, where appropriate, utilize such regional arrangements or agencies for enforcement action under its authority. But no enforcement action shall be taken under regional arrangements or by regional agencies without the authorization of the Security Council, with the exception of measures against any enemy state, as defined in paragraph 2 of this Article, provided for pursuant to Article 107 or in regional arrangements directed against renewal of aggressive policy on the part of any such state, until such time as the Organization may, on request of the Governments concerned, be charged with the responsibility for preventing further aggression by such a state.

2. The term enemy state as used in paragraph 1 of this Article applies to any state which during the Second World War has been an enemy of any signatory of the present Charter.

Article 54

The Security Council shall at all times be kept fully informed of activities undertaken or in contemplation under regional arrangements or by regional agencies for the maintenance of international peace and security.

CHAPTER IX

International Economic and Social Cooperation

Article 55

With a view to the creation of conditions of stability and well-being which are necessary for peaceful and friendly relations among nations based on respect for the principle of equal rights and self-determination of peoples, the United Nations shall promote:

   a. higher standards of living, full employment, and conditions of economic and social progress and development;
   b. solutions of international economic, social, health, and related problems; and international cultural and educational cooperation; and

    c. universal respect for, and observance of, human rights and fundamental freedoms for all without distinction as to race, sex, language, or religion.

Article 56

All Members pledge themselves to take joint and separate action in cooperation with the Organization for the achievement of the purposes set forth in Article 55.

Article 57

1. The various specialized agencies, established by intergovernmental agreement and having wide international responsibilities, as defined in their basic instruments, in economic, social, cultural, educational, health, and related fields, shall be brought into relationship with the United Nations in accordance with the provisions of Article 63.

2. Such agencies thus brought into relationship with the United Nations are hereinafter referred to as specialized agencies.

Article 58

The Organization shall make recommendations for the coordination of the policies and activities of the specialized agencies.

Article 59

The Organization shall, where appropriate, initiate negotiations among the states concerned for the creation of any new specialized agencies required for the accomplishment of the purposes set forth in Article 55.

Article 60

Responsibility for the discharge of the functions of the Organization set forth in this Chapter shall be vested in the General Assembly and, under the authority of the General Assembly, in the Economic and Social Council, which shall have for this purpose the powers set forth in Chapter X.

CHAPTER X

The Economic and Social Council

Composition

Article 61

1. The Economic and Social Council shall consist of eighteen Members of the United Nations elected by the General Assembly.

2. Subject to the provisions of paragraph 3, six members of the Economic and Social Council shall be elected each year for a term of three years. A retiring member shall be eligible for immediate re-election.

3. At the first election, eighteen members of the Economic and Social Council shall be chosen. The term of office of six members so chosen shall expire at the end of one year, and of six other members at the end of two years, in accordance with arrangements made by the General Assembly.

4. Each member of the Economic and Social Council shall have one representative.

Functions and Powers

Article 62

1. The Economic and Social Council may make or initiate studies and reports with respect to international economic, social, cultural, educational, health, and

related matters and may make recommendations with respect to any such matters to the General Assembly, to the Members of the United Nations, and to the specialized agencies concerned.

2. It may make recommendations for the purpose of promoting respect for, and observance of, human rights and fundamental freedoms for all.

3. It may prepare draft conventions for submission to the General Assembly, with respect to matters falling within its competence.

4. It may call, in accordance with the rules prescribed by the United Nations, international conferences on matters falling within its competence.

Article 63

1. The Economic and Social Council may enter into agreements with any of the agencies referred to in Article 57, defining the terms on which the agency concerned shall be brought into relationship with the United Nations. Such agreements shall be subject to approval by the General Assembly.

2. It may coordinate the activities of the specialized agencies through consultation with and recommendations to such agencies and through recommendations to the General Assembly and to the Members of the United Nations.

Article 64

1. The Economic and Social Council may take appropriate steps to obtain regular reports from the specialized agencies. It may make arrangements with the Members of the United Nations and with the specialized agencies to obtain reports on the steps taken to give effect to its own recommendations and to recommendations on matters falling within its competence made by the General Assembly.

2. It may communicate its observations on these reports to the General Assembly.

Article 65

The Economic and Social Council may furnish information to the Security Council and shall assist the Security Council upon its request.

Article 66

1. The Economic and Social Council shall perform such functions as fall within its competence in connection with the carrying out of the recommendations of the General Assembly.

2. It may, with the approval of the General Assembly, perform services at the request of Members of the United Nations and at the request of specialized agencies.

3. It shall perform such other functions as are specified elsewhere in the present Charter or as may be assigned to it by the General Assembly.

Voting

Article 67

1. Each member of the Economic and Social Council shall have one vote.

2. Decisions of the Economic and Social Council shall be made by a majority of the members present and voting.

Procedure

Article 68

The Economic and Social Council shall set up commissions in economic and social fields and for the promotion of human rights, and such other commissions as may be required for the performance of its functions.

Article 69

The Economic and Social Council shall invite any Member of the United Nations to participate, without vote, in its deliberations on any matter of particular concern to that Member.

Article 70

The Economic and Social Council may make arrangements for representatives of the specialized agencies to participate, without vote, in its deliberations and in those of the commissions established by it, and for its representatives to participate in the deliberations of the specialized agencies.

Article 71

The Economic and Social Council may make suitable arrangements for consultation with non-governmental organizations which are concerned with matters within its competence. Such arrangements may be made with international organizations and, where appropriate, with national organizations after consultation with the Member of the United Nations concerned.

Article 72

1. The Economic and Social Council shall adopt its own rules of procedure, including the method of selecting its President.

2. The Economic and Social Council shall meet as required in accordance with its rules, which shall include provision for the convening of meetings on the request of a majority of its members.

CHAPTER XI

Declaration Regarding Non-Self-Governing Territories

Article 73

Members of the United Nations which have or assume responsibilities for the administration of territories whose peoples have not yet attained a full measure of self-government recognize the principle that the interests of the inhabitants of these territories are paramount, and accept as a sacred trust the obligation to promote to the utmost, within the system of international peace and security established by the present Charter, the well-being of the inhabitants of these territories, and, to this end:

  a. to ensure, with due respect for the culture of the peoples concerned, their political, economic, social, and educational advancement, their just treatment, and their protection against abuses;

  b. to develop self-government, to take due account of the political aspirations of the peoples, and to assist them in the progressive development of their free political institutions, according to the particular circumstances of each territory and its peoples and their varying stages of advancement;

  c. to further international peace and security;

  d. to promote constructive measures of development, to encourage research, and to cooperate with one another and, when and where appropriate, with specialized international bodies with a view to the practical achievement of the social, economic, and scientific purposes set forth in this Article; and

  e. to transmit regularly to the Secretary-General for information purposes, subject to such limitation as security and constitutional considerations may require, statistical and other information of a technical nature relating to economic, social, and educational conditions in the territories for which they are respectively responsible other than those territories to which Chapters XII and XIII apply.

Article 74

Members of the United Nations also agree that their policy in respect of the territories to which this Chapter applies, no less than in respect of their metropolitan areas, must be based on the general principle of good-neighborliness, due account being taken of the interests and well-being of the rest of the world, in social, economic, and commercial matters.

CHAPTER XII

International Trusteeship System

Article 75

The United Nations shall establish under its authority an international trusteeship system for the administration and supervision of such territories as may be placed thereunder by subsequent individual agreements. These territories are hereinafter referred to as trust territories.

Article 76

The basic objectives of the trusteeship system, in accordance with the Purposes of the United Nations laid down in Article 1 of the present Charter, shall be:

a. to further international peace and security;
b. to promote the political, economic, social, and educational advancement of the inhabitants of the trust territories, and their progressive development towards self-government or independence as may be appropriate to the particular circumstances of each territory and its peoples and the freely expressed wishes of the peoples concerned, and as may be provided by the terms of each trusteeship agreement;
c. to encourage respect for human rights and for fundamental freedoms for all without distinction as to race, sex, language, or religion, and to encourage recognition of the interdependence of the peoples of the world; and
d. to ensure equal treatment in social, economic, and commercial matters for all Members of the United Nations and their nationals, and also equal treatment for the latter in the administration of justice, without prejudice to the attainment of the foregoing objectives and subject to the provisions of Article 80.

Article 77

1. The trusteeship system shall apply to such territories in the following categories as may be placed thereunder by means of trusteeship agreements:

a. territories now held under mandate;
b. territories which may be detached from enemy states as a result of the Second World War; and
c. territories voluntarily placed under the system by states responsible for their administration.

2. It will be a matter for subsequent agreement as to which territories in the foregoing categories will be brought under the trusteeship system and upon what terms.

Article 78

The trusteeship system shall not apply to territories which have become Members of the United Nations, relationship among which shall be based on respect for the principle of sovereign equality.

Article 79

The terms of trusteeship for each territory to be placed under the trusteeship system, including any alteration or amendment, shall be agreed upon by the states directly concerned, including the mandatory power in the case of territories held under mandate by a Member of the United Nations, and shall be approved as provided for in Articles 83 and 85.

Article 80

1. Except as may be agreed upon in individual trusteeship agreements, made under Articles 77, 79, and 81, placing each territory under the trusteeship system, and until such agreements have been concluded, nothing in this Chapter shall be construed in or of itself to alter in any manner the rights whatsoever of any states or any peoples or the terms of existing international instruments to which Members of the United Nations may respectively be parties.

2. Paragraph 1 of this Article shall not be interpreted as giving grounds for delay or postponement of the negotiation and conclusion of agreements for placing mandated and other territories under the trusteeship system as provided for in Article 77.

Article 81

The trusteeship agreement shall in each case include the terms under which the trust territory will be administered and designate the authority which will exercise the administration of the trust territory. Such authority, hereinafter called the administering authority, may be one or more states or the Organization itself.

Article 82

There may be designated, in any trusteeship agreement, a strategic area or areas which may include part or all of the trust territory to which the agreement applies, without prejudice to any special agreement or agreements made under Article 43.

Article 83

1. All functions of the United Nations relating to strategic areas, including the approval of the terms of the trusteeship agreements and of their alteration or amendment, shall be exercised by the Security Council.

2. The basic objectives set forth in Article 76 shall be applicable to the people of each strategic area.

3. The Security Council shall, subject to the provisions of the trusteeship agreements and without prejudice to security considerations, avail itself of the assistance of the Trusteeship Council to perform those functions of the United Nations under the trusteeship system relating to political, economic, social, and educational matters in the strategic areas.

Article 84

It shall be the duty of the administering authority to ensure that the trust territory shall play its part in the maintenance of international peace and security. To this end the administering authority may make use of volunteer forces, facilities, and assistance from the trust territory in carrying out the obligations towards the Security Council undertaken in this regard by the administering authority, as well as for local defense and the maintenance of law and order within the trust territory.

Article 85

1. The functions of the United Nations with regard to trusteeship agreements for all areas not designated as strategic, including the approval of the terms of the trusteeship agreements and of their alteration or amendment, shall be exercised by the General Assembly.

2. The Trusteeship Council, operating under the authority of the General Assembly, shall assist the General Assembly in carrying out these functions.

CHAPTER XIII

The Trusteeship Council

Composition

Article 86

1. The Trusteeship Council shall consist of the following Members of the United Nations:

    a. those Members administering trust territories;

    b. such of those Members mentioned by name in Article 23 as are not administering trust territories; and

    c. as many other Members elected for three-year terms by the General Assembly as may be necessary to ensure that the total number of members of the Trusteeship Council is equally divided between those Members of the United Nations which administer trust territories and those which do not.

2. Each member of the Trusteeship Council shall designate one specially qualified person to represent it therein.

Functions and Powers

Article 87

The General Assembly and, under its authority, the Trusteeship Council, in carrying out their functions, may:

    a. consider reports submitted by the administering authority;

    b. accept petitions and examine them in consultation with the administering authority;

    c. provide for periodic visits to the respective trust territories at times agreed upon with the administering authority; and

    d. take these and other actions in conformity with the terms of the trusteeship agreements.

Article 88

The Trusteeship Council shall formulate a questionnaire on the political, economic, social, and educational advancement of the inhabitants of each trust territory, and the administering authority for each trust territory within the competence of the General Assembly shall make an annual report to the General Assembly upon the basis of such questionnaire.

Voting

Article 89

1. Each member of the Trusteeship Council shall have one vote.

2. Decisions of the Trusteeship Council shall be made by a majority of the members present and voting.

Procedure

Article 90

1. The Trusteeship Council shall adopt its own rules of procedure, including the method of selecting its President.

2. The Trusteeship Council shall meet as required in accordance with its rules, which shall include provision for the convening of meetings on the request of a majority of its members.

Article 91

The Trusteeship Council shall, when appropriate, avail itself of the assistance of the Economic and Social Council and of the specialized agencies in regard to matters with which they are respectively concerned.

CHAPTER XIV

The International Court of Justice

Article 92

The International Court of Justice shall be the principal judicial organ of the United Nations. It shall function in accordance with the annexed Statute, which is based upon the Statute of the Permanent Court of International Justice and forms an integral part of the present Charter.

Article 93

1. All Members of the United Nations are *ipso facto* parties to the Statute of the International Court of Justice.

2. A state which is not a Member of the United Nations may become a party to the Statute of the International Court of Justice on conditions to be determined in each case by the General Assembly upon the recommendation of the Security Council.

Article 94

1. Each Member of the United Nations undertakes to comply with the decision of the International Court of Justice in any case to which it is a party.

2. If any party to a case fails to perform the obligations incumbent upon it under a judgment rendered by the Court, the other party may have recourse to the Security Council, which may, if it deems necessary, make recommendations or decide upon measures to be taken to give effect to the judgment.

Article 95

Nothing in the present Charter shall prevent Members of the United Nations from entrusting the solution of their differences to other tribunals by virtue of agreements already in existence or which may be concluded in the future.

Article 96

1. The General Assembly or the Security Council may request the International Court of Justice to give an advisory opinion on any legal question.

2. Other organs of the United Nations and specialized agencies, which may at any time be so authorized by the General Assembly, may also request advisory opinions of the Court on legal questions arising within the scope of their activities.

CHAPTER XV

The Secretariat

Article 97

The Secretariat shall comprise a Secretary-General and such staff as the Organization may require. The Secretary-General shall be appointed by the General Assembly upon the recommendation of the Security Council. He shall be the chief administrative officer of the Organization.

Article 98

The Secretary-General shall act in that capacity in all meetings of the General Assembly, of the Security Council, of the Economic and Social Council, and of the Trusteeship Council, and shall perform such other functions as are entrusted to him by these organs. The Secretary-General shall make an annual report to the General Assembly on the work of the Organization.

Article 99

The Secretary-General may bring to the attention of the Security Council any matter which in his opinion may threaten the maintenance of international peace and security.

Article 100

1. In the performance of their duties the Secretary-General and the staff shall not seek or receive instructions from any government or from any other authority external to the Organization. They shall refrain from any action which might reflect on their position as international officials responsible only to the Organization.

2. Each Member of the United Nations undertakes to respect the exclusively international character of the responsibilities of the Secretary-General and the staff and not to seek to influence them in the discharge of their responsibilities.

Article 101

1. The staff shall be appointed by the Secretary-General under regulations established by the General Assembly.

2. Appropriate staffs shall be permanently assigned to the Economic and Social Council, the Trusteeship Council, and, as required, to other organs of the United Nations. These staffs shall form a part of the Secretariat.

3. The paramount consideration in the employment of the staff and in the determination of the conditions of service shall be the necessity of securing the highest standards of efficiency, competence, and integrity. Due regard shall be paid to the importance of recruiting the staff on as wide a geographical basis as possible.

CHAPTER XVI

Miscellaneous Provisions

Article 102

1. Every treaty and every international agreement entered into by any Member of the United Nations after the present Charter comes into force shall as soon as possible be registered with the Secretariat and published by it.

2. No party to any such treaty or international agreement which has not been

registered in accordance with the provisions of paragraph 1 of this Article may invoke that treaty or agreement before any organ of the United Nations.

Article 103

In the event of a conflict between the obligations of the Members of the United Nations under the present Charter and their obligations under any other international agreement, their obligations under the present Charter shall prevail.

Article 104

The Organization shall enjoy in the territory of each of its Members such legal capacity as may be necessary for the exercise of its functions and the fulfilment of its purposes.

Article 105

1. The Organization shall enjoy in the territory of each of its Members such privileges and immunities as are necessary for the fulfilment of its purposes.

2. Representatives of the Members of the United Nations and officials of the Organization shall similarly enjoy such privileges and immunities as are necessary for the independent exercise of their functions in connection with the Organization.

3. The General Assembly may make recommendations with a view to determining the details of the application of paragraphs 1 and 2 of this Article or may propose conventions to the Members of the United Nations for this purpose.

CHAPTER XVII

Transitional Security Arrangements

Article 106

Pending the coming into force of such special agreements referred to in Article 43 as in the opinion of the Security Council enable it to begin the exercise of its responsibilities under Article 42, the parties to the Four-Nation Declaration, signed at Moscow, October 30, 1943, and France, shall, in accordance with the provisions of paragraph 5 of that Declaration, consult with one another and as occasion requires with other Members of the United Nations with a view to such joint action on behalf of the Organization as may be necessary for the purpose of maintaining international peace and security.

Article 107

Nothing in the present Charter shall invalidate or preclude action, in relation to any state which during the Second World War has been an enemy of any signatory to the present Charter, taken or authorized as a result of that war by the Governments having responsibility for such action.

CHAPTER XVIII

Amendments

Article 108

Amendments to the present Charter shall come into force for all Members of the United Nations when they have been adopted by a vote of two thirds of the members of the General Assembly and ratified in accordance with their respective constitutional processes by two thirds of the Members of the United Nations, including all the permanent members of the Security Council.

Article 109

1. A General Conference of the Members of the United Nations for the purpose of reviewing the present Charter may be held at a date and place to be fixed by a two-thirds vote of the members of the General Assembly and by a vote of any seven members of the Security Council. Each Member of the United Nations shall have one vote in the conference.

2. Any alteration of the present Charter recommended by a two-thirds vote of the conference shall take effect when ratified in accordance with their respective constitutional processes by two thirds of the Members of the United Nations including all the permanent members of the Security Council.

3. If such a conference has not been held before the tenth annual session of the General Assembly following the coming into force of the present Charter, the proposal to call such a conference shall be placed on the agenda of that session of the General Assembly, and the conference shall be held if so decided by a majority vote of the members of the General Assembly and by a vote of any seven members of the Security Council.

CHAPTER XIX

Ratification and Signature

Article 110

1. The present Charter shall be ratified by the signatory states in accordance with their respective constitutional processes.

2. The ratifications shall be deposited with the Government of the United States of America, which shall notify all the signatory states of each deposit as well as the Secretary-General of the Organization when he has been appointed.

3. The present Charter shall come into force upon the deposit of ratifications by the Republic of China, France, the Union of Soviet Socialist Republics, the United Kingdom of Great Britain and Northern Ireland, and the United States of America, and by a majority of the other signatory states. A protocol of the ratifications deposited shall thereupon be drawn up by the Government of the United States of America which shall communicate copies thereof to all the signatory states.

4. The states signatory to the present Charter which ratify it after it has come into force will become original Members of the United Nations on the date of the deposit of their respective ratifications.

Article 111

The present Charter, of which the Chinese, French, Russian, English, and Spanish texts are equally authentic, shall remain deposited in the archives of the Government of the United States of America. Duly certified copies thereof shall be transmitted by that Government to the Governments of the other signatory states.

IN FAITH WHEREOF the representatives of the Governments of the United Nations have signed the present Charter.

DONE at the city of San Francisco the twenty-sixth day of June, one thousand nine hundred and forty-five.

STATUTE OF THE INTERNATIONAL COURT OF JUSTICE

Article 1

THE INTERNATIONAL COURT OF JUSTICE established by the Charter of the United Nations as the principal judicial organ of the United Nations shall be constituted and shall function in accordance with the provisions of the present Statute.

CHAPTER I

Organization of the Court

Article 2

The Court shall be composed of a body of independent judges, elected regardless of their nationality from among persons of high moral character, who possess the qualifications required in their respective countries for appointment to the highest judicial offices, or are jurisconsults of recognized competence in international law.

Article 3

1. The Court shall consist of fifteen members, no two of whom may be nationals of the same state.

2. A person who for the purposes of membership in the Court could be regarded as a national of more than one state shall be deemed to be a national of the one in which he ordinarily exercises civil and political rights.

Article 4

1. The members of the Court shall be elected by the General Assembly and by the Security Council from a list of persons nominated by the national groups in the Permanent Court of Arbitration, in accordance with the following provisions.

2. In the case of Members of the United Nations not represented in the Permanent Court of Arbitration, candidates shall be nominated by national groups appointed for this purpose by their governments under the same conditions as those prescribed for members of the Permanent Court of Arbitration by Article 44 of the Convention of The Hague of 1907 for the pacific settlement of international disputes.

3. The conditions under which a state which is a party to the present Statute but is not a Member of the United Nations may participate in electing the members of the Court shall, in the absence of a special agreement, be laid down by the General Assembly upon recommendation of the Security Council.

Article 5

1. At least three months before the date of the election, the Secretary-General of the United Nations shall address a written request to the members of the Permanent Court of Arbitration belonging to the states which are parties to the

present Statute, and to the members of the national groups appointed under Article 4, paragraph 2, inviting them to undertake, within a given time, by national groups, the nomination of persons in a position to accept the duties of a member of the Court.

2. No group may nominate more than four persons, not more than two of whom shall be of their own nationality. In no case may the number of candidates nominated by a group be more than double the number of seats to be filled.

Article 6

Before making these nominations, each national group is recommended to consult its highest court of justice, its legal faculties and schools of law, and its national academies and national sections of international academies devoted to the study of law.

Article 7

1. The Secretary-General shall prepare a list in alphabetical order of all the persons thus nominated. Save as provided in Article 12, paragraph 2, these shall be the only persons eligible.

2. The Secretary-General shall submit this list to the General Assembly and to the Security Council.

Article 8

The General Assembly and the Security Council shall proceed independently of one another to elect the members of the Court.

Article 9

At every election, the electors shall bear in mind not only that the persons to be elected should individually possess the qualifications required, but also that in the body as a whole the representation of the main forms of civilization and of the principal legal systems of the world should be assured.

Article 10

1. Those candidates who obtain an absolute majority of votes in the General Assembly and in the Security Council shall be considered as elected.

2. Any vote of the Security Council, whether for the election of judges or for the appointment of members of the conference envisaged in Article 12, shall be taken without any distinction between permanent and non-permanent members of the Security Council.

3. In the event of more than one national of the same state obtaining an absolute majority of the votes both of the General Assembly and of the Security Council, the eldest of these only shall be considered as elected.

Article 11

If, after the first meeting held for the purpose of the election, one or more seats remain to be filled, a second and, if necessary, a third meeting shall take place.

Article 12

1. If, after the third meeting, one or more seats still remain unfilled, a joint conference consisting of six members, three appointed by the General Assembly and three by the Security Council, may be formed at any time at the request of either the General Assembly or the Security Council, for the purpose of choosing by the vote of an absolute majority one name for each seat still vacant, to submit to the General Assembly and the Security Council for their respective acceptance.

2. If the joint conference is unanimously agreed upon any person who fulfils the

required conditions, he may be included in its list, even though he was not included in the list of nominations referred to in Article 7.

3. If the joint conference is satisfied that it will not be successful in procuring an election, those members of the Court who have already been elected shall, within a period to be fixed by the Security Council, proceed to fill the vacant seats by selection from among those candidates who have obtained votes either in the General Assembly or in the Security Council.

4. In the event of an equality of votes among the judges, the eldest judge shall have a casting vote.

Article 13

1. The members of the Court shall be elected for nine years and may be re-elected; provided, however, that of the judges elected at the first election, the terms of five judges shall expire at the end of three years and the terms of five more judges shall expire at the end of six years.

2. The judges whose terms are to expire at the end of the above-mentioned initial periods of three and six years shall be chosen by lot to be drawn by the Secretary-General immediately after the first election has been completed.

3. The members of the Court shall continue to discharge their duties until their places have been filled. Though replaced, they shall finish any cases which they may have begun.

4. In the case of the resignation of a member of the Court, the resignation shall be addressed to the President of the Court for transmission to the Secretary-General. This last notification makes the place vacant.

Article 14

Vacancies shall be filled by the same method as that laid down for the first election, subject to the following provision: the Secretary-General shall, within one month of the occurrence of the vacancy, proceed to issue the invitations provided for in Article 5, and the date of the election shall be fixed by the Security Council.

Article 15

A member of the Court elected to replace a member whose term of office has not expired shall hold office for the remainder of his predecessor's term.

Article 16

1. No member of the Court may exercise any political or administrative function, or engage in any other occupation of a professional nature.

2. Any doubt on this point shall be settled by the decision of the Court.

Article 17

1. No member of the Court may act as agent, counsel, or advocate in any case.

2. No member may participate in the decision of any case in which he has previously taken part as agent, counsel, or advocate for one of the parties, or as a member of a national or international court, or of a commission of enquiry, or in any other capacity.

3. Any doubt on this point shall be settled by the decision of the Court.

Article 18

1. No member of the Court can be dismissed unless, in the unanimous opinion of the other members, he has ceased to fulfil the required conditions.

2. Formal notification thereof shall be made to the Secretary-General by the Registrar.

3. This notification makes the place vacant.

Article 19

The members of the Court, when engaged on the business of the Court, shall enjoy diplomatic privileges and immunites.

Article 20

Every member of the Court shall, before taking up his duties, make a solemn declaration in open Court that he will exercise his powers impartially and conscientiously.

Article 21

1. The Court shall elect its President and Vice-President for three years; they may be re-elected.

2. The Court shall appoint its Registrar and may provide for the appointment of such other officers as may be necessary.

Article 22

1. The seat of the Court shall be established at The Hague. This, however, shall not prevent the Court from sitting and exercising its functions elsewhere whenever the Court considers it desirable.

2. The President and the Registrar shall reside at the seat of the Court.

Article 23

1. The Court shall remain permanently in session, except during the judicial vacations, the dates and duration of which shall be fixed by the Court.

2. Members of the Court are entitled to periodic leave, the dates and duration of which shall be fixed by the Court, having in mind the distance between The Hague and the home of each judge.

3. Members of the Court shall be bound, unless they are on leave or prevented from attending by illness or other serious reasons duly explained to the President, to hold themselves permanently at the disposal of the Court.

Article 24

1. If, for some special reason, a member of the Court considers that he should not take part in the decision of a particular case, he shall so inform the President.

2. If the President considers that for some special reason one of the members of the Court should not sit in a particular case, he shall give him notice accordingly.

3. If in any such case the member of the Court and the President disagree, the matter shall be settled by the decision of the Court.

Article 25

1. The full Court shall sit except when it is expressly provided otherwise in the present Statute.

2. Subject to the condition that the number of judges available to constitute the Court is not thereby reduced below eleven, the Rules of the Court may provide for allowing one or more judges, according to circumstances and in rotation, to be dispensed from sitting.

3. A quorum of nine judges shall suffice to constitute the Court.

Article 26

1. The Court may from time to time form one or more chambers, composed of three or more judges as the Court may determine, for dealing with particular categories of cases; for example, labour cases and cases relating to transit and communications.

2. The Court may at any time form a chamber for dealing with a particular case. The number of judges to constitute such a chamber shall be determined by the Court with the approval of the parties.

3. Cases shall be heard and determined by the chambers provided for in this Article if the parties so request.

Article 27

A judgment given by any of the chambers provided for in Articles 26 and 29 shall be considered as rendered by the Court.

Article 28

The chambers provided for in Articles 26 and 29 may, with the consent of the parties, sit and exercise their functions elsewhere than at The Hague.

Article 29

With a view to the speedy despatch of business, the Court shall form annually a chamber composed of five judges which, at the request of the parties, may hear and determine cases by summary procedure. In addition, two judges shall be selected for the purpose of replacing judges who find it impossible to sit.

Article 30

1. The Court shall frame rules for carrying out its functions. In particular, it shall lay down rules of procedure.*

2. The Rules of the Court may provide for assessors to sit with the Court or with any of its chambers, without the right to vote.

Article 31

1. Judges of the nationality of each of the parties shall retain their right to sit in the case before the Court.

2. If the Court includes upon the Bench a judge of the nationality of one of the parties, any other party may choose a person to sit as judge. Such person shal be chosen preferably from among those persons who have been nominated as candidates as provided in Articles 4 and 5.

3. If the Court includes upon the Bench no judge of the nationality of the parties, each of these parties may proceed to choose a judge as provided in paragraph 2 of this Article.

4. The provisions of this Article shall apply to the case of Articles 26 and 29. In such cases, the President shall request one or, if necessary, two of the members of the Court forming the chamber to give place to the members of the Court of the nationality of the parties concerned, and, failing such, or if they are unable to be present, to the judges specially chosen by the parties.

5. Should there by several parties in the same interest, they shall, for the purpose of the preceding provisions, be reckoned as one party only. Any doubt upon this point shall be settled by the decision of the Court.

6. Judges chosen as laid down in paragraphs 2, 3, and 4 of this Article shall fulfil the conditions required by Articles 2, 17 (paragraph 2), 20, and 24 of the present Statute. They shall take part in the decision on terms of complete equality with their colleagues.

Article 32

1. Each member of the Court shall receive an annual salary.

2. The President shall receive a special annual allowance.

* Not reproduced. For text of the Rules of Court, see Sh. Rosenne, *The International Court of Justice* (Leyden, 1957), 543-61.

3. The Vice-President shall receive a special allowance for every day on which he acts as President.

4. The judges chosen under Article 31, other than members of the Court, shall receive compensation for each day on which they exercise their functions.

5. These salaries, allowances, and compensation shall be fixed by the General Assembly. They may not be decreased during the term of office.

6. The salary of the Registrar shall be fixed by the General Assembly on the proposal of the Court.

7. Regulations made by the General Assembly shall fix the conditions under which retirement pensions may be given to members of the Court and to the Registrar, and the conditions under which members of the Court and the Registrar shall have their travelling expenses refunded.

8. The above salaries, allowances, and compensation shall be free of all taxation.

Article 33

The expenses of the Court shall be borne by the United Nations in such a manner as shall be decided by the General Assembly.

CHAPTER II

Competence of the Court

Article 34

1. Only states may be parties in cases before the Court.

2. The Court, subject to and in conformity with its Rules, may request of public international organizations information relevant to cases before it, and shall receive such information presented by such organizations on their own initiative.

3. Whenever the construction of the constituent instrument of a public international organization or of an international convention adopted thereunder is in question in a case before the Court, the Registrar shall so notify the public international organization concerned and shall communicate to it copies of all the written proceedings.

Article 35

1. The Court shall be open to the states parties to the present Statute.

2. The conditions under which the Court shall be open to other states shall, subject to the special provisions contained in treaties in force, be laid down by the Security Council, but in no case shall such conditions place the parties in a position of inequality before the Court.

3. When a state which is not a Member of the United Nations is a party to a case, the Court shall fix the amount which that party is to contribute towards the expenses of the Court. This provision shall not apply if such state is bearing a share of the expenses of the Court.

Article 36

1. The jurisdiction of the Court comprises all cases which the parties refer to it and all matters specially provided for in the Charter of the United Nations or in treaties and conventions in force.

2. The states parties to the present Statute may at any time declare that they recognize as compulsory *ipso facto* and without special agreement, in relation to any other state accepting the same obligation, the jurisdiction of the Court in all legal disputes concerning:

a. the interpretation of a treaty;
b. any question of international law;
c. the existence of any fact which, if established, would constitute a breach of an international obligation;
d. the nature or extent of the reparation to be made for the breach of an international obligation.

3. The declarations referred to above may be made unconditionally or on condition of reciprocity on the part of several or certain states, or for a certain time.

4. Such declarations shall be deposited with the Secretary-General of the United Nations, who shall transmit copies thereof to the parties to the Statute and to the Registrar of the Court.

5. Declarations made under Article 36 of the Statute of the Permanent Court of International Justice and which are still in force shall be deemed, as between the parties to the present Statute, to be acceptances of the compulsory jurisdiction of the International Court of Justice for the period which they still have to run and in accordance with their terms.

6. In the event of a dispute as to whether the Court has jurisdiction, the matter shall be settled by the decision of the Court.

Article 37

Whenever a treaty or convention in force provides for reference of a matter to a tribunal to have been instituted by the League of Nations, or to the Permanent Court of International Justice, the matter shall, as between the parties to the present Statute, be referred to the International Court of Justice.

Article 38

1. The Court, whose function is to decide in accordance with international law such disputes as are submitted to it, shall apply:

a. international conventions, whether general or particular, establishing rules expressly recognized by the contesting states;
b. international custom, as evidence of a general practice accepted as law;
c. the general principles of law recognized by civilized nations;
d. subject to the provisions of Article 59, judicial decisions and the teachings of the most highly qualified publicists of the various nations, as subsidiary means for the determination of rules of law.

2. This provision shall not prejudice the power of the Court to decide a case *ex aequo et bono*, if the parties agree thereto.

CHAPTER III

Procedure

Article 39

1. The official languages of the Court shall be French and English. If the parties agree that the case shall be conducted in French, the judgment shall be delivered in French. If the parties agree that the case shall be conducted in English, the judgment shall be delivered in English.

2. In the absence of an agreement as to which language shall be employed, each party may, in the pleadings, use the language which it prefers; the decision of the Court shall be given in French and English. In this case the Court shall at the same time determine which of the two texts shall be considered as authoritative.

3. The Court shall, at the request of any party, authorize a language other than French or English to be used by that party.

Article 40

1. Cases are brought before the Court, as the case may be, either by the notification of the special agreement or by a written application addressed to the Registrar. In either case the subject of the dispute and the parties shall be indicated.

2. The Registrar shall forthwith communicate the application to all concerned.

3. He shall also notify the Members of the United Nations through the Secretary-General, and also any other states entitled to appear before the Court.

Article 41

1. The Court shall have the power to indicate, if it considers that circumstances so require, any provisional measures which ought to be taken to preserve the respective rights of either party.

2. Pending the final decision, notice of the measures suggested shall forthwith be given to the parties and to the Security Council.

Article 42

1. The parties shall be represented by agents.

2. They may have the assistance of counsel or advocates before the Court.

3. The agents, counsel, and advocates of parties before the Court shall enjoy the privileges and immunities necessary to the independent exercise of their duties.

Article 43

1. The procedure shall consist of two parts: written and oral.

2. The written proceedings shall consist of the communication to the Court and to the parties of memorials, counter-memorials and, if necessary, replies; also all papers and documents in support.

3. These communications shall be made through the Registrar, in the order and within the time fixed by the Court.

4. A certified copy of every document produced by one party shall be communicated to the other party.

5. The oral proceedings shall consist of the hearing by the Court of witnesses, experts, agents, counsel, and advocates.

Article 44

1. For the service of all notices upon persons other than the agents, counsel, and advocates, the Court shall apply direct to the government of the state upon whose territory the notice has to be served.

2. The same provision shall apply whenever steps are to be taken to procure evidence on the spot.

Article 45

The hearing shall be under the control of the President or, if he is unable to preside, of the Vice-President; if neither is able to preside, the senior judge present shall preside.

Article 46

The hearing in Court shall be public, unless the Court shall decide otherwise, or unless the parties demand that the public be not admitted.

Article 47

1. Minutes shall be made at each hearing and signed by the Registrar and the President.

2. These minutes alone shall be authentic.

Article 48

The Court shall make orders for the conduct of the case, shall decide the form and time in which each party must conclude its arguments, and make all arrangements connected with the taking of evidence.

Article 49

The Court may, even before the hearing begins, call upon the agents to produce any document or to supply any explanations. Formal note shall be taken of any refusal.

Article 50

The Court may, at any time, entrust any individual, body, bureau, commission, or other organization that it may select, with the task of carrying out an enquiry or giving an expert opinion.

Article 51

During the hearing any relevant questions are to be put to the witnesses and experts under the conditions laid down by the Court in the rules of procedure referred to in Article 30.

Article 52

After the Court has received the proofs and evidence within the time specified for the purpose, it may refuse to accept any further oral or written evidence that one party may desire to present unless the other side consents.

Article 53

1. Whenever one of the parties does not appear before the Court, or fails to defend its case, the other party may call upon the Court to decide in favor of its claim.

2. The Court must, before doing so, satisfy itself, not only that it has jurisdiction in accordance with Articles 36 and 37, but also that the claim is well founded in fact and law.

Article 54

1. When, subject to the control of the Court, the agents, counsel, and advocates have completed their presentation of the case, the President shall declare the hearing closed.

2. The Court shall withdraw to consider the judgment.

3. The deliberations of the Court shall take place in private and remain secret.

Article 55

1. All questions shall be decided by a majority of the judges present.

2. In the event of an equality of votes, the President or the judge who acts in his place shall have a casting vote.

Article 56

1. The judgment shall state the reasons on which it is based.

2. It shall contain the names of the judges who have taken part in the decision.

Article 57

If the judgment does not represent in whole or in part the unanimous opinion of the judges, any judge shall be entitled to deliver a separate opinion.

Article 58

The judgment shall be signed by the President and by the Registrar. It shall be read in open Court, due notice having been given to the agents.

Article 59

The decision of the Court has no binding force except between the parties and in respect of that particular case.

Article 60

The judgment is final and without appeal. In the event of dispute as to the meaning or scope of the judgment, the Court shall construe it upon the request of any party.

Article 61

1. An application for revision of a judgment may be made only when it is based upon the discovery of some fact of such a nature as to be a decisive factor, which fact was, when the judgment was given, unknown to the Court and also to the party claiming revision, always provided that such ignorance was not due to negligence.

2. The proceedings for revision shall be opened by a judgment of the Court expressly recording the existence of the new fact, recognizing that it has such a character as to lay the case open to revision, and declaring the application admissible on this ground.

3. The Court may require previous compliance with the terms of the judgment before it admits proceedings in revision.

4. The application for revision must be made at latest within six months of the discovery of the new fact.

5. No application for revision may be made after the lapse of ten years from the date of the judgment.

Article 62

1. Should a state consider that it has an interest of a legal nature which may be affected by the decision in the case, it may submit a request to the Court to be permitted to intervene.

2. It shall be for the Court to decide upon this request.

Article 63

1. Whenever the construction of a convention to which states other than those concerned in the case are parties is in question, the Registrar shall notify all such states forthwith.

2. Every state so notified has the right to intervene in the proceedings; but if it uses this right, the construction given by the judgment will be equally binding upon it.

Article 64

Unless otherwise decided by the Court, each party shall bear its own costs.

CHAPTER IV

Advisory Opinions

Article 65

1. The Court may give an advisory opinion on any legal question at the request of whatever body may be authorized by or in accordance with the Charter of the United Nations to make such a request.

2. Questions upon which the advisory opinion of the Court is asked shall be laid before the Court by means of a written request containing an exact statement of the question upon which an opinion is required, and accompanied by all documents likely to throw light upon the question.

Article 66

1. The Registrar shall forthwith give notice of the request for an advisory opinion to all states entitled to appear before the Court.

2. The Registrar shall also, by means of a special and direct communication, notify any state entitled to appear before the Court or international organization considered by the Court, or, should it not be sitting, by the President, as likely to be able to furnish information on the question, that the Court will be prepared to receive, within a time limit to be fixed by the President, written statements, or to hear, at a public sitting to be held for the purpose, oral statements relating to the question.

3. Should any such state entitled to appear before the Court have failed to receive the special communication referred to in paragraph 2 of this Article, such state may express a desire to submit a written statement or to be heard; and the Court will decide.

4. States and organizations having presented written or oral statements or both shall be permitted to comment on the statements made by other states or organizations in the form, to the extent, and within the time limits which the Court, or, should it not be sitting, the President, shall decide in each particular case. Accordingly, the Registrar shall in due time communicate any such written statements to states and organizations having submitted similar statements.

Article 67

The Court shall deliver its advisory opinions in open Court, notice having been given to the Secretary-General and to the representatives of Members of the United Nations, of other states and of international organizations immediately concerned.

Article 68

In the exercise of its advisory functions the Court shall further be guided by the provisions of the present Statute which apply in contentious cases to the extent to which it recognizes them to be applicable.

CHAPTER V

Amendment

Article 69

Amendments to the present Statute shall be effected by the same procedure as is provided by the Charter of the United Nations for amendments to that Charter,

subject however to any provisions which the General Assembly upon recommendation of the Security Council may adopt concerning the participation of states
which are parties to the present Statute but are not Members of the United
Nations.

Article 70

The Court shall have power to propose such amendments to the present Statute
as it may deem necessary, through written communications to the Secretary-
General, for consideration in conformity with the provisions of Article 69.

[Here follow the signatures]

PARTIES TO THE STATUTE

(a) *Original members of Charter and Statute, in force from 24 October 1945*

Argentina, Australia, Belgium, Bolivia, Brazil, Byelorussian Soviet Socialist
Republic, Canada, Chile, China, Colombia, Costa Rica, Cuba, Czechoslovakia,
Denmark, Dominican Republic, Ecuador, El Salvador, Ethiopia, France, Greece,
Guatemala, Haiti, Honduras, India, Iran, Iraq, Lebanon, Liberia, Luxembourg,
Mexico, Netherlands, New Zealand, Nicaragua, Norway, Panama, Paraguay,
Peru, Philippines, Poland, Saudi Arabia, South Africa, Syria,* Turkey, Ukrai-
nian Soviet Socialist Republic, Union of Soviet Socialist Republics, United
Arab Republic (Egypt), United Kingdom of Great Britain and Northern
Ireland, United States of America, Uruguay, Venezuela, Yugoslavia.

(b) *States admitted to membership in the United Nations in accordance with Article 4 of
the Charter*

State	Date of the decision of the General Assembly
Afghanistan	19 November 1946
Albania	14 December 1955
Algeria	8 October 1962
Austria	14 December 1955
Bulgaria	14 December 1955
Burma	19 April 1948
Burundi	18 September 1962
Cambodia	14 December 1955
Cameroun	20 September 1960
Central African Republic	20 September 1960
Ceylon	14 December 1955
Chad	20 September 1960
Congo (Brazzaville)	20 September 1960
Congo (Leopoldville)	20 September 1960
Cyprus	20 September 1960
Dahomey	20 September 1960
Federation of Malaya	17 September 1957

*Syria was an original member of the United Nations from 24 October 1945.
From 21 February 1958 until October, 1961, Syria and Egypt joined to form
the United Arab Republic, a single member of the United Nations. On 13 October 1961 Syria, having resumed its status as an independent State, also
resumed its separate membership in the Organization.

State	Date of the decision of the General Assembly
Finland	14 December 1955
Gabon	20 September 1960
Ghana	8 March 1957
Guinea	12 December 1958
Hungary	14 December 1955
Iceland	19 November 1946
Indonesia	28 September 1950
Ireland	14 December 1955
Israel	11 May 1949
Italy	14 December 1955
Ivory Coast	20 September 1960
Jamaica	18 September 1962
Japan	18 December 1956
Jordan	14 December 1955
Laos	14 December 1955
Libya	14 December 1955
Madagascar	20 September 1960
Mali	28 September 1960
Mauretania	27 October 1961
Mongolia	27 October 1961
Morocco	12 November 1956
Nepal	14 December 1955
Niger	20 September 1960
Nigeria	7 October 1960
Pakistan	30 September 1947
Portugal	14 December 1955
Romania	14 December 1955
Rwanda	18 September 1962
Senegal	28 September 1960
Sierra Leone	27 September 1961
Somalia	20 September 1960
Spain	14 December 1955
Sudan	12 November 1956
Sweden	19 November 1946
Tanganyika	14 December 1961
Thailand	16 December 1946
Togo	20 September 1960
Trinidad and Tobago	18 September 1962
Tunisia	12 November 1956
Uganda	25 October 1962
Upper Volta	20 September 1960
Yemen	30 September 1947

(c) *Other States parties to the Statute*

Liechtenstein as from 29 March 1950.
San Marino as from 18 February 1954.
Switzerland as from 28 July 1948.
Japan as from 2 April 1954 until admission to U.N.

Appendix 3

COMPOSITION OF THE COURT

(A) *Permanent Court of International Justice*

First Period, 1922-30

R. ALTAMIRA y Crevea	Spain
D. ANZILOTTI (President, 1928-30)	Italy
R. BARBOSA (d. 1 March 1923)	Brazil
A. S. de BUSTAMENTE y Sirven	Cuba
Viscount FINLAY (d. 9 March 1929)	U.K.
H. FROMAGEOT (from 19 September 1929)	France
H. M. HUBER (President, 1925-7, Vice-President 1928-31)	Switzerland
C. E. HUGHES (8 September 1928-15 February 1930)	U.S.A.
C. J. B. HURST (from 19 September 1929)	U.K.
F. B. KELLOG (from 25 September 1930)	U.S.A.
B. C. J. LODER (President, 1922-4)	Netherlands
J. B. MOORE (resigned 11 April 1928)	U.S.A.
D. G. G. NYHOLM	Denmark
Y. ODA	Japan
E. d. S. PESSÔA (from 10 September 1923)	Brazil
C. A. WEISS (Vice-President 1922-8, d. 31 August 1928)	France

Deputy-Judges

F. V. N. BEICHMANN	Norway
D. NEGULESCO	Rumania
WANG Ch'ung-hui	China
M. YOVANOVITCH	Yugoslavia

Second Period, 1931-45

M. ADATCI (President 1931-3, d. 28 December 1934)	Japan
R. ALTAMIRA y Crevea	Spain
D. ANZILOTTI	Italy
A. S. de BUSTAMENTE y Sirven	Cuba
CHENG Tien-Hsi (from 8 October 1936)	China
R. W. ERICH (from 26 September 1938)	Finland
W. J. M. van EYSINGA	Netherlands
H. FROMAGEOT	France
J. G. GUERRERO (Vice-President, 1931-36, President, 1936-46)	El Salvador
Åke HAMMARSKJÖLD (from 8 October 1936, d. 7 July 1937)	Sweden
M. O. HUDSON (from 8 October 1936)	U.S.A.
C. J. B. HURST (President 1934-6, Vice-President 1936-46)	U.K.
F. B. KELLOG (to 9 September 1935)	U.S.A.
H. NAGAOKA (from 17 September 1935 to 15 January 1942)	Japan
D. NEGULESCO	Rumania

E. ROLIN-JAEQUEMYNS (d. 11 July 1936)   Belgium
M. C. J. ROSTWOROWSKI (d. 24 March 1940)   Poland
W. SCHÜCKING (d. 25 August 1935)   Germany
F. J. URRUTIA (to 9 January 1942)   Colombia
Ch. de VISSCHER (from 27 May 1937)   Belgium
WANG Ch'ung-hui (to 15 January 1936)   China

Deputy-Judges

(Post abolished on 1 February 1936)

R. W. ERICH   Finland
J. C. d. MATTA   Portugal
M. NOVACOVITCH   Yugoslavia
J. REDLICH   Austria

(B) *International Court of Justice*

(Judges in order of Precedence)

First Period, 1946-9 and Second Period, 1949-52

*** J. G. GUERRERO (President 1946-9, Vice-President 1949-52)   El Salvador
*** J. BASDEVANT (Vice-President 1946-9, President 1949-52)   France
*** A. ALVAREZ   Chile
 ** I. FABELA   Mexico
 ** G. H. HACKWORTH   U.S.A.
  * B. WINIARSKI   Poland
  * M. ZORIČIĆ   Yugoslavia
 ** Ch. de VISSCHER   Belgium
*** Sir A. McNAIR   U.K.
 ** H. KLAESTAD   Norway
  * A. H. BADAWI   Egypt
 ** S. B. KRYLOV   U.S.S.R.
  * J. E. READ   Canada
  * HSU MO   China
*** J. AZEVEDO (d. 7 May 1951)   Brazil
**** L. CARNEIRO (from 6 December 1951)   Brazil

   * Elected for three-year term expiring on 6 February 1949.
  ** Elected for six-year term expiring on 6 February 1952.
 *** Elected for nine-year term expiring on 6 February 1955.
**** Elected for remainder of predecessor's term.

Third Period, 1952-5

Sir A. McNAIR (President)   U.K.
J. G. GUERRERO (Vice-President)   El Salvador
A. ALVAREZ   Chile
J. BASDEVANT   France
G. H. HACKWORTH   U.S.A.
B. WINIARSKI   Poland

M. Zoričić	Yugoslavia
H. Klaestad	Norway
A. H. Badawi	Egypt
J. E. Read	Canada
Hsu Mo	China
L. Carneiro	Brazil
Sir B. Rau (d. 30 November 1953)	India
E. C. Armand-Ugon	Uruguay
S. A. Golunsky (to 25 July 1953)	U.S.S.R.
F. I. Kojevnikov (from 27 November 1953)	U.S.S.R.
Sir M. Zafrulla Khan (from 7 October 1954)	Pakistan

Fourth Period, 1955-8

G. H. Hackworth (President)	U.S.A.
A. H. Badawi (Vice-President)	Egypt
J. G. Guerrero	El Salvador
J. Basdevant	France
B. Winiarski	Poland
M. Zoričić	Yugoslavia
H. Klaestad	Norway
J. E. Read	Canada
Hsu Mo (d. 28 June 1956)	China
E. C. Armand-Ugon	Uruguay
F. I. Kojevnikov	U.S.S.R.
Sir M. Zafrulla Khan	Pakistan
Sir H. Lauterpacht	U.K.
L. M. Moreno Quintana	Argentina
R. Córdova	Mexico
V. K. Wellington Koo (from 11 January 1957)	China

Fifth Period, 1958-61

H. Klaestad (President)	Norway
Sir M. Zafrulla Khan (Vice-President)	Pakistan
J. G. Guerrero (d. 25 November 1958)	El Salvador
J. Basdevant	France
G. H. Hackworth	U.S.A.
B. Winiarski	Poland
A. H. Badawi	United Arab Republic
E. G. Armand-Ugon	Uruguay
F. I. Kojevnikov	U.S.S.R.
Sir H. Lauterpacht (d. 8 May 1960)	U.K.
L. M. Moreno Quintana	Argentina
R. Córdova	Mexico
V. K. Wellington Koo	China
J. Spiropoulos	Greece
Sir Percy Spender	Australia
R. J. Alfaro (from 29 September 1959)	Panama
Sir Gerald Fitzmaurice (from 16 November 1960)	U.K.

APPENDIX 3

Sixth Period, 1961-4

B. Winiarski (President)	Poland
R. J. Alfaro (Vice-President)	Panama
J. Basdevant	France
A. H. Badawi	U.A.R.
L. M. Moreno Quintana	Argentina
R. Córdova	Mexico
V. K. Wellington Koo	China
J. Spiropoulos	Greece
Sir Percy Spender	Australia
Sir Gerald Fitzmaurice	U.K.
V. M. Koretsky	U.S.S.R.
K. Tanaka	Japan
J. L. Bustamente y Rivero	Peru
P. C. Jessup	U.S.A.
G. Morelli	Italy

JUDICIAL STATISTICS

(A) *Permanent Court of International Justice*

Year	New Cases filed	Advisory Opinions	Judgments	Orders (since 1926)	Cases Dis-continued	Removed from List by Court
1922	4	3				
1923	5	5	2			
1924	5	1	2			
1925	5	3	3		1	
1926	3	1	1	2		
1927	5	1	4	4		
1928	6	2	2	17		
1929			3	8	2	
1930	2	2		7		
1931	8	4		12		
1932	7	3	3	19		
1933	3		2	17	5	
1934	1		2	2		
1935	4	2		6		
1936	3		1	14	1	
1937	2		3	11		
1938	2		1	12	1	
1939	1		3	4		
1940				2		
1941						
1942						
1943						
1944						
1945					2	
Total	66	27	32	137	12	

(B) *The International Court of Justice*

Year	New Cases filed	Advisory Opinions	Judgments	Orders	Cases Discontinued	Removed from List by Court
1946						
1947	2			3		
1948	1	1	1	3		
1949	6	1	2	9		
1950	4	4	2	7	1	
1951	4	1	2	11		
1952			3	8		
1953	3		3	5		
1954	3	1	1	10	1	2
1955	8	1	1	3		
1956		2		9		4
1957	6		2	9		
1958	3		1	19		1
1959	4		3	12	1	1
1960	2	1	2	6	2	
1961	2		1	9	1	
Total	48	12	24	123	6	8

Note: The figures for the Permanent Court are taken from M. Hudson, *The Permanent Court of International Justice, 1920-1942*, p. 779. (Corrected on the basis of the Sixteenth Report of the Permanent Court (E/16), pp. 92-197.) For the above figures, preliminary objections and requests for interim measures of protection are not included as "new cases". Requests for interpretation of judgments (two by the Permanent Court and one by the present Court) are so listed. The general List of the Permanent Court contained 79 folios, and that of the present Court 50 folios to October of 1962.

THE AUTHORITY TO REQUEST ADVISORY OPINIONS

(a) *Organs authorized directly by the Charter*

By Article 96, paragraph 1, of the Charter, the following organs are authorized to request an advisory opinion on any legal question: the General Assembly, the Security Council.

(b) *Organs authorized by the General Assembly*

By Article 96, paragraph 2, of the Charter, organs of the United Nations and specialized agencies may be authorized by the General Assembly to request advisory opinions on legal questions arising within the scope of their activities.
The following organs of the United Nations have been so authorized:

Organ	Scope of Authority	General Assembly Resolution
Economic and Social Council	All legal questions arising within the scope of the activities of the Council (including legal questions concerning mutual relationships of the United Nations and the Specialized Agencies).	89 (I) of 11 December 1946
Trusteeship Council	Legal questions arising within the scope of its activities.	171 B (II) of 14 December 1947
Interim Committee	Legal questions arising within the scope of the Committee's activities.	196 (III) of 3 December 1948 and 295 (IV) of 21 November 1949
Committee on Applications for Review of Administrative Tribunal Judgments	For the purpose of Article 11 of the Statute of the United Nations Administrative Tribunal.	957 (X) of 8 November 1955

The following specialized agencies have been authorized to request advisory opinions on legal questions arising within the scope of their *activities*, other than questions concerning the mutual relationships of that specialized agency and the United Nations or other specialized agencies. In each case, when requesting an opinion the specialized agency has to inform ECOSOC. The terms of the authorization are contained in the relationship agreement (see p. 42 above), and the authorization of the General Assembly itself appears in the resolution by which the relationship agreement was approved.

Agency	Organs	Article of Relationship Agreement	Resolution of General Assembly
I.L.O.	Conference. Governing Body when authorized by Conference.	IX	50 (I) of 14 December 1946
F.A.O.	Conference. Executive Committee when acting in pursuance of an authorization by the Conference.	IX	50 (I)
UNESCO	General Conference. Executive Board acting in pursuance of an authorization by the Conference.	IX	50 (I)
I.C.A.O.	Assembly or Council.	X	50 (I)
I.B.R.D.	The Bank.	VIII	124 (II) of 15 November 1947
I.D.A.	The Association.	I	1594 (XV) of 27 March 1961
I.M.F.	The Fund.	VIII	124 (II)
I.M.C.O.	Assembly. Council acting in pursuance of an authorization by the Assembly.	IX	204 (III) of 18 November 1948
I.F.C.	The Corporation.	I	1116 (XI) of 20 February 1957

The following specialized agencies have similarly been authorized to request advisory opinions on legal questions arising within the scope of their *competence*, other than questions concerning the mutual relationships of the specialized agency and the United Nations or other specialized agencies. In each case the specialized agency shall inform ECOSOC of the request.

Agency	Organs	Article of Relationship Agreement	Resolution of General Assembly
W.H.O.	Health Assembly. Executive Board acting in pursuance of an authorization by the Health Assembly.	X	124 (II)
I.T.U.	Plenipotentiary Conference. Administrative Council acting in pursuance of an authorization by the Plenipotentiary Conference.	VII	124 (II)
W.M.O.	Congress.	VII	531 (VI) of 20 December 1951

The International Atomic Energy Agency has been authorized by Resolution 1146 (XII) of 14 November 1957 to request advisory opinions on legal questions arising within the scope of its activities other than questions concerning the relationship between the Agency and the United Nations or any specialized agency. By Article X of the relationship agreement, the United Nations will take the necessary action to enable the General Conference or the Board of Governors to seek such advisory opinions. This agreement was approved by Resolution 1145 (XII) of 14 December 1957.

Although the Organization of American States is not authorized to request advisory opinions, Article LI of the American Treaty on Pacific Settlement (the Pact of Bogotá) of 1948 enables the parties concerned in the solution of a controversy to petition the General Assembly or the Security Council to request an advisory opinion on any legal question. Such petition shall be submitted through the Council of the Organization.

NOTE ON BIBLIOGRAPHY

The publications of the Permanent Court of International Justice (P.C.I.J.) were organized in the following Series:

  A. Judgments and Orders. Nos. 1-24 (1922-30).

  B. Advisory opinions. Nos. 1-18 (1922-30).

These were amalgamated in 1931 to form

  A/B. Judgments, orders and advisory opinions. Nos. 40-80 (1931-40).

  C. Acts and Documents relating to judgments and advisory opinions (Pleadings). Nos. 1-19 (1922-30), 52-88 (1931-45).

  D. Acts and Documents concerning the organization of the Court. Nos. 1-6 (1922-40).

  E. Annual Reports. Nos. 1-16 (1925-45).

  F. General Indexes. Nos. 1-4 (1922-36).

The publications of the International Court of Justice (I.C.J.) are organized as follows:

  Reports (Rep.)

  Reports of judgments, advisory opinions and orders. Annual since 1948.

  Pleadings

  Pleadings, oral arguments and documents. One or more volumes, containing the Court record, for each case.

  Acts

  Acts and documents concerning the organization of the Court.

  One volume only to date, containing the basic texts (including the Rules of Court (1946)).

  Yearbook

  Yearbook of the International Court of Justice, covering the period 16 July-15 July. Annual since 1946-7.

All the above are in bilingual editions except Series E and the Yearbook (*Annuaire*), which are published in separate English and French editions.

The International Court and its work is probably the subject of more learned comment than any other international organ, and it is not practicable in these pages to give any bibliographical indications other than those cited in the text (see Index of Names). A general bibliography on the Court, prepared by the Court's librarian, will be found in Chapter IX of the Reports of the Permanent Court and of the Yearbooks of the present Court. This bibliography is highly classified and fully indexed. About 300 titles a year are added to it.

The abbreviation R.A.D.I. used in the Notes refers to the *Recueil des Cours* of the Academy of International Law, which is also situated in the Peace Palace at The Hague. The abbreviation O.R. refers to the *Official Records* of the various organs of the United Nations.

INDEX OF NAMES

Adatci, M., 213
Alfaro, R. J., 215
Altamira y Crevea, R., 213
Alvarez, A., 214
Anzilotti, D., 213
Araya, R. R., 68
Armand-Ugon, E. C., 69, 70, 131, 214-5
Attlee, C. R., 177
Azevedo, J., 46, 214

Badawi, A. H., 118, 131, 214-5
Bainton, R., 28
Barbosa, R., 213
Barros Jarpa, E., 69
Bartoš, M., 69
Basdevant, J., 131, 214-5
Baxter, R. R., 68
Beichmann, F. V. N., 213
Bos, M., 29
Bourquin, M., 103
Bozeman, A. B., 27
Briggs, H. W., 95
Bruns, V., 30
Bustamente y Rivero, J. L., 69, 70, 216
Bustamente y Sirven, A. S. de, 213

Carlston, K. S., 29
Carneiro, L., 214
Castrén, E., 69
Chagla, M. A. C., 116, 118, 131
Chan Nay Chow, 27
Chatterjee, H., 27
Cheng, Tien-Hsi, 213
Córdova, R., 215

Eppstein, J., 27
Erich, R. W., 214
Eysinga, W. J. M. van, 213

Fabela, I., 214
Fernandes, M., 116, 118, 131
Finlay, Viscount, 213
Fisher, H. A. L., 28
Fitzmaurice, Sir Gerald, 215
Flor, M. E., 69

Fox, H., 29
François, J. P. A., 28
Frankfurter, F., 96
Fromageot, H., 213

Golunsky, S. A., 214
Grotius, H., 11
Guerrero, J. C., 9, 213, 214
Guggenheim, P., 69, 103

Hackworth, G. H., 69, 115, 214-5
Hadwen, J. G., 68
Hambro, E., 30, 136
Hammarskjöld, Å., 213
Hsu Mo, 214
Huber, Max, 68, 121, 213
Hudson, M. O., 26, 28, 29, 95, 136, 213, 218
Hughes, C. E., 213
Hurewitz, J. C., 177
Hurst, Sir Cecil, 213

Jenks, C. W., 29
Jessup, P., 69, 216

Kaufmann, J., 68
Kellog, F. B., 213
Khadduri, M., 27
Klaestad, H., 69, 118, 126, 131, 214-5
Kojevnikov, F. I., 69, 118, 131, 215
Koo, Wellington, 131, 215
Koretsky, V., 69, 215
Krylov, S. B., 214

Lalive, P., 103
Lapradelle, A. G. de, 28
Latimer, H., 177
Lauterpacht, Sir Hersch, 28, 30, 96, 136, 215
Loder, B. C. J., 213

Macadam, I. S., 177
Matine-Daftary, A., 69
Matta, J. C. de, 214
Mérignhac, A., 29

Moore, J. B., 27, 28, 213
Morelli, G., 69, 216
Moreno Quintana, L. M., 131, 215
McNair, Lord, 66, 214

Nagaoka, H., 213
Negulesco, D., 213
Nicholas, II, Tsar, 14
Nisot, J., 69
Novacovitch, M., 214
Nyholm, D. G. G., 213

Pal, R., 69
Pessôa, E. d. S., 213
Petrén, S., 69
Phillipson, C., 27
Politis, N., 28, 29
Potiemkine, V., 28
Prodjodikoro, W., 69

Raeder, A., 27
Ralston, J., 27, 29
Rau, Sir Benegal, 214
Read, J. E., 214-5
Rechid, A., 27
Redlich, J., 214
Rolin, H., 103
Rolin-Jaequemyns, E., 214
Rosenne, Sh., 30, 96, 136, 204
Rostworowski, M. C. J., 214
Rudzinski, A. W., 69

Sapena Pastor, R., 69
Schücking, W., 214
Scott, J. B., 28
Simpson, J. L., 29
Sørensen, M., 69
Soskice, Sir Frank, 103
Spender, Sir Percy 131, 215-6
Spiropoulos, J., 131, 215-6

Tanaka, K., 69, 216
Taube, M., 27
Ténékidès, G., 27
Tod, M., 27
Tunkin, G., 69

Urrutia, F. J., 214
Usteri, E., 27

Visscher, Ch. de, 214

Waldock, Sir Humphrey, 103
Wang, Ch'ung-kui, 214
Weiss, C. A., 213
Winiarski, B., 131, 214-6
Witenberg, J. C., 29

Yovanovitch, M., 213

Zafrulla Khan, Sir, 69, 215
Zoričić, M., 214-5

INDEX OF CASES

Acquisition of Polish Nationality, 29
Administrative Tribunal of I.L.O., 46, 159-60
Administrative Tribunal of U.N., 159
Admission into U.N., 91, 141-3
Aerial Incident Cases, 95, 160-1
Aerial Incident of 27 July 1955, 95, 96, 136, 164-6
Alabama, The, 13
Ambatielos, 95, 153-4
Anglo-Iranian Oil Co., 44, 66, 83, 85, 88, 95, 154-6, 172
Antarctica, 95, 161
Asylum, 77, 95, 146-8

Barcelona Traction etc., 95, 167
Bay of Fundy, 28
Bienne-Beppet arbitration, 27
Borchgrave, 30

Chorzów Factory, 29
Compagnie du Port, etc., 95, 158
Competence of General Assembly –
See Admission into U.N.,
Corfu Channel, 44, 80, 95, 126, 138-41, 145, 158.
Customs Union, 24

Danzig and the I.L.O., 30
Danzig Legislative Decrees, 30

Eastern Carelia, 30, 96
Eastern Greenland, 29.
Electricité de Beyrouth, 95, 158
European Commission of the Danube, 30
Exchange of Greek and Turkish Populations, 30

Fisheries, 83, 144-6, 172
Free Zones, 95
French Nationals in Egypt, 95, 146
Frontier between Turkey and Iraq, 30, 96
Frontier Lands, 95, 166

Genocide Convention, 46, 152-3
German Interests in Polish Upper Silesia, 29
German Minority Schools in Upper Silesia, 30
German Settlers in Poland, 29
Greco-Bulgarian Communities, 30
Guardianship Convention of 1902, 162-3

Haya de la Torre, 95
And see *Asylum* case
Honduras-Nicaragua Frontier, 95, 166-7, 172

Interhandel, 95, 96, 163-4, 173
Interpretation of Greco-Bulgarian Agreement of 1927, 30
Interpretation of Greco-Turkish Protocol of 1926, 30
Interpretation of Peace Treaties with Bulgaria, Hungary and Rumania, 46, 91, 148-9, 177

Jaworzina (Polish-Czechoslovakian Frontier), 30
Jurisdiction of Danzig Courts, 29

Lighthouses, 30
Lotus, The, 30, 176

Maritime Safety Committee of I.M.C.O., 46, 167, 173, 178
Mavrommatis Palestine Concessions, 30
Memel Statute, 30
Minority Schools in Albania, 30
Minority Schools in Upper Silesia, 29
Minquiers and Ecrehos, 95, 101, 156
Monastery of Saint Naoum, 30
Monetary Gold, 95, 96, 157-8, 173

Northern Cameroons, 95, 168, 173
Norwegian Loans, 161-2
Nottebohm, 95, 157, 173

Oscar Chinn, 30

Passamaquoddy Bay, 28
Phosphates in Morocco, 30 177
Polish Agrarian Reform, 30
Polish Postal Service in Danzig, 29
Polish War Vessels in Danzig, 30
Prince von Pless, 30

Railway Traffic between Poland and
   Lithuania, 30
Reparation for Injuries Suffered by
   U.N., 95, 143-4.
Reservations –
See Genocide Convention.
Right of Passage, 83, 96, 98-137, 162,
   172
River Oder Commission, 30

South-West Africa, 39, 93, 95, 151, 173
South-West Africa – Oral Hearings,
   46, 151
South-West Africa Voting Procedure,
   46, 96, 151
South-West Africa (Status), 150-2

Temple of Preah Vihear, 96, 168
Treatment of Polish Nationals in
   Danzig, 30
Treaty of Neuilly (Art. 4), 30
Tunis and Morocco Nationality De-
   crees, 30

U.S. Nationals in Morocco, 152

Wimbledon, The, 29

GENERAL INDEX

Act of Algeciras (1906), 152, 177
Acting-President (and see President of Court), 63, 116
Admissibility of Claim –
  See jurisdiction, disputes over
Advisory Opinions, 21, 24, 31, 42, 89-94, 136, 141-2, 142-3, 148-9, 150-2, 153, 159-60, 167-8, 169, 219-21
Advocates, 103, 110-2
Agent, 102, 103, 104, 107, 110-2, 114, 118, 155
Albania, 44, 138-40, 158
Amphictyonies, Delphic, 12
Application instituting proceedings, 101, 102, 104, 106, 113, 131, 138, 144, 146, 155, 157, 160, 161, 166, 167, 168
Arbitration, 12, 13, 14-9, 20, 28, 29, 40, 158, 167
  – Award, see judgment.
  – Procedure, 18-9, 28, 86, 106
  – Treaties of, 18
  – Tribunal (and see Permanent Court of Arbitration), 15
Arbitrators (and see Judges), 15, 16, 18, 19
Argentina, 54, 68, 80, 161, 175
Australia, 54, 96, 175, 176, 178
Austria, 21, 24, 54

Belgium, 54, 96, 103, 167, 175, 178
Brazil, 13, 54
Bulgaria, 148-9, 164-6, 176, 177, 178
Byelorussian S.S.R., 175, 176, 177, 178
Byzantium, 12

Cambodia, 96, 168
Cameroun, 168
Canada, 54, 96, 175, 177, 178
Central American Court of Justice, 29
Chambers of Court, 66-7
Chile, 80, 161, 177
China, 27, 33, 50, 51, 54, 96, 175, 176, 177, 178
Claims Commissions, 13, 28
Colombia, 54, 96, 146-8

Compromis –
  See Special Agreement
Compromissory clause –
  See Special Agreement
Concert of Europe, 15, 19
Conciliation, 12, 19, 129
Costs, 116, 134
Counsel –
  See Advocates
Counter-Memorial –
  See Written pleadings
Court (and see Permanent Court of International Justice), 15, 19, 21, 84
  – Composition (and see Judges), 15, 20, 23, 49-55, 62, 63-6, 115-6, 120, 125-6, 213-6
  – Financial matters, 23, 31, 44-5, 47
  – Statistics, 83, 87, 168-9, 218
  – Statute of, 34, 35, 49-50, 52-4, 200-11
    – Parties to, 211-2
Cuba, 54, 147-8
Czechoslovakia, 161, 175, 176, 178

Decision –
  See Advisory Opinions, judgments
  – *Ex aequo et bono*, 129-30, 147
Default procedure, 107, 126-7, 140
Deliberations of Court, 62, 98, 116-8, 120-3, 131
Denmark, 54, 96, 178
Diplomatic Privileges, 67-8
Disputes, international, pacific settlement of, 11, 73, 170
  – justiciability of, 16, 39
  – legal, 17, 20-1, 74, 80-3
Dissenting opinions, 19, 98, 116, 118, 120-3, 131-2, 142
Documents, filing of –
  See Written pleadings
Domestic jurisdiction, reservation of, 82, 108, 162, 164, 166
Dominican Republic, 96
Drafting Committee (Court's), 62, 117-8

Dumbarton Oaks Proposals (1944), 34, 45, 82

Ecuador, 177
Egypt, 54, 96, 143, 146, 176
Equality of the Parties, 19, 105
Ethiopia, 151
European Organization for Nuclear Research, 97
Experts appointed by Court, 139, 140
Extra-judicial activities, 32, 63, 135, 156

Facts, statement of, 101, 102, 116
Finland, 54, 96
Food and Agriculture Organization, 41, 97, 220
France, 50, 54, 95, 96, 103, 146, 152, 156, 158, 159, 162, 175, 176, 177, 178

General List, 104
Geneva Conference on Law of the Sea (1958), 78, 95, 145, 174, 176
Germany, 16, 21, 24, 26, 28, 54
Greece, 11, 12, 27, 54, 153-4, 175, 177
Guatemala, 157, 175, 177

Hague Conferences (1899, 1907) – See Hague Conventions
Hague Conventions (1899, 1907), 14-19, 20, 21, 28, 50, 55
Hague, The, 17, 22, 62, 104-5
Haiti, 96
Honduras, 96, 166-7, 175
Hungary, 148-9, 160-1, 176

India, 27, 54, 61, 95, 96, 98-137, 175, 176, 178
Individual opinions – See Dissenting opinions
Informal Inter-Allied Committee (1943-4), 33-4, 45, 70
Institute of International Law, 20, 68
Interim measures of protection, 44, 84-5, 110, 115, 155, 164
Inter-American Juridical Committee, 33
International Atomic Energy Agency, 41, 97, 220-21
International Bank for Reconstruction and Development, 41, 220

International Civil Aviation Organization, 41, 96, 97, 220
International Development Association, 41, 220
International Finance Corporation, 41, 220
International Labour Organization, 24, 41, 42, 94, 97, 159-60, 177, 220
International law, 12, 26, 123, 127-30, 173
International Law Commission, 28, 137, 145, 153
International Maritime Consultative Organization, 41, 42, 93, 167-8, 178, 220
International Monetary Fund, 41, 220
International Prize Court, 29
International Telecommunication Organization, 41, 97, 220
Intervention, 104, 109, 147-8
Iran, 44, 154-6
Iraq, 174, 177
Ireland, 178
Islam, 11, 27
Israel, 96, 143, 144, 164-6, 176, 177
Italy, 13, 54, 158, 178

Japan, 51, 54, 76, 96, 178
Jay Treaty (1794), 13
Jordan, 143, 177
Judges (and see Arbitrators) 48-70
 – Election, 20, 22, 29, 35, 48, 56-61
 – Emoluments, 44, 62
 – Independence, 19, 29, 61-2
 – Nationality, 49, 63-6
 – Nomination, 54, 55-6, 68
 – Number, 48, 54, 62, 116, 126
 – Pensions, 38, 44-5
 – Precedence, 63
 – Qualifications, 48-55, 66
 – Term of Office, 48, 65
 – Voting, 63, 116-7
Judges ad hoc, 63-6, 116, 155, 166, 167
Judgment, 14, 19, 104, 112, 113, 116, 118-20, 131-4
 – Drafts of, (see Deliberations, Drafting Committee)
 – Effect of, 123, 133-4
 – Execution of, 31, 42-4, 158
 – Final and binding, 19, 129, 165
 – Interpretation of, 134, 147
 – Reasons for, 64, 113, 116
 – Revision of, 134
Judicial precedents, 127-9

Jurisdiction (and see Advisory Opinions, Special Agreement), 15-6, 23, 26, 73-97, 101, 113, 126-7, 133
– Compulsory, 15, 16, 20, 23, 26, 35, 73, 74, 76, 80-3, 86, 89, 99, 123, 152, 155, 157, 162, 163, 164, 165, 168
– Disputes over, 18, 85-9, 107, 108-9, 110, 114-5, 118-20, 133, 139, 154, 155-6, 157, 158, 162, 164, 165, 168

Languages, official, 102, 106, 111, 118
Law applied by Court –
See International law
League of Nations, 19-22, 31, 32, 35, 50, 69, 77, 78, 80-2, 91, 150-1
– Covenant of, 20, 21, 22, 23, 29, 43, 81, 90
– Dissolution of, 36
Lebanon, 158-9
Liberia, 95, 96, 151, 168, 173, 178
Liechtenstein, 75, 96, 157
Lithuania, 25
Litigation, international, parties to, 74-6, 90
– Individuals as, 74, 94, 95
– International Organizations as, 75
Locarno Agreements (1925), 25
Luxembourg, 96

Macedonia, 12
Mediation, 12, 19, 129
Memorial –
See Written pleadings
Merits, 73, 109, 119, 123-6, 130-1
Mexico, 54, 95, 96, 177, 178

Netherlands, The, 20, 54, 68, 96, 162-3, 177, 178
New Zealand, 96
Nicaragua, 96, 166-7
Non liquet, 137
Norway, 54, 83, 96, 144-5, 161-2, 178

Organization of American States, 42, 166-7, 177, 221
Oral Pleadings, 19, 98, 109-12, 115, 125

Pakistan, 54, 95, 96
Panama, 54, 96, 169, 178
Permanent Court of Arbitration (and see Hague Conventions), 16-9, 22, 28, 55

Permanent Court of International Justice (and see Court), 21, 22-7, 29, 32-3, 34, 35, 43, 67, 68-9, 77, 78, 80-3, 84, 87, 91, 103, 104, 117, 144, 154, 165, 169-75
– Statistics of, 24, 25, 217
– Statute of, 21, 22-7, 86
Peru, 54, 146-8
Philippines, 96, 177, 178
Poland, 24, 54, 175, 176, 177, 178
Portugal, 54, 96, 98-137,178
Preliminary objections –
See Jurisdiction, disputes over.
President of Court, 32, 44, 58, 62-3, 68, 104, 111, 116-8, 125-6, 135, 156
Procedure, 19, 23, 98-137
Proceedings, institution of, (and see Application instituting proceedings, Special Agreement), 101
Public International Organizations (and see Specialized Agencies), 41
Publications, Court's, 135, 136, 222

Récusation, 62, 70
Registrar, 44, 62, 67, 101, 103-4, 106, 110, 116
Rejoinder –
See Written pleadings
Reply –
See Written pleadings
Res judicata, –
See Judgment, effect of, execution of
Rome, 12, 27
Rules of Court, 23
Rumania, 54, 148-9, 176, 178
Russia –
See U.S.S.R.

Salvador, 54, 96, 176
San Francisco Conference (1945), 31-6, 46, 57, 75, 90, 91, 173
San Marino, 75
Separate opinions, –
See Dissenting opinions
Settlement out of Court, 127, 159, 167
South Africa, 93, 95, 96, 150-2, 176, 178
Spain, 54, 167, 178
Special Agreement, 17, 41, 76-80, 101, 106, 113, 139, 145, 156, 166
Specialized Agencies (and see individual agencies), 37, 41-3, 46, 67, 75, 90
States entitled to appear before Court, 22, 74-6
States not parties to Statute, 22, 36, 67

Statute –
  See International Court, Permanent
    Court of International Justice
Submissions, 105, 107, 112-5, 116, 123,
  124, 130-1
Sudan, 96
Sweden, 54, 96, 126-7, 162-3, 177
Switzerland, 13, 20, 54, 75, 96, 103,
  163-4, 178

Thailand, 96, 168, 178
Time-limits, 105, 107, 109, 123-6
Turkey, 96, 177

Ukrainian S.S.R., 175, 176, 177, 178
UNESCO, 41, 42, 93, 97, 159-60, 177,
  220
United Arab Republic –
  See Egypt
United Kingdom, 13, 28, 33, 43-4, 50,
  54, 59, 66, 80, 83, 95, 96, 138-40,
  144-5, 153-4, 154-6, 158, 161, 164-6,
  169, 173, 175, 176, 177, 178
United Nations, 27, 31-47, 51-2, 75,
  91, 143, 149, 175, 176, 177, 178
  – Administrative Tribunal, 40, 93,
    94, 96-7, 159-60, 219-20
  – Charter, 31-44, 85, 173, 179-99
  – Committee on Contributions, 45
  – Economic and Social Council, 31,
    42, 68, 75, 93, 219
  – General Assembly, 28, 31, 35, 38,
    41, 44-5, 46, 48, 56-61, 68, 69, 90,
    140, 141-2, 143-4, 145, 149, 150-2,
    170, 219, 220, 221
  – Joint Staff Pension Fund, 45, 97

  – Non-members of, and Court, 36,
    43, 45, 57, 75, 99, 138
  – Security Council, 31, 35, 38, 43-4,
    46, 48, 56-61, 69, 76, 77, 85, 90,
    93, 138-40, 141-2, 155, 170, 172,
    175, 219, 221
  – Tax Equalization Scheme, 45, 47
  – Trusteeship Council, 68, 93, 219
United States, 13, 20, 25, 28, 33, 35,
  50, 54, 80, 82, 91, 95, 96, 152, 158,
  160-1, 163-4, 164-6, 175, 176, 177,
  178
Universal Postal Union, 41, 46
U.S.S.R. 14, 25, 28, 33, 35, 50, 54,
  78, 80, 82, 91, 138-41, 149, 160-1
  174, 175, 176
Upper Volta, 178
Uruguay, 54, 96

Venezuela, 174
Vice-President –
  See President
Vienna Conference on Diplomatic
  Relations (1961), 95

Washington Treaty (1871), 13
Washington Committee of Jurists
  (1945), 34-5, 46, 56
Witnesses, 112, 139
World Health Organization, 41, 97,
  220
World Meteorological Organization,
  41, 97, 220
Written pleadings, 19, 98, 105-8, 109,
  110, 123-5

Yugoslavia, 54, 175, 176.